Artificial Intelligence Applications Using ChatGPT in Education:

Case Studies and Practices

Muhammad Shahzad Aslam
School of Traditional Chinese Medicine, Xiamen University Malaysia, Malaysia

Saima Nisar
School of Computing, UUM College of Arts and Sciences, University Utara Malaysia, Sintok, Malaysia

A volume in the Advances in Educational Technologies and Instructional Design (AETID) Book Series

IGI Global
PUBLISHER of TIMELY KNOWLEDGE

Published in the United States of America by
IGI Global
Information Science Reference (an imprint of IGI Global)
701 E. Chocolate Avenue
Hershey PA, USA 17033
Tel: 717-533-8845
Fax: 717-533-8661
E-mail: cust@igi-global.com
Web site: http://www.igi-global.com

Library of Congress Cataloging-in-Publication Data

Names: Aslam, Muhammad Shahzad, 1985- author. | Nisar, Saima, 1988- author.

Title: Artificial intelligence applications using ChatGPT in education : case studies and practices / Authored by Muhammad Shahzad Aslam, Saima Nisar.
Description: Hershey, PA : Information Science Reference, [2023] | Includes bibliographical references and index. | Summary: "ChatGPT is recently introduce Artificial intelligence (AI) tool that uses large language model (LLM). It was developed by OpenAI and released in November 2022. Chatbots that use natural language AI, like ChatGPT, use enormous volumes of text data to anticipate words or phrases in a certain context. However, there is lack of knowledge on how to use such tool? What is the acceptability of AI tools in current era? What is the application of ChatGPT in medical education? How to use ChatGPT effectively and is there moral and ethical issues user faces when use ChatGPT?"-- Provided by publisher.
Identifiers: LCCN 2023025876 (print) | LCCN 2023025877 (ebook) | ISBN 9781668493007 (hardcover) | ISBN 9781668493045 (paperback) | ISBN 9781668493014 (ebook)
Subjects: LCSH: Artificial intelligence--Educational applications. | ChatGPT. | Natural language generation (Computer science)--Computer programs. | Artificial intelligence--Educational applications--Case studies. | ChatGPT--Case studies.
Classification: LCC LB1028.43 .A86 2023 (print) | LCC LB1028.43 (ebook) | DDC 371.33/463--dc23/eng/20230607
LC record available at https://lccn.loc.gov/2023025876
LC ebook record available at https://lccn.loc.gov/2023025877

British Cataloguing in Publication Data
A Cataloguing in Publication record for this book is available from the British Library.

All work contributed to this book is new, previously-unpublished material.
The views expressed in this book are those of the authors, but not necessarily of the publisher.

For electronic access to this publication, please contact: eresources@igi-global.com.

Advances in Educational Technologies and Instructional Design (AETID) Book Series

Lawrence A. Tomei
Robert Morris University, USA

ISSN:2326-8905
EISSN:2326-8913

MISSION

Education has undergone, and continues to undergo, immense changes in the way it is enacted and distributed to both child and adult learners. In modern education, the traditional classroom learning experience has evolved to include technological resources and to provide online classroom opportunities to students of all ages regardless of their geographical locations. From distance education, Massive-Open-Online-Courses (MOOCs), and electronic tablets in the classroom, technology is now an integral part of learning and is also affecting the way educators communicate information to students.

The **Advances in Educational Technologies & Instructional Design (AETID) Book Series** explores new research and theories for facilitating learning and improving educational performance utilizing technological processes and resources. The series examines technologies that can be integrated into K-12 classrooms to improve skills and learning abilities in all subjects including STEM education and language learning. Additionally, it studies the emergence of fully online classrooms for young and adult learners alike, and the communication and accountability challenges that can arise. Trending topics that are covered include adaptive learning, game-based learning, virtual school environments, and social media effects. School administrators, educators, academicians, researchers, and students will find this series to be an excellent resource for the effective design and implementation of learning technologies in their classes.

COVERAGE

- Social Media Effects on Education
- Adaptive Learning
- Game-Based Learning
- Collaboration Tools
- Instructional Design Models
- Virtual School Environments
- K-12 Educational Technologies
- Digital Divide in Education
- Web 2.0 and Education
- Educational Telecommunications

IGI Global is currently accepting manuscripts for publication within this series. To submit a proposal for a volume in this series, please contact our Acquisition Editors at Acquisitions@igi-global.com or visit: http://www.igi-global.com/publish/.

The Advances in Educational Technologies and Instructional Design (AETID) Book Series (ISSN 2326-8905) is published by IGI Global, 701 E. Chocolate Avenue, Hershey, PA 17033-1240, USA, www.igi-global.com. This series is composed of titles available for purchase individually; each title is edited to be contextually exclusive from any other title within the series. For pricing and ordering information please visit http://www.igi-global.com/book-series/advances-educational-technologies-instructional-design/73678. Postmaster: Send all address changes to above address.

Titles in this Series

For a list of additional titles in this series, please visit: http://www.igi-global.com/book-series/

Handbook of Research on Innovative Frameworks and Inclusive Models for Online Learning
Jared Keengwe (University of North Dakota, USA)
Information Science Reference • © 2023 • 412pp • H/C (ISBN: 9781668490723) • US $270.00

Technology Management and Its Social Impact on Education
P.C. Lai (University of Malaya, Malaysia)
Information Science Reference • © 2023 • 316pp • H/C (ISBN: 9781668491034) • US $215.00

Handbook of Research on Advancing Equity and Inclusion Through Educational Technology
Paula Escudeiro (ISEP, Polytechnic of Porto, Portugal & GILT, ATHENA European University, Portugal) Nuno Escudeiro (ISEP, Polytechnic of Porto, Portugal & GILT, ATHENA European University, Portugal) and Oscar Bernardes (ISEP, Polytechnic of Porto, Portugal & University of Aveiro, Portugal & GILT, ATHENA European University, Portugal)
Information Science Reference • © 2023 • 446pp • H/C (ISBN: 9781668468685) • US $270.00

Third-Space Exploration in Education
Candace Kaye (New Mexico State University, USA) and Jeanette Haynes Writer (New Mexico State University, USA)
Information Science Reference • © 2023 • 331pp • H/C (ISBN: 9781668484029) • US $215.00

STEM Education Approaches and Challenges in the MENA Region
Fatimah Alhashem (Gulf University for Science and Technology, Kuwait) Heather Pacheco-Guffrey (Bridgewater State University, USA) and Jacquelynne Anne Boivin (Bridgewater State University, USA)
Information Science Reference • © 2023 • 306pp • H/C (ISBN: 9781668468838) • US $215.00

IGI Global
PUBLISHER of TIMELY KNOWLEDGE

701 East Chocolate Avenue, Hershey, PA 17033, USA
Tel: 717-533-8845 x100 • Fax: 717-533-8661
E-Mail: cust@igi-global.com • www.igi-global.com

We strongly believe that the book is dedicated to some prominent mathematicians from ancient Greece: Archimedes, then Persian mathematician: Al-Khwarizmi, who is often called the "father of algebra," and the Indian mathematician: Aryabhata, who is known for his work on algebra and trigonometry, Greek mathematician: Euclid. We must remember the father of the Internet, Dr Vint Cerf and Robert Kahn, who worked on the transmission Control Protocol/ Internet Protocol (TCP/IP), the primary communication protocol that underlies the entire Internet. Lastly, a most profound dedication to John McCarthy, an American computer scientist who coined the term "artificial intelligence" in 1955 and was one of the founders of the field of Artificial intelligence.

Table of Contents

Detailed Table of Contents

Artificial intelligence (AI) is gaining increasing prominence in the field of education, yet comprehensive investigations into its underlying patterns, research limitations, and potential applications remain scarce. ChatGPT, an AI-powered platform developed by the AI research and deployment company OpenAI, allows users to input text instructions and receive prompt textual responses based on its machine learning-driven interactions with online information sources. This study aims to assess the efficacy of ChatGPT in addressing student-centered medical inquiries pertaining to pharmacology, thereby examining its relevance as a self-study resource to enhance the learning experiences of students. Specifically, the study encompasses various domains of pharmacology, such as pharmacokinetics, mechanism of action, clinical uses, adverse effects, contraindications, and drug-drug interactions. The findings demonstrate that ChatGPT provides pertinent and accurate answers to these questions.

In this chapter, the authors explore the pedagogical implication of (ChatGPT) using content analysis. It has several applications in education, teaching, and research. The authors have performed the content analysis to observe the perception of the ChatGPT tool among the general population. The research uses the keywords "ChatGPT and pedagogy" and searches webpages, news articles, white papers, and university guidelines. The researchers use qualitative methodology to create the word cloud of the context extracted from included web pages. The authors have identified ChatGPT as an opportunity to use it as a learning tool, and everyone, including students and teachers, can take help from the application. Teachers are concerned about the increasing prevalence of plagiarism and academic misconduct. ChatGPT is a productive tool for brainstorming and developing the content outline. The reliability of ChatGPT is a question; everyone must use the tool carefully and vet their search from a reliable source or original source of knowledge and information.

In this chapter, the authors use a adapted technology acceptance model (ATAM) to examined the extent to which undergraduate students perceived ChatGPT to be a resource that is useful and easy to use. A pilot study was performed from different discipline of undergraduate students exploring their perceptions of ChatGPT as part of their research process. A statistical analysis was performed using Smart-PLS 4.0. The current study confirmed the use of adapted technology acceptance model for predicting undergraduate student use of ChatGPT.

In this chapter, the authors have compared two applications (ChatGPT and Google Scholar) used among the students and scholars. The researchers have collected the data from Google trends from the past 90 days to compare ChatGPT and Google Scholar. The search criteria were focused on education, from the website and YouTube. ChatGPT was launched on November 30, 2022 by San Francisco–based OpenAI. The results have found an increasing web search trend of ChatGPT from 19th December 2022 till 15th March 2023 with an average percentage of 27.71%. Google Scholar is a well-known tool among scholars, academician, and students. The study found a fluctuating result between the same timeline for web search with an average percentage of 71.71%. The study has found a surprising decreasing YouTube search trends of Google Scholar (10.45%) compared with ChatGPT (35.74%).

In this chapter, the authors present an appropriate use of prompt engineering in ChatGPT in developing a hypothetical case study for students in understanding basic medical science. In artificial intelligence, particularly in natural language processing, the idea of prompt engineering is used. In prompt engineering, the task description that the AI is expected to complete is incorporated into the input, for example, as a question. Students and teachers can develop hypothetical case studies for their learning of the subjects such as pathology, pharmacology, Western medical diagnostic, and internal medicine. The chapter provided the structure of composing the prompt with a hypothetical case study of peptic ulcer disease of a 45 year of women that underwent endoscopy for H. pylori detection.

In this chapter, the authors present a practical application of ChatGPT in teaching pedagogy to improve traditional Chinese medicine student engagement in the subjects pharmacology and pathology. ChatGPT is a conversational AI model developed by OpenAI. It is based on the GPT (generative pre-trained transformer) architecture, specifically GPT-3.5, which is the third iteration of the GPT series. GPT-3.5 is a state-of-the-art language model that has been trained on a vast amount of text data from the internet. The authors presented a teaching plan that involve the use of ChatGPT. The authors bring the idea of "bring your own paper" (BYOP) that could help students and teachers to improve student critical thinking and does allow the use with student's own device (BYOD).

It is true that our beliefs are formed through personal experiences, upbringing, cultural influences, education, and other external factors, and we do not have direct control over our beliefs. Our belief is not entirely under our conscious control. Let's put questions on the ethical use of ChatGPT in education. Why are people fearful of adopting the new technology such as artificial intelligence? The recent launch of ChatGPT, an AI tool, led to banned in several institutions after hearing about its potential as creating content and generating a wide range of textual output. So, how, or can, we inspire the institutions to change their beliefs by not banning the tool? How can we morally use ChatGPT with values, principles, and norms that govern ethical behavior?

ChatGPT's extensive and strong capabilities make it useful for various applications, such as scholarly research, content creation, and language translation. Natural language processing is revolutionized by its capacity to produce human-like writing and deliver pertinent information quickly and accurately. Artificial intelligence aids in class material preparation can improve the efficiency, accessibility, engagement, personalization, and collaboration of the teaching and learning process. As technology evolves, it will likely become an even more essential academic tool. Academics can benefit greatly from ChatGPT's ability to provide content suited to particular subject matter or writing styles. It enables individuals to provide instructional materials that are more precise, pertinent, and consistent with their own preferred writing style. The accessibility of ChatGPT is a major advantage for academics, as it allows them to create class materials quickly and conveniently from anywhere with an internet connection.

The current study reviews the challenges of using ChatGPT within medical education to address challenges and proposed solutions given by experts in the medical field. The scoping review uses PubMED using Levac, Colquhoun, and O'Brien's Framework as a reference. A total of 13 studies, out of 102 communication, viewpoints, comments, editorials, brief reports, and letters were included and reviewed. Two reviewers independently conducted the selection process, and the decision was consensually made. The study excluded the review, original, and irrelevant articles. The scoping review did identify concerns about the ethical and rational use of ChatGPT. Several experts have raised questions on how to use ChatGPT so that it does not violate the epistemological methods, which generally involve the critical examination of the sources, methods, and justifications for knowledge claims.

ChatGPT has emerged as a ubiquitous tool across various age groups in contemporary times. Its widespread adoption is evident as individuals continually engage with it throughout the day, employing diverse prompts and pushing the boundaries of its capabilities. This current research seeks to investigate the perceptions and attitudes of the general populace concerning their usage of ChatGPT in their daily lives. The researcher obtained secondary data from prominent social question-and-answer platforms, predominantly from Quora and Reddit, to achieve this objective. The research centred on three key research questions (RQ), using them as a foundation to uncover pertinent themes and corresponding quotes from users. Employing a convenient method, the researcher efficiently identified noteworthy user quotes, enriching the study with valuable insights.

ChatGPT, an advanced language model based on the GPT-3.5 architecture developed by OpenAI, has garnered significant attention and widespread discussions across various domains. Students, educators, professionals, and businesses alike are engaging in dialogues about the capabilities and potential applications of this cutting-edge technology. The objective of the study is to seek current research directions of ChatGPT by looking at various pre-print servers. The current research surrounding ChatGPT demonstrates a growing interest in its application within the context of medical examination boards. Researchers have observed the potential of ChatGPT as a beneficial tool in supporting medical assessments and evaluations. Other research directions include literature synthesis and clinical decision.

An AI application called ChatGPT has spurred discussions about how it can affect education. The researcher used the PESTEL analysis framework to understand the political, economic, social, technological, environmental, and legal aspects of ChatGPT in education and research. The political aspect observed leaned towards the left orientation. The economic aspect is loosely inclined towards increased productivity and efficiency. The social aspect is directed towards improved social services sectors. The environmental aspect raised concerns about carbon emissions and is yet not explored in detail by researchers, leading to a clear research gap. Last, the authors discuss the legal impact of ChatGPT on the population, and there is an unclear picture towards the AI laws and regulations. There is a need for research to differentiate traditional AI and generative AI. Moreover, generative AI must subclassify before developing the policy for all stakeholders. In conclusion, the responsible use of ChatGPT will benefit the productivity of the general population.

with time. The current chapter has attempted to find solutions for incorporating ChatGPT in teaching pathology. The teacher uses a rational approach to suggest some tips in case the reader does not want to adopt ChatGPT in teaching methods. The authors believe a mixed approach is better and more rational in using ChatGPT in pathology, particularly for students of traditional Chinese medicine who face difficulty with language and understanding Western medicine theories, which contrast with traditional Chinese medicine philosophy.

Foreword

The book *Artificial Intelligence Applications Using ChatGPT in Education: Case Studies and Practices* delves into a topic relevant to academicians and researchers. With the launch of ChatGPT by OpenAI in November 2022, the field of artificial intelligence has witnessed significant advancements. The current book did cover some important topics such as the pedagogical implications of ChatGPT in education, ChatGPT acceptance and use among undergraduate students, a comparative analysis of Scholar Google and ChatGPT use, the epistemology of ChatGPT and a PubMed scoping review on ChatGPT focused on medical education. This book explores the current landscape and provides valuable insights into practical implementation, such as using Prompt engineering in ChatGPT. The book thoroughly examines the advantages of leveraging ChatGPT in education while also documenting the concerns surrounding its potential for irrational or improper use. Addressing these crucial aspects offers a comprehensive exploration of the benefits and potential challenges associated with incorporating ChatGPT into educational contexts. However, the current book may need another volume in the future where it proposes practical solutions to addressing the copyright concern in generating the creativity and innovation in various fields such as entertainment and media. ChatGPT has the potential to write the whole script with the relevant prompt tool, which is a concern and needs further research.

Kashif Nisar
Swinburne University of Technology, Australia

Preface

ChatGPT is recently introduce Artificial intelligence (AI) tool that uses large language model (LLM). It was developed by OpenAI and released in November 2022. Chatbots that use natural language AI, like ChatGPT, use enormous volumes of text data to anticipate words or phrases in a certain context. However, there is lack of knowledge on how to use such tool? What is the acceptability of AI tools in current era? What is the application of ChatGPT in medical education? How to use ChatGPT effectively and is there moral and ethical issues user faces when use ChatGPT?

These all questions that many people think and the current book has efforted to address all questions in each chapter.

THE CHALLENGES

The challenge of establishing a rational use of ChatGPT among traditional Chinese medicine (TCM) students.

The challenge in understanding an awareness on the rational use of ChatGPT in medical education.

The challenging in establishing the acceptance of ChatGPT among students and compare with another tool.

The challenge of developing methods and concept in extracting accurate information through ChatGPT.

ORGANIZATION OF THE BOOK

The book is organized into 15 chapters. A brief description of each of the chapters follows:

Chapter 1 discusses about the use of ChatGPT as a tool for T&CM students in studying Pharmacology.

Chapter 2 explores the pedagogical Implications of ChatGPT in education.

Chapter 3 discusses the ChatGPT acceptance and use among undergraduate students.

Chapter 4 compares the use of ChatGPT and Google Scholar worldwide.

Chapter 5 gives an understanding about the prompt Engineering in ChatGPT tool in generating questions and related answers.

Chapter 6 develops the idea on Bring Your Own Paper (BYOP) involving ChatGPT to enhance Traditional Chinese Medicine (TCM) student's engagement in Pharmacology.

Chapter 7 emphasizes on the ethical and morality of ChatGPT in context to Epistemology.

Chapter 8 unleashed the potential of ChatGPT with given authors own perspective.

Chapter 9 briefs about advancing the Role of ChatGPT in Medical Education using PubMED scoping review methodology.

Chapter 10 discusses the perceptions and attitudes of the general population concerning their usage of ChatGPT in their daily lives.

Chapter 11 analyzed the pre-print manuscript on ChatGPT in context to current research in medical education research and discuss the trends using ChatGPT.

Chapter 12 is understanding the PESTEL analysis framework to discuss the political, economic, social, technological, environmental, and legal aspects of ChatGPT in education and research.

Chapter 13 provides the conceptual model of potential increase risk of Cyberchondriasis after post-ChatGPT era.

Chapter 14 discusses the current policy guideline post-ChatGPT era in education, Research and Public administration.

Chapter 15 explains case studies and educates the reader on how to use ChatGPT effectively in Pathology education to Traditional and complementary medicine students.

Muhammad Shahzad Aslam
School of Traditional Chinese Medicine, Xiamen University Malaysia, Malaysia

Saima Nisar
School of Computing, UUM College of Arts and Sciences, University Utara Malaysia, Sintok, Malaysia

Acknowledgment

We want to express our heartfelt gratitude to all we have enjoyed working with during this and other related projects. Our heartfelt thanks to the IGI Global team for supporting us in writing the book right from the beginning at every stage. Their supervision was instrumental in completing the different phases of this journey.

We especially want to thank our supervisors Prof. IR. Dr Muhammad Syarhabil Ahmad and late Prof. Dr Wan Rozaini Bt Sheik Osman and co-supervisor Prof. Dr Awang Soh Mamat and Dr Alawiyah Bt Abd Wahab, for their expert guidance and unwavering support throughout the research and writing process. Their encouragement and constructive feedback have been invaluable to us.

We are particularly grateful to the students who participated in the study that forms the basis of one of the chapters of this book. Their willingness to share their experiences and perspectives was essential to our research, and we sincerely appreciate their contributions.

Finally, we would like to acknowledge the support of our families and loved ones, who have been our constant encouragement and inspiration throughout our academic careers.

Introduction

The education sector is changing dramatically in today's quickly expanding digital landscape. Innovative technologies such as artificial intelligence and natural language processing are changing how we teach, learn, and engage with educational content. ChatGPT emerges as a valuable tool in this environment, combining the capabilities of advanced language models with the special demands of educators and learners.

ChatGPT is an artificial intelligence-powered conversational bot developed to help and improve the educational experience. ChatGPT, created by OpenAI, harnesses the massive information it has gained from analyzing a wide range of texts, including books, papers, and websites, until its training deadline in September 2021. It can hold natural, human-like conversations, making it a great resource for information, assistance, and support for students, teachers, and educational institutions.

Our book's major purpose is to facilitate personalized and interactive learning experiences. ChatGPT can address various educational topics, from mathematics and physics to literature and history, by leveraging its enormous knowledge base and language understanding capabilities. It may help clarify complex topics, provide explanations, examples, and even problem-solving assistance, making it an excellent virtual companion for learners of all ages.

Our book consists of chapters such as evaluating the efficacy of ChatGPT as a valuable resource for pharmacology studies in traditional and complementary medicine education; exploring the pedagogical implications of ChatGPT in education: pedagogical perspective; ChatGPT acceptance and use among undergraduate students; ChatGPT or Google scholar?: which tool is trending?; how to use prompt engineering for ChatGPT in medical education?; Bring Your Own Paper (BYOP) involving ChatGPT to enhance traditional Chinese medicine students' engagement in pharmacology and the epistemology of ChatGPT; and lastly, discuss the opinion on ChatGPT use in education.

While ChatGPT can provide vital insights and support, it should not be used in place of real teachers and mentors. Instead, it is intended to augment and supplement the existing educational ecosystem, empowering educators and students. ChatGPT aims to provide assistance, promote discovery, and arouse interest, ultimately cultivating a lifelong love of learning.

Let us use the power of AI and human collaboration to unleash new possibilities in education as we embark on this educational journey together. ChatGPT is here to assist in navigating the huge sea of information, create deeper comprehension, and empower us to attain our best potential.

Let us get started with ChatGPT in Education on this transforming learning journey!

Chapter 1
Evaluating the Efficacy of ChatGPT as a Valuable Resource for Pharmacology Studies in Traditional and Complementary Medicine (T&CM) Education

ABSTRACT

Artificial intelligence (AI) is gaining increasing prominence in the field of education, yet comprehensive investigations into its underlying patterns, research limitations, and potential applications remain scarce. ChatGPT, an AI-powered platform developed by the AI research and deployment company OpenAI, allows users to input text instructions and receive prompt textual responses based on its machine learning-driven interactions with online information sources. This study aims to assess the efficacy of ChatGPT in addressing student-centered medical inquiries pertaining to pharmacology, thereby examining its relevance as a self-study resource to enhance the learning experiences of students. Specifically, the study encompasses various domains of pharmacology, such as pharmacokinetics, mechanism of action, clinical uses, adverse effects, contraindications, and drug-drug interactions. The findings demonstrate that ChatGPT provides pertinent and accurate answers to these questions.

DOI: 10.4018/978-1-6684-9300-7.ch001

BACKGROUND

Artificial intelligence's (AI) advantages haven't been fully tapped into in education. The technological and pedagogical expertise of teachers in AI is crucial for the successful integration of AI into education (Celik, 2023). Artificial intelligence (AI) refers to the simulation of human intellect in devices that have been designed to think and behave like people. These robots can carry out activities that ordinarily need human intellect, including as comprehending language, identifying pictures, and making judgements. They are created to learn, reason, and solve problems in a way that is similar to human cognition (O'Connor & ChatGPT, 2023).

ChatGPT allows users to enter text prompts and rapidly generates text responses drawn from its knowledge acquired via machine learning in engagement with the internet. AI platform called ChatGPT is made available to the public in 2022 for free use (Pavlik, 2023). Beyond the academic community, there has been a lot of interest in the release of ChatGPT, a language model that can produce writing that seems real and human-like. ChatGPT is trained on a large dataset of human conversations and can be used to create responses to a wide range of topics and prompts. The chatbot can be used for customer service, content creation, and language translation tasks, creating replies in multiple languages (Aydin & Karaarslan, 2022).

METHODOLOGY

ChatGPT were tested from selected question prepared from pharmacology (Lippincott's Illustrated Reviews Series), fifth edition in Unit VII (chemotherapeutic drug) (Harvey et al., 2011). The unit was selected randomly and the questions were prepared in different domain of drug's pharmacokinetics, mechanism of action, clinical uses, adverse effect, contraindications and drug-drug interactions. Some of the questions were ask from already available text book to test the response of ChatGPT. List of questions prepared to test ChatGPT were given in table 1.

Table 1. List of questions prepared to test ChatGPT

Domain	Drug Selected/ Drug Class	Questions Prepared
1. Pharmacokinetics	Telavancin Erythromycin	1.1. What is the half-life of telavancin? 1.2. What is the half-life of erythromycin?
2. Mechanism of Action	Penicillins Vancomycin Macrolides	2.1. How do Penicillins interfere with bacterial cell wall synthesis? 2.2. How does vancomycin prevent the transglycosylation step in peptidoglycan polymerization? 2.3. Do macrolides act as bactericidal action? 2.4. What is the mode of action of acyclovir?
3. Clinical uses	Cefepime Cefotaxime Clindamycin	3.1. Cefepime is active against which microorganism? 3.2. An elderly diabetic patient is admitted to the hospital with pneumonia. The sputum culture stains for a gram-negative rod. The patient is started on IV ampicillin. Two days later, the patient is not improving, and the microbiology laboratory reports the organism to be a β-lactamase-producing H. influenza. What course of treatment? 3.3. A patient with a gunshot wound to the abdomen, which has resulted in the spillage of intestinal contents, is brought to the emergency room. Which antibiotic would effectively treat infection due to Bacteroides fragilis?
4. Adverse drug effects	Telavancin Tetracycline Minocycline Gentamicin	4.1. What are the adverse effects of telavancin? 4.2. What are the effects of tetracycline on calcified tissues? 4.3. Minocycline produces which kind of adverse effect on the vestibular system? 4.4. What are the adverse effects of aminoglycosides? 4.5. A pregnant woman was hospitalized and catheterized with a Foley catheter. She developed a urinary tract infection caused by Pseudomonas aeruginosa and was treated with gentamicin. Which adverse effects were a risk to the fetus when the woman was on gentamicin? 4.6. Tinnitus, dizziness, blurred vision, and headache indicate toxicity to which antimalarial drugs?
5. Contraindications	Tetracycline	5.1. Tetracyclines are contraindicated under which conditions?
6.Drug-drug interactions	Chloramphenicol Isoniazid Rifampin Ketoconazole Interferon	6.1. Does Chloramphenicol blocks the metabolism of other drugs? 6.2. Isoniazid produces drug interactions with which drugs? 6.3. What is the action of rifampin with cytochrome P450 enzymes? 6.4. Ketoconazole can potentiate the toxicities of which drugs? 6.5. Interferon may potentiate the myelosuppression with which drug?

RESULTS AND DISCUSSION

The answer of the given questions inside the methodology were compared with Lippincott's illustrated reviews. Lippincott's has stated telavancin and erythromycin half-life of 7 to 9 hours and 2 hours respectively. The results on half-life of telavancin and erythromycin using ChatGPT were presented in Figure 1.1 and Figure 1.2.

Figure 1. Pedagogical suggestions in the word cloud

Figure 2. What is the half-life of erythromycin?

When we ask the question about penicillin mechanism of action from ChatGPT then the results were similar to Lippincott which stated that the penicillins interfere with the last step of bacterial cell wall synthesis (transpeptidation or cross-linkage), resulting in exposure of the osmotically less stable membrane. Cell lysis can then occur, either through osmotic pressure or through the activation of autolysins. Similarly, ChatGPT answered vancomycin mechanism in a similar manner as given before about penicillin mechanism. Lippincott stated the mechanism as vancomycin inhibits synthesis of bacterial cell wall phospholipids as well as peptidoglycan polymerization in a time-dependant fashion by binding to the D-Ala-D-Ala side chain of the precursor pentapeptide, which prevents the transglycosylation step in peptidoglycan polymerization, thus weakening the cell wall and damaging the underlying cell membrane. When question ask about macrolides bactericidal action the ChatGPT elaborate it in detail. The results on various questions using ChatGPT about mechanism of action were presented in Figures 3, 4, 5, and 6.

The question about cefepime antimicrobial activity were asked by ChatGPT and they explain it with list of gram-negative and gram-positive bacteria. The response was brief as given in the screenshot but it was found that ChatGPT may produce different answer when the same questions were asked. Lippincott has stated cefepime as classified as a fourth-generation cephalosporin and must be administered parenterally. Cefepime has a wide antibacterial spectrum, being active against streptococci and staphylococci (but only those that are methicillin susceptible). Cefepime is also effective against aerobic gram-negative organisms, such as Enterobacter species, E. coli, K. pneumoniae, P. mirabilis, and P. aeruginosa. When selecting an antibiotic that is active against P. aeruginosa, clinicians should refer to their local antibiograms (laboratory testing for the sensitivity of an isolated bacterial strain to different antibiotics) for direction. The answer about given case studies were clinical and multiple drug combinations were provided. The results on various questions about clinical uses of various drugs were presented in Figures 7, 8, and 9.

Figure 3. How do penicillins interfere with bacterial cell wall synthesis?

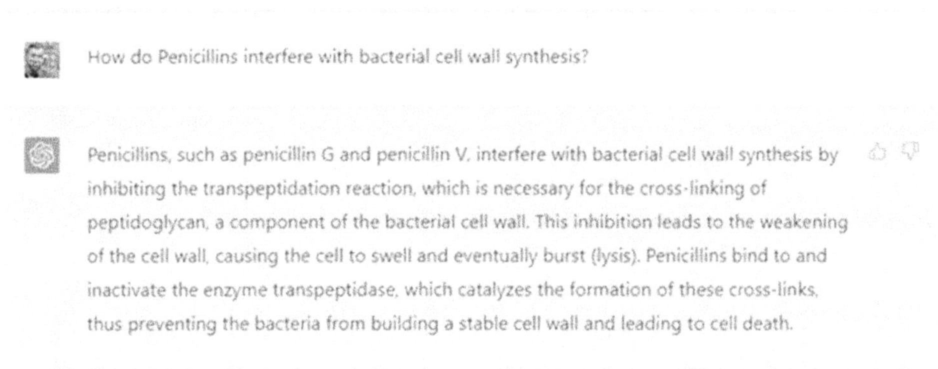
How do Penicillins interfere with bacterial cell wall synthesis?

Penicillins, such as penicillin G and penicillin V, interfere with bacterial cell wall synthesis by inhibiting the transpeptidation reaction, which is necessary for the cross-linking of peptidoglycan, a component of the bacterial cell wall. This inhibition leads to the weakening of the cell wall, causing the cell to swell and eventually burst (lysis). Penicillins bind to and inactivate the enzyme transpeptidase, which catalyzes the formation of these cross-links, thus preventing the bacteria from building a stable cell wall and leading to cell death.

Figure 4. How does vancomycin prevent the transglycosylation step in peptidoglycan polymerization?

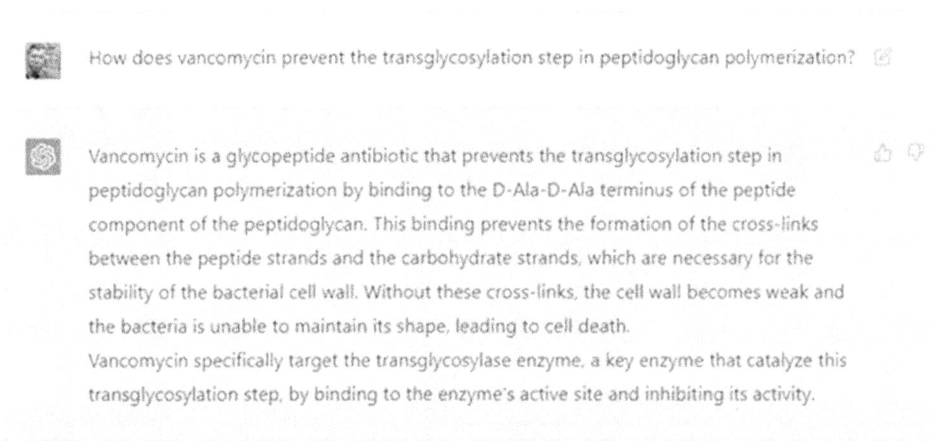
How does vancomycin prevent the transglycosylation step in peptidoglycan polymerization?

Vancomycin is a glycopeptide antibiotic that prevents the transglycosylation step in peptidoglycan polymerization by binding to the D-Ala-D-Ala terminus of the peptide component of the peptidoglycan. This binding prevents the formation of the cross-links between the peptide strands and the carbohydrate strands, which are necessary for the stability of the bacterial cell wall. Without these cross-links, the cell wall becomes weak and the bacteria is unable to maintain its shape, leading to cell death.
Vancomycin specifically target the transglycosylase enzyme, a key enzyme that catalyze this transglycosylation step, by binding to the enzyme's active site and inhibiting its activity.

Figure 5. Do macrolides act as bactericidal action?

Do macrolides act as bactericidal action?

Macrolides, such as erythromycin, azithromycin, and clarithromycin, are generally considered to have bacteriostatic action, meaning they inhibit the growth of bacteria rather than killing them outright. They do this by binding to the 50S ribosomal subunit of bacteria, which prevents the formation of the initiation complex required for protein synthesis. This inhibition of protein synthesis leads to the inhibition of cell growth and multiplication.

However, under certain conditions such as high concentration of the antibiotic, macrolides can have bactericidal action, killing the bacteria. This is because they can cause the accumulation of misfolded proteins and the inhibition of the ribosomal activity, which can lead to the induction of stress response and eventually cell death. Also, macrolides can act as a time-dependent manner in which the prolonged exposure to the antibiotic will increase the chances of killing the bacteria.

Figure 6. What is the mode of action of acyclovir?

What is the mode of action of acyclovir?

Acyclovir is an antiviral medication that is used to treat infections caused by certain types of viruses, including herpes simplex virus (HSV) and varicella-zoster virus (VZV). It works by targeting a specific enzyme, called viral DNA polymerase, that is essential for the replication of the viral DNA.

Acyclovir is a prodrug, which means it is inactive until it is converted into its active form by a viral enzyme called thymidine kinase. This enzyme is present in infected cells but not in normal cells. Once acyclovir is converted into its active form, it is able to bind to the viral DNA polymerase, which is responsible for replicating the viral DNA. This binding leads to the termination of the viral DNA chain, preventing the virus from replicating and spreading to new cells.

Acyclovir primarily acts as a chain terminator of viral DNA. And it has a high affinity for the viral DNA polymerase than the host DNA polymerase. This allows acyclovir to selectively target the virus without harming the host cells.

Figure 7. Cefepime is active against which microorganism?

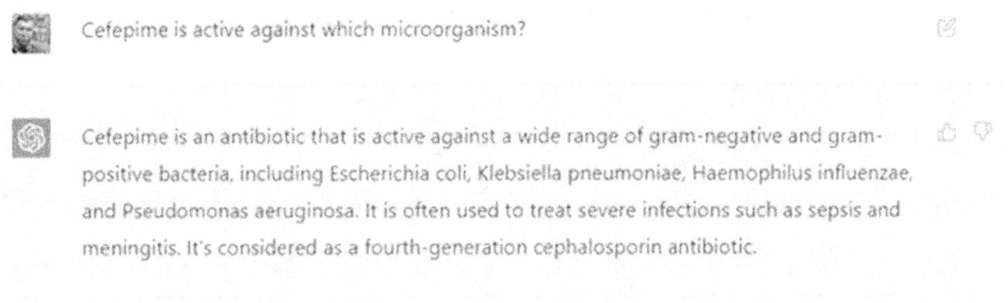

Figure 8. An elderly diabetic patient is admitted to the hospital with pneumonia. The sputum culture stains for a gram-negative rod. The patient is started on IV ampicillin. Two days later, the patient is not improving, and the microbiology laboratory reports the organism to be a β-lactamase-producing H. influenza. What course of treatment?

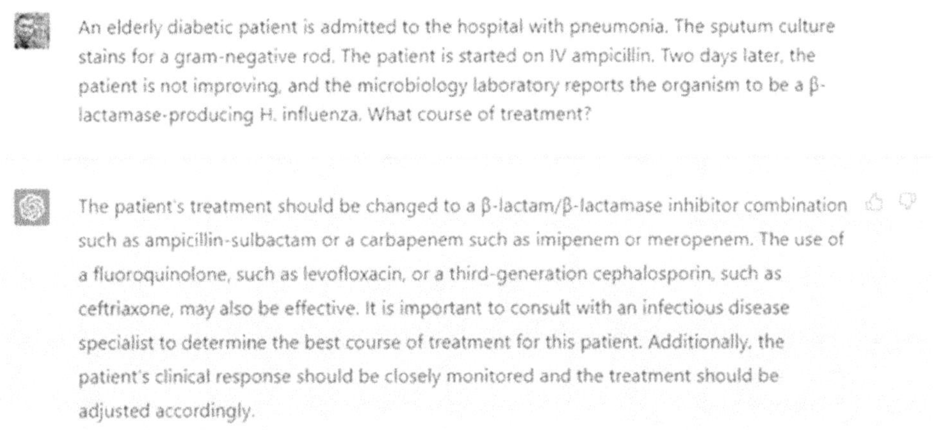

There were six questions asked about the adverse effect of various drugs and the results were consistent with Lippincott. The results on various questions about adverse effects of various drugs were presented in Figures 10, 11, 12, 13, 14, and 15.

Figure 9. A patient with a gunshot wound to the abdomen, which has resulted in the spillage of intestinal contents, is brought to the emergency room. Which antibiotic would effectively treat infection due to Bacteroides fragilis?

A patient with a gunshot wound to the abdomen, which has resulted in the spillage of intestinal contents, is brought to the emergency room. Which antibiotic would effectively treat infection due to Bacteroides fragilis?

Bacteroides fragilis is a gram-negative anaerobic bacteria that is commonly found in the intestinal tract. A patient with a gunshot wound to the abdomen, which has resulted in the spillage of intestinal contents, may be at risk of infection due to Bacteroides fragilis. Effective antibiotics for treating infections due to Bacteroides fragilis include metronidazole and piperacillin-tazobactam. Other antibiotics such as clindamycin, tigecycline and carbapenems may also be effective. However, it is important to note that the choice of antibiotic will depend on the susceptibility of the specific strain of Bacteroides fragilis and the overall health of the patient. A culture and sensitivity test should be done to identify the specific bacteria and its susceptibility to antibiotics before starting any treatment.

Figure 10. What are the adverse effects of telavancin?

What are the adverse effects of telavancin?

Common adverse effects of telavancin include nausea, diarrhea, headache, and injection site reactions. Other possible side effects include kidney dysfunction, decreased white blood cell count, and increased blood levels of creatinine and potassium. Telavancin can also cause allergic reactions, which can be serious in rare cases. It is important to consult a healthcare provider if you experience any serious or persistent side effects while taking telavancin.

Figure 11. What are the effects of tetracycline on calcified tissues?

What are the effects of tetracycline on calcified tissues?

Tetracycline is known to cause discoloration and inhibition of growth in developing teeth and bones. This is because the drug binds to calcium, which is a crucial component of these tissues. Long-term use or high doses of tetracycline can lead to the formation of brownish or grayish discolorations in the teeth, as well as decreased bone growth. These effects are more common in children and adolescents, whose bones and teeth are still developing. It is important to note that these effects may not be reversible and can be permanent.

Figure 12. Minocycline produces which kind of adverse effect on the vestibular system?

Minocycline produces which kind of adverse effect on the vestibular system?

Minocycline can cause vestibular adverse effects such as dizziness and vertigo.

Figure 13. What are the adverse effects of aminoglycosides?

What are the adverse effects of aminoglycosides?

Aminoglycosides are a class of antibiotics that can cause several adverse effects, including:

- Ototoxicity (damage to the ears), which can result in hearing loss or ringing in the ears
- Nephrotoxicity (damage to the kidneys), which can lead to kidney failure
- Neuromuscular toxicity, which can cause muscle weakness or twitching
- Allergic reactions, such as rash or hives
- Gastrointestinal symptoms, such as nausea, vomiting, and diarrhea
- Injection site reactions
- Blood dyscrasias (abnormalities of blood cells)
- Vestibular toxicity, resulting in dizziness or vertigo

It's important to note that these side effects are generally rare, but can occur in certain individuals or with prolonged use of the medication.

Figure 14. A pregnant woman was hospitalized and catheterized with a Foley catheter. She developed a urinary tract infection caused by Pseudomonas aeruginosa and was treated with gentamicin. Which adverse effects were a risk to the fetus when the woman was on gentamicin?

A pregnant woman was hospitalized and catheterized with a Foley catheter. She developed a urinary tract infection caused by Pseudomonas aeruginosa and was treated with gentamicin. Which adverse effects were a risk to the fetus when the woman was on gentamicin?

Gentamicin is an aminoglycoside antibiotic that can cross the placenta and potentially cause adverse effects to the fetus. The potential risks include ototoxicity (damage to the auditory system) and nephrotoxicity (damage to the kidneys). It is important to monitor the fetal well-being and consider alternative antibiotics if necessary.

Figure 15. Tinnitus, dizziness, blurred vision, and headache indicate toxicity to which antimalarial drugs?

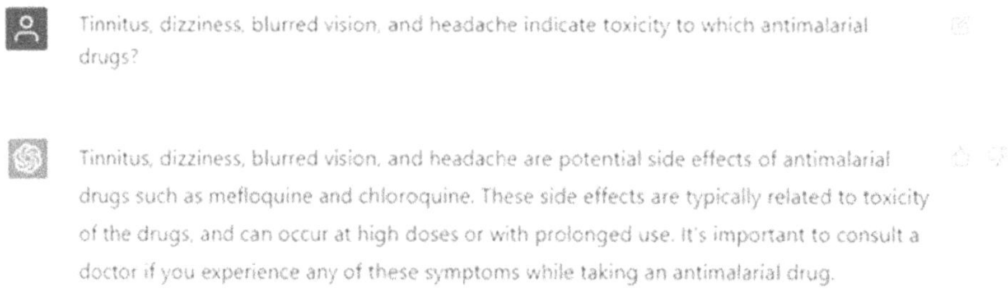
Tinnitus, dizziness, blurred vision, and headache indicate toxicity to which antimalarial drugs?

Tinnitus, dizziness, blurred vision, and headache are potential side effects of antimalarial drugs such as mefloquine and chloroquine. These side effects are typically related to toxicity of the drugs, and can occur at high doses or with prolonged use. It's important to consult a doctor if you experience any of these symptoms while taking an antimalarial drug.

Lippincott has stated about tetracycline contraindicated to renally impaired patients except doxycycline. Accumulation of tetracyclines may aggravate preexisting azotemia (a higher-thannormal level of urea or other nitrogen-containing compounds in the blood) by interfering with protein synthesis, thus promoting amino acid degradation. The tetracyclines should not be employed in pregnant or breast-feeding women or in children less than 8 years of age. The result about tetracycline contraindications produced by ChatGPT were presented in table 5.1.

Figure 16. Tetracyclines are contraindicated under which conditions?

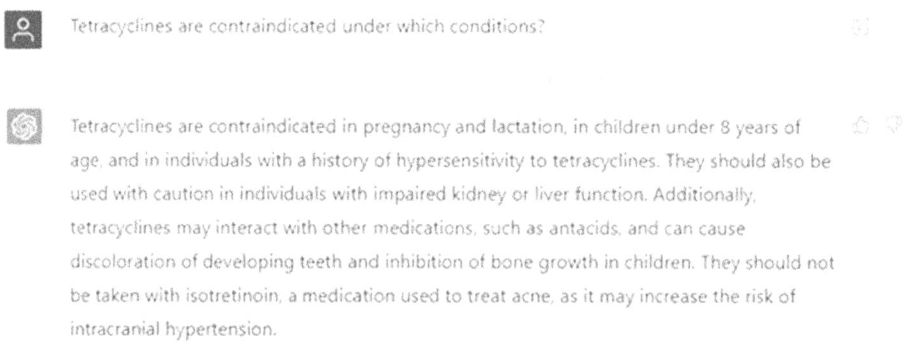
Tetracyclines are contraindicated under which conditions?

Tetracyclines are contraindicated in pregnancy and lactation, in children under 8 years of age, and in individuals with a history of hypersensitivity to tetracyclines. They should also be used with caution in individuals with impaired kidney or liver function. Additionally, tetracyclines may interact with other medications, such as antacids, and can cause discoloration of developing teeth and inhibition of bone growth in children. They should not be taken with isotretinoin, a medication used to treat acne, as it may increase the risk of intracranial hypertension.

During investigation to compare the drug interaction given in Lippincott and ChatGPT, it was found that the question on chloramphenicol effect on drug metabolism on other drugs were not completely address. The results on various questions about different drug interactions were presented in Figures 17, 18, 19, 20, and 21.

Figure 17. Does Chloramphenicol block the metabolism of other drugs?

Does Chloramphenicol blocks the metabolism of other drugs?

Chloramphenicol is a broad-spectrum antibiotic that has been known to interact with other drugs by inhibiting the metabolism of certain drugs through the inhibition of CYP450 enzymes, specifically CYP3A4, CYP2C9, and CYP2C19. This can lead to increased blood levels of those drugs and potentially increased risk of side effects. It is important to inform your healthcare provider of any other medications you are taking before starting treatment with chloramphenicol.

Figure 18. Isoniazid produces drug interactions with which drugs?

Isoniazid produces drug interactions with which drugs?

Isoniazid can interact with a variety of drugs, including but not limited to:

- Rifampin: reduces the effectiveness of isoniazid
- Antidepressants (such as fluoxetine and sertraline): increases the risk of a dangerous condition called serotonin syndrome
- Acetaminophen: increases the risk of liver damage
- Ethambutol: increases the risk of optic neuritis (inflammation of the optic nerve)
- Warfarin: increases the risk of bleeding
- Pyrazinamide: increases the risk of liver damage
- Griseofulvin: reduces the effectiveness of isoniazid
- Phenytoin: increases the risk of side effects of isoniazid, such as liver damage
- Methotrexate: increases the risk of side effects of isoniazid, such as liver damage

It is important to inform your doctor and pharmacist of all medications you are taking to avoid potential drug interactions.

Figure 19. What is the action of rifampin with cytochrome P450 enzymes?

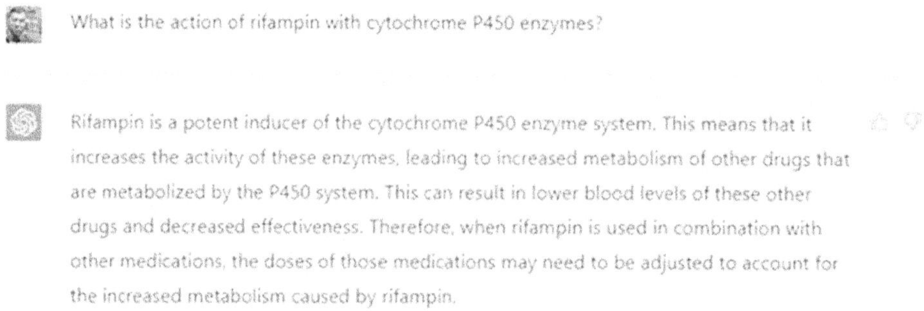

The rapid advancement of computing technologies has facilitated the implementation of Artificial Intelligence (AI) in education applications (Hwang et al., 2020). AI can be used outside of typical computer settings and is widely accessible through inexpensive smart gadgets, making it widely available to the general public (Alam, 2021). A new pre-trained language model chatGPT was launched on Nov 30, 2022 (Zhang et al., 2022). Pre-trained language models have achieved striking success in natural language processing (NLP), leading to a paradigm shift from supervised learning to pre-training followed by fine-tuning (Wang et al., 2022).

Pharmacology is one the difficult subject for undergraduate students in allied health science as they inability to see the linkages between pharmacology theory and clinical practise. Previous research on ungraduate nursing students has shown that students frequently divide their understanding of pharmacology into scientific principles (such as the mechanisms of actions of drugs, distribution throughout the body, and metabolism by the liver or kidney) and nursing principles (assessing the patient's ability to consume the medication, preparing the medication for administration) (Manias et al., 1999; Manias et al., 2000). ChatGPT is new AI assisted language model that is trained for dialogues. There are several manuscripts endorsed the effectiveness of ChatGPT in medical education (Gilson et al., 2023; Lyu et al., 2023; Sharma et al., 2023; Hariri, 2023; Zhi et al., 2023). Figure 20 illustrate the brief summary of use of ChatGPT in various medical field.

Figure 20. Literature evidence of the effectiveness of ChatGPT in medical education

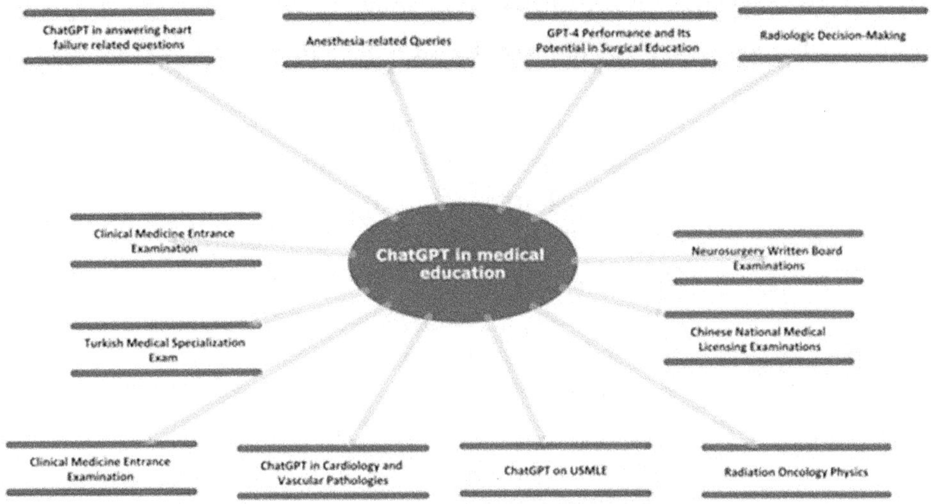

The current study observes good accuracy in practicing pharmacology questions for undergraduate students. T&CM students who face difficulty in learning the subject pharmacology can use it as self-learning method to practice the questions. However, there is still need of some improvement in ChatGPT to addressed more complexed questions, cross-disciplinary answer and research-based question.

When Yee Hui Yeo et al., assess the capabilities of ChatGPT in delivering accurate and consistent information, personalized guidance, and emotional support for individuals with cirrhosis and hepatocellular carcinoma (HCC). The researcher gauged ChatGPT's effectiveness and revealed that ChatGPT demonstrated a strong ability to provide detailed insights about cirrhosis (achieving 79.1% accuracy) and HCC (achieving 74.0% accuracy). However, a smaller proportion of its responses (47.3% for cirrhosis and 41.1% for HCC) were considered comprehensive. Notably, the model's performance excelled in conveying fundamental knowledge, lifestyle recommendations, and treatment insights, while it showed comparatively weaker performance in areas like diagnosis and preventive medicine. In terms of addressing quality metric-related questions, ChatGPT answered accurately in 76.9% of cases but struggled to specify decision-making thresholds and treatment durations. The model also demonstrated limited familiarity with regional guideline variations, particularly regarding HCC screening criteria. Nevertheless, it stood out in providing practical, well-rounded advice for patients and caregivers, guiding them on next steps and coping strategies following a new diagnosis (Yeo et al., 2023).

Jialin Liu, Changyu Wang, and Siru Liu has demonstrated that ChatGPT has its prowess in intelligent question-answering, offering dependable insights into diseases and medical inquiries. Furthermore, its application extends to medical documentation, where ChatGPT has showcased its efficacy in producing patient clinical letters, radiology reports, medical notes, and discharge summaries. This multifaceted utilization contributes to enhanced efficiency and precision for healthcare practitioners. However, they concluded in their work to take cautious and proactive in addressing potential risks when using ChatGPT to ensure the safety and quality of patient care (Liu et al., 2023).

Figure 21. Grade of responses by the ChatGPT language model to questions related to (a) cirrhosis and (b) hepatocellular carcinoma (HCC). The percentage of responses being graded as comprehensive, correct but inadequate, mixed with correct and incorrect/outdated data, and completely incorrect were provided. GPT, generative pre-trained transformer.
Source: Yeo et al. (2023)

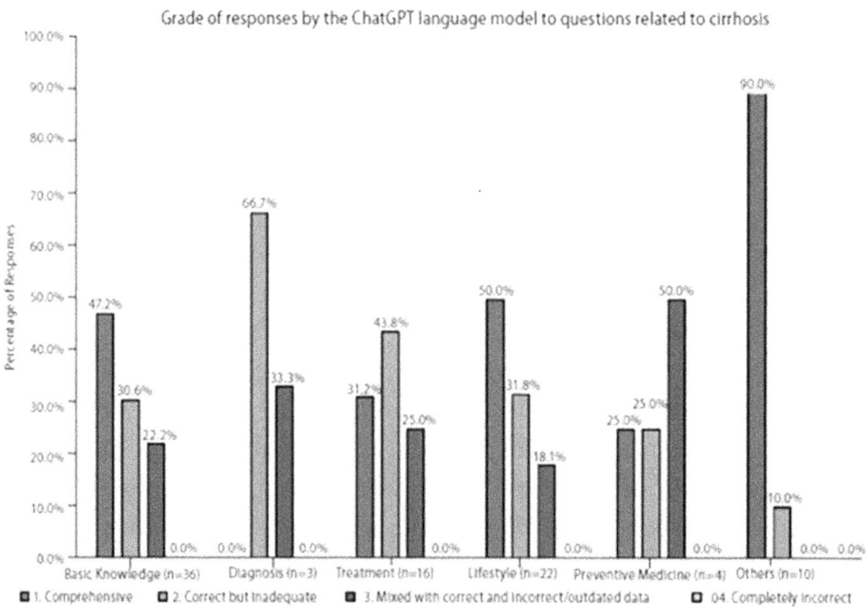

A

Figure 22. ChatGPT effectiveness in clinical practice
Source: Adapted from Liu et al. (2023)

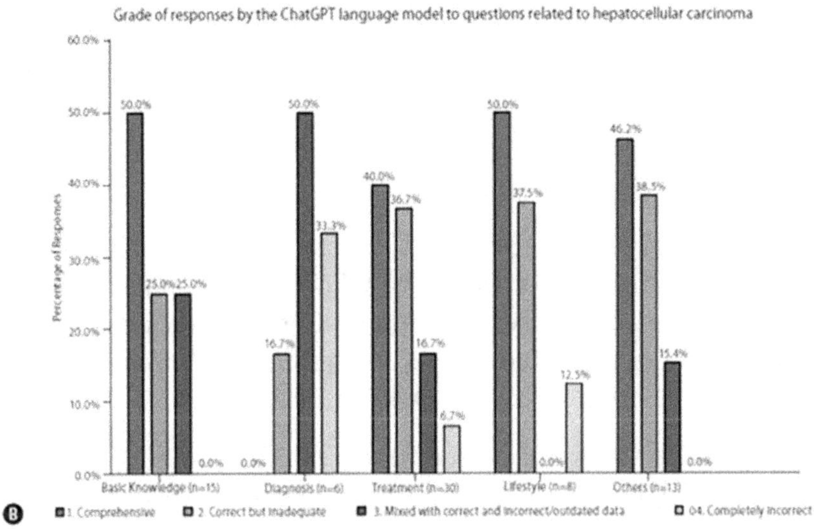

CONCLUSION

ChatGPT an indeed a good tool for self-studying T&CM students studying pharmacology. If the website includes reference or source under each answer stated, then students can prepare their own notes without consultation of the book. ChatGPT can work as quick guide for students in a short time. The answer given on each question were good and comprehensive for T&CM students. The authors observe that the content may not be enough for the researcher and may need more details such as mechanism of action and cross-disciplinary approach to every question. There is indeed need of deeper integration of scholarly literature such as PubMED and other scholar google so that T&CM students will receive deeper knowledge.

REFERENCES

Alam, A. (2021). Possibilities and Apprehensions in the Landscape of Artificial Intelligence in Education. *2021 International Conference on Computational Intelligence and Computing Applications (ICCICA)*, 1–8. 10.1109/ICCICA52458.2021.9697272

Aydin, Ö., & Karaarslan, E. (2022). OpenAI ChatGPT Generated Literature Review : Digital Twin in Healthcare. In *Emerging Computer Technologies 2* (Vol. 2). İzmir Akademi Dernegi. doi:10.2139srn.4308687

Celik, I. (2023). Towards Intelligent-TPACK: An empirical study on teachers' professional knowledge to ethically integrate artificial intelligence (AI)-based tools into education. *Computers in Human Behavior*, *138*, 107468. doi:10.1016/j.chb.2022.107468

Gilson, A., Safranek, C. W., Huang, T., Socrates, V., Chi, L., Taylor, R. A., & Chartash, D. (2023). How Does ChatGPT Perform on the United States Medical Licensing Examination? The Implications of Large Language Models for Medical Education and Knowledge Assessment. *JMIR Medical Education*, *9*, e45312. doi:10.2196/45312 PMID:36753318

Hariri, W. (2023). Analyzing the Performance of ChatGPT in Cardiology and Vascular Pathologies. doi:/v1www.researchsquare.com/article/rs-2782768/v1 doi:10.21203/rs.3.rs-2782768

Hwang, G.-J., Xie, H., Wah, B. W., & Gašević, D. (2020). Vision, challenges, roles and research issues of Artificial Intelligence in Education. *Computers and Education: Artificial Intelligence*, *1*, 100001. doi:10.1016/j.caeai.2020.100001

Liu, J., Wang, C., & Liu, S. (2023). Utility of ChatGPT in Clinical Practice. *Journal of Medical Internet Research*, *25*, e48568. doi:10.2196/48568 PMID:37379067

Lyu, Q., Tan, J., Zapadka, M. E., Ponnatapura, J., Niu, C., Myers, K. J., Wang, G., & Whitlow, C. T. (2023). Translating Radiology Reports into Plain Language using ChatGPT and GPT-4 with Prompt Learning: Promising Results, Limitations, and Potential. *Visual Computing for Industry, Biomedicine, and Art*, *6*(1), 9. Advance online publication. doi:10.118642492-023-00136-5 PMID:37198498

Manias, E., Bullock, S., & Bennett, R. (1999). A computer-assisted learning program in pharmacology: Integrating scientific and nursing knowledge. *Contemporary Nurse*, *8*(2), 23–29. doi:10.5172/conu.1999.8.2.23 PMID:11096792

Manias, E., Bullock, S., & Bennett, R. (2000). Formative evaluation of a computer-assisted learning program in pharmacology for nursing students. *Computer Nurse, 18*(6), 265–271. https://pubmed.ncbi.nlm.nih.gov/11105400/

O'Connor, S., & Chat, G. P. T.ChatGPT. (2023). Open artificial intelligence platforms in nursing education: Tools for academic progress or abuse? *Nurse Education in Practice*, *66*, 103537. doi:10.1016/j.nepr.2022.103537 PMID:36549229

Pavlik, J. V. (2023). *Collaborating With ChatGPT: Considering the Implications of Generative Artificial Intelligence for Journalism and Media Education*. doi:10.1177/10776958221149577

Sharma, P., Thapa, K., Thapa, D., Dhakal, P., Upadhaya, M. D., Adhikari, S., & Khanal, S. R. (2023). Performance of ChatGPT on USMLE: Unlocking the Potential of Large Language Models for AI-Assisted Medical Education. https://arxiv.org/abs/2307.00112

Wang, H., Li, J., Wu, H., Hovy, E., & Sun, Y. (2022). Pre-Trained Language Models and Their Applications. *Engineering (Beijing)*. Advance online publication. doi:10.1016/j.eng.2022.04.024

Yeo, Y. H., Samaan, J. S., Ng, W. H., Ting, P.-S., Trivedi, H., Vipani, A., Ayoub, W., Yang, J. D., Liran, O., Spiegel, B., & Kuo, A. (2023). Assessing the performance of ChatGPT in answering questions regarding cirrhosis and hepatocellular carcinoma. *Clinical and Molecular Hepatology*, *29*(3), 721–732. doi:10.3350/cmh.2023.0089 PMID:36946005

Zhang, B., Ding, D., & Jing, L. (2022). How would Stance Detection Techniques Evolve after the Launch of ChatGPT? https://doi.org/https://doi.org/10.48550/arXiv.2212.14548

Zhi, T., Lei, L., Renyuan, W., & Song, G. (2023). Performance of ChatGPT on Chinese National Medical Licensing Examinations: A Five-Year Examination Evaluation Study for Physicians, Pharmacists and Nurses. https://doi.org/https://doi.org/10.1101/2023.07.09.23292415

Chapter 2
Exploring the Pedagogical Implications of ChatGPT in Education:
Pedagogical Perspective

ABSTRACT

In this chapter, the authors explore the pedagogical implication of (ChatGPT) using content analysis. It has several applications in education, teaching, and research. The authors have performed the content analysis to observe the perception of the ChatGPT tool among the general population. The research uses the keywords "ChatGPT and pedagogy" and searches webpages, news articles, white papers, and university guidelines. The researchers use qualitative methodology to create the word cloud of the context extracted from included web pages. The authors have identified ChatGPT as an opportunity to use it as a learning tool, and everyone, including students and teachers, can take help from the application. Teachers are concerned about the increasing prevalence of plagiarism and academic misconduct. ChatGPT is a productive tool for brainstorming and developing the content outline. The reliability of ChatGPT is a question; everyone must use the tool carefully and vet their search from a reliable source or original source of knowledge and information.

DOI: 10.4018/978-1-6684-9300-7.ch002

BACKGROUND

ChatGPT is a public tool developed by OpenAI using Generative Pretrained Transformer (GPT) (Lund & Wang, 2023; Rudolph et al., 2023). While the previous class of AI models have primarily been Deep Learning (DL) models, designed to learn and recognize patterns in data, Large Language Model (LLM) was developed recently by OpenAI. It is a new type of AI algorithm trained to predict the likelihood of a given sequence of words based on the context of the words that come before it. As a result, if LLMs are trained on enough text data, they can produce novel word sequences. ChatGPT is powered by GPT3.5, an LLM trained on the OpenAI 175B parameter foundation model and a large corpus of text data from the Internet via reinforcement and supervised learning methods.

ChatGPT is useful in education. Several articles have been published to endorse its efficiency in education. For example, ChatGPT demonstrated a high level of concordance and insight in United States Medical Licensing Exam (USMLE), which consists of three exams: Step 1, Step 2CK, and Step 3. Without any extra instruction or reinforcement, ChatGPT passed all three exams with a score at or around the passing mark (Kung et al., 2023). Another study has confirmed the efficiency of ChatGPT in answering the questions in the USMLE (Gilson et al., 2023).

The term "digital era" refers to the period in history characterized by the widespread use and integration of digital technologies in various aspects of society, including communication, commerce, education, and entertainment. The current technological revolution has reached all social classes and its educative use by teachers has not gone unnoticed. The introduction of 2.0 tools has become a reality in many classrooms. In order to evaluate the digital competence of teachers, different dimensions must be considered, including knowledge and educative use (Guillén-Gámez et al., 2021).

The objective of the current study is to understand the pedagogical implications of ChatGPT in education from current available online resources. The research questions include the following items.

1. What are the advantages and disadvantages of using ChatGPT in education?
2. How to utilize the potential pedagogical ChatGPT in education?

3. What are the current online resource suggestions for using ChatGPT in education?

METHODOLOGY

The researcher uses a systematic sampling method to collect the data from a google search using the keywords "chatgpt and pedagogy" from the news articles, white papers, webpages and university guidelines. The information was retrieved on 19th February 2023, and a total of fifty-five webpages were identified. The information was screened manually, and relevant website pages were included based on given above research questions (Table 1). Irrelevant web pages, a language other than English, content that was not relevant to our research questions, and closed-access content were excluded. The website search using google is not stable and keeps changing every day. As a result, information retrieved on 18th February 2023 was included in the study. The information was extracted manually by reading the content, and the answers to focused questions were identified as given in Table 1. A total of twenty-five webpages were included to study the research questions, whereas thirty webpages were excluded. Text-driven content analyses are conducted by a researcher from the presented texts in Table 1 and developed word cloud (Zygomatic, 2003).

RESULTS AND DISCUSSION

Dr. Grace Aguiling-Dalisay, president of the Center for Educational Measurement, said that AI, specifically the "AI chat program ChatGPT, should open up more opportunities instead of being an avenue for cheating and plagiarism" (Red Mendoza, 2023). A Bloomberg Opinion column asserted that ChatGPT "AI will almost certainly help kill the college essay" (Gilliard & Rorabaugh, 2023). The University of Utah is developing and revising policies for its students using AI tools such as ChatGPT. According to them, "Students should seek guidance from their instructors before utilizing AI generative tools for assignments." If students choose to use these tools in some capacity related to creative work, they must make evident any portion of the work generated by the AI tool and which AI tool they used". "An individual faculty member may craft specific policies and communicate via syllabi and/or Canvas relating to the use of such tools in their courses. Please note that this is interim guidance as we continue to explore and understand the possibilities and challenges of these tools" (Hagood, 2023). Sarah Parsons, Hannah Davis, Rene Caputo and Miranda Welsh have written their opinion in "THE CHRONICLES," "If we view chatGPT as a tool, rather than a threat, maybe (just maybe) a future world with ChatGPT will be a world with more "good" writers." Michael Bugeja, a regular contributor at Poynter has given a piece of suggestion to the lecturer, "In the wake of AI chatbots, professors are scrambling to find replacements for the term paper. Let's hope they abandon it and focus on reading" (Bugeja, 2023). A list of Pedagogical implications has been given in Table 1. Figure 1 and Figure 2 has extracted the word cloud and summary from the suggestions given by various writer of the content included in current manuscript.

FUTURE RESEARCH DIRECTIONS

It is essential to assess the reliability of the content given by ChatGPT. The UNICEF had published the report titled as "Safer Chatbots Implementation Guide" and aims to bring awareness about implementation guidelines by offering established and validated frameworks for integrating enhanced safety protocols into all chatbots that cater to users in potentially precarious situations. This is particularly relevant for individuals like girls and women, as well as vulnerable children in contexts such as refugees and migrants (Unicef, 2022).

There is a needs much upgradation of ChatGPT, such as the real-time update of content. The speed of developing new knowledge and new information has increased. Therefore, the researchers need to develop the real-time update of knowledge given by ChatGPT. Moreover, including sources or citations in answering any questions requires time. If anyone asks questions using the tool, the application must provide the source of information. If ChatGPT creates new content, then there must be the inclusion of a watermark/symbol/pattern that represents the writing source ChatGPT. Although there is some

Table 1. Pedagogical implications of ChatGPT

Source	Benefits	Disadvantages	Suggestions	Reference
Kevin Roose, The New York times	ChatGPT will be an effective teaching tool, improving student cognitive capacity and it is not possible to block the application	-	Do not ban ChatGPT, live it with the adaptation of technology	(Roose, 2023)
Ames Southworth, University affairs	-	ChatGPT has the potential to disrupt our ability to think. It has the potential to write a literature review.	It is suggested to avoid generic essay. Implementation of ethical ChatGPT to incorporate it into teaching and learning using extensive feedback and revision process.	(Southworth, 2023)
Teachers College Newsroom, Columbia University	ChatGPT help teachers plan lessons and grade papers.	Cheating	Teacher design more active, culturally relevant learning environments.	(Newsroom, 2023)
Brett Henebery, The educator	ChatGPT can be used for tasks such as answering questions, generating and rewording text, and even writing code.	ChatGPT could affect the critical thinking.	Striking the right balance between fundamentals and advance use of artificial intelligence.	(Henebery, 2023)
Vineeta Dwivedi, The Hindu businessline	Teachers can use it to create educational content and question banks for quizzes and exams. ChatGPT helps in providing personal tutoring.	Loss of basic cognitive skills	Teachers are advice to ask assignment related to personal reflection, creative thinking. Students should have guidelines for adequately citing sources. The institutions must develop policy on rational use of ChatGPT.	(Dwivedi, 2023)
Ethan Steinberg, The Tufts Daily	ChatGPT was used to develop the software program, abilities to compose essays and generate ideas.	Plagiarism issues	Teachers suggest to their respective institutions to develop the policy on ChatGPT use.	(Steinberg, 2023)
Hope 103.2 Network	Easily accessible and user-friendly.	-	The teacher asked students to complete their assignment at the site and hand-written assignments could be a solution. Development of real-time feedback on assignment.	(Annonymous, 2023)

continues on following page

Table 1. Continued

Source	Benefits	Disadvantages	Suggestions	Reference
Kelsey Goodwin, W&L Magazine	ChatGPT helps in research tasks by providing writing support, generating citations, answering questions related to specific fields of study.	ChatGPT could develop misleading information. ChatGPT produces predicting information, based upon large dataset.	The teachers can asked students assignments that are of practical value such as video projects, podcast assignments, and research such as interview methods or data generation.	(Goodwin, 2023)
João Paulo Meneses, Macau business	ChatGPT use as personal assistant to quickly and easily produce work.	Plagiarism issues	Teacher re-evaluate pedagogical approaches.	(Meneses, 2023)
Adam Au, South China Morning Post	-	Cheating, wrong answers, weak analysis, displacing our ability to think, create and collaborate	Teachers may design exercises for students to analyze the AI-assembled products to improve their critical thinking. Implementation of in-class assessments for students.	(Au, 2023)
Larry Ferlazzo, EdW	ChatGPT can develop historical biographies; develop essays of different kind; teachers can generate lesion plan	Bias information, cheating	Teacher can asked the students to use hand written essays.	(Ferlazzo, 2023)
Dartmouth	ChatGPT could be useful to get students to think in new ways about writing and examine what goes into writing a good essay.	Mis-information	Development of coherent policy between different discipline.	(Dartmouth, 2023)
Nandini Sircar, Khaleej Times	Biggest drivers of human productivity	Stunt critical thinking	Assignments and all assessments (tests) will need to take place during class time	(Sircar, 2023)
John Villasenor, Scientific American	Clear, long-form answers to complex questions	ChatGPT answer could be doubtful in quality, accuracy and originality	Hand written essays, ethically and productively use of ChatGPT	(Villasenor, 2023)
Dawn Gilmore, Anitra Nottingham, Marcelo Zerwes, RMIT University	Creating written content, creating a course outline, draft scripts for videos and podcasts	Cheating	Putting pedagogy first than technology will help in solving the problem	(Gilmore et al., 2023)
Chris gilliard and Pete rorabaugh, Slate	Educators have to adapt discussions, activities, and assessments to the changed environment that it creates.	Plagiarism	Plagiarism detector software such as GPTZero and Student surveillance	(Gilliard & Rorabaugh, 2023)

continues on following page

Table 1. Continued

Source	Benefits	Disadvantages	Suggestions	Reference
T. Chase Hagood, The University of Utah	Automate content generation in multiple categories	Increase in cases of academic misconduct due to improper citation or attribution when using tools like ChatGPT.	Revising policies on AI to uplift educational integrity	(Hagood, 2023)
Brandon Paykamian, govtech	ChatGPT can solve complex questions and even write coherent essays.	Academic dishonesty	Faculty just need to adapt to different learning styles	(Paykamian, 2023)
Robert Hunt and Drew Dickens, The Dallas Morning news	ChatGPT has the ability to handle complex task.	Cheating and plagiarism	Introducing subjectivity into the testing and grading process	(Hunt & Dickens, 2023)
Adam Voigt	ChatGPT can write essays or complete tasks such as a student's homework.	Academic integrity compromised	Flipped learning	(Voigt, 2023)
Julian Hartman-Sigall, the daily princetonian	Human-like text responses	Academic integrity compromised	ChatGPT could incorporate into lessons and compare with human written content and AI written content	(Hartman-Sigall, 2023)
Phillip Sitter, Ames Tribune	ChatGPT is part of a new generation of AI systems called "large language models" that can converse, generate readable text on demand and even produce novel images and video based on what they've learned from a vast database of digital books, online writings and other media.	Plagiarism	Institutions need to develop policies and procedures around AI and how faculty might use the technology.	(Sitter, 2023)
Sarah Parsons, Hannah Davis, Rene Caputo and Miranda Welsh, The chronicles	Brainstorming, outlining, or thesis writing phase, may be of some use.	Plagiarism Academic integrity compromised	Use ChatGPT as a tool	(Parsons et al., 2023)
Michael Bugeja, Poynter	ChatGPT can compose essays	Academic dihonesty	Written assignment could replace it with reading paper book and real time discussions. Flip teaching	(Bugeja, 2023)
Vijay Victor, deccan herald	AI-powered content generators	Plagiarism	The long-term plan should be a phased integration of AI into the curriculum and a shift from pedagogy and andragogy to heutagogy, or more student-centered and student-led instructional strategies.	(Victor, 2023)

Figure 1. Pedagogical suggestions in the word cloud

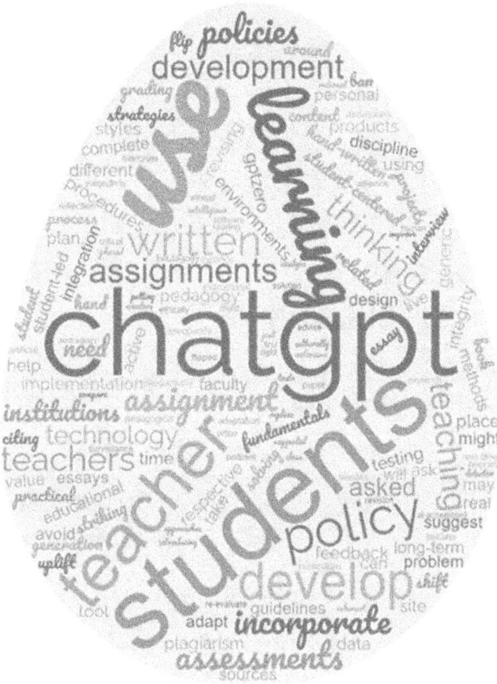

Figure 2. Summary of pros and cons of pedagogical implication of ChatGPT in education

Pros	Cons
ChatGPT is an effective Teaching tool.	ChatGPT may declince critical thinking.
ChatGPT helps in improving cognition.	ChatGPT could become a tool to Cheats.
Helps teacher to devlop lession plan and grading the assessment.	Loss of basic cognitive functions
ChGPT helps in rewriting, generating code in computer programming	Plagariarsm issues
ChatGPT is easy to access and use	Missleading information
ChatGPT provide personal assisgance	Academic dishonesty
Improve the productivity	
ChatGPT can solve complex problems	
ChatGPT helps in Brainstorming	

Figure 3. Challenges and ethical implication of ChatGPT
Source: UNESCO (2023)

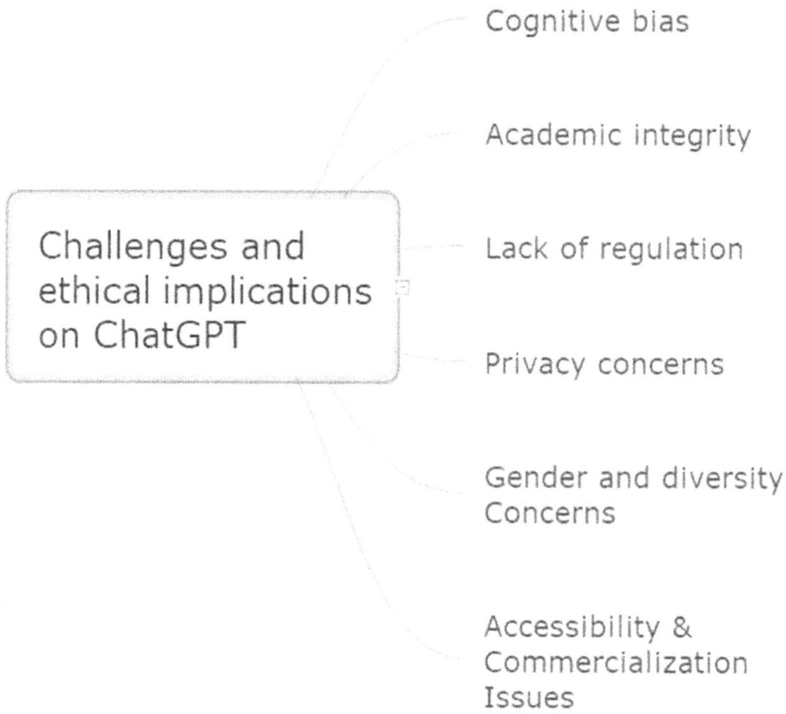

available tool to catch ChatGPT content, nerveless, these tools can crack easily, and we cannot rely on them.

CONCLUSION

ChatGPT is a good tool in all disciplines as its works like a language calculator. There is no need to be fearful of the potential harm caused by ChatGPT. Including a new tool allows an academician to upgrade the pedagogical methodology such as real-time assessment, paper assessment and flip classroom environment. Time is needed to get rid of old pedagogy and advance it to a practical approach. Moreover, there is a need for the inclusion of subjective-based learning. Subjective-based learning will involve the introspective of the students. Therefore, affective and psychomotor learning methodologies must be preferred over cognitive learning.

REFERENCES

Anonymous. (2023). *How ChatGPT Will Impact the Future of Education.* Hope 103.2. https://hope1032.com.au/stories/life/education/2023/how-chatgpt-will-impact-the-future-of-education/

Au, A. (2023). *Inevitable rise of ChatGPT and other AI tools must be managed rather than resisted.* South China Morning Post. https://www.scmp.com/comment/opinion/article/3208914/inevitable-rise-chatgpt-and-other-ai-tools-must-be-managed-rather-resisted

Bugeja, M. (2023). *If AI kills the essay, I will be a pallbearer at the funeral.* Poynter. https://www.poynter.org/commentary/2023/will-chatgpt-kill-term-papers-essays/

Dartmouth. (2023). *ChatGPT Gets Dartmouth Talking*. Dartmouth. https://home.dartmouth.edu/news/2023/02/chatgpt-gets-dartmouth-talking

Dwivedi, V. (2023). Teaching in times of ChatGPT. *The Hindu Businessline.* https://www.thehindubusinessline.com/opinion/teaching-in-times-of-chatgpt/article66522426.ece

Ferlazzo, L. (2023). *Educators Need to Get With the AI Program. ChatGPT, More Specifically.* Education Week. https://www.edweek.org/teaching-learning/opinion-educators-need-to-get-with-the-ai-program-chatgpt-more-specifically/2023/01

Gilliard, C., & Rorabaugh, P. (2023). *You're Not Going to Like How Colleges Respond to ChatGPT.* Slate. https://slate.com/technology/2023/02/chat-gpt-cheating-college-ai-detection.html

Gilmore, D., Nottingham, A., Zerwes, M., & University, R. (2023). *ChatGPT as a course content creator.* RMIT University. https://www.timeshighereducation.com/campus/chatgpt-and-learning-design-what-online-content-creation-opportunities-does-it-offer

Gilson, A., Safranek, C. W., Huang, T., Socrates, V., Chi, L., Taylor, R. A., & Chartash, D. (2023). How Does ChatGPT Perform on the United States Medical Licensing Examination? The Implications of Large Language Models for Medical Education and Knowledge Assessment. *JMIR Medical Education, 9*(1), e45312. doi:10.2196/45312 PMID:36753318

Goodwin, K. (2023). W&L Dialogues on the Future of AI. *W&L Magazine*. https://columns.wlu.edu/wl-dialogues-on-the-future-of-ai/

Guillén-Gámez, F. D., Mayorga-Fernández, M., Bravo-Agapito, J., & Escribano-Ortiz, D. (2021). Analysis of Teachers' Pedagogical Digital Competence: Identification of Factors Predicting Their Acquisition. *Technology, Knowledge and Learning*, *26*(3), 481–498. doi:10.100710758-019-09432-7

Hagood, T. C. (2023). *ChatGPT message to faculty*. The University of Utah. https://attheu.utah.edu/facultystaff/chatgpt-message-to-faculty/

Hartman-Sigall, J. (2023). *University declines to ban ChatGPT, releases faculty guidance for its usage*. The Princetonian. https://www.dailyprincetonian.com/article/2023/01/university-declines-ban-chatgpt-releases-faculty-guidance-for-usage

Henebery, B. (2023). *How schools can strike the right balance with ChatGPT*. The Educator K/12. https://www.theeducatoronline.com/k12/news/how-schools-can-strike-the-right-balance-with-chatgpt/281845

Hunt, R., & Dickens, D. (2023). *ChatGPT isn't going to make us slaves; uninspired education might*. The Dallas Morning News. https://www.dallasnews.com/opinion/commentary/2023/02/04/chatgpt-isnt-going-to-make-us-slaves-uninspired-education-might/

Kung, T. H., Cheatham, M., Medenilla, A., Sillos, C., De Leon, L., Elepaño, C., Madriaga, M., Aggabao, R., Diaz-Candido, G., Maningo, J., & Tseng, V. (2023). Performance of ChatGPT on USMLE: Potential for AI-assisted medical education using large language models. *PLOS Digital Health*, *2*(2), e0000198. doi:10.1371/journal.pdig.0000198 PMID:36812645

Lund, B. D., & Wang, T. (2023). Chatting about ChatGPT: how may AI and GPT impact academia and libraries? *Library Hi Tech News*. doi:10.1108/LHTN-01-2023-0009

Meneses, J. P. (2023). *We spoke with ChatGPT about Macau*. Macau Business. https://www.macaubusiness.com/we-spoke-with-chatgpt-about-macau/

Newsroom, T. C. (2023). *Navigating the Risks and Rewards of ChatGPT*. Columbia University. https://www.tc.columbia.edu/articles/2023/january/navigating-the-risks-and-rewards-of-chatgpt/

Parsons, S., Davis, H., Caputo, R., & Welsh, M. (2023). *A conversation among Duke Thompson Writing Program faculty about ChatGPT.* The Chronicle. https://www.dukechronicle.com/article/2023/01/013123-parsons-davis-caputo-welsh-chat-gpt

Paykamian, B. (2023). *Higher Ed Reactions to ChatGPT Run the Gamut.* Government Technology. https://www.govtech.com/education/higher-ed/higher-ed-reactions-to-chatgpt-run-the-gamut

Red Mendoza. (2023). *Experts – AI not a threat, but can be used as complement | The Manila Times.* The Manila Times. https://www.manilatimes.net/2023/02/19/news/national/experts-ai-not-a-threat-but-can-be-used-as-complement/1879314

Roose, K. (2023). *Don't Ban ChatGPT in Schools. Teach With It.* The New York Times. https://www.nytimes.com/2023/01/12/technology/chatgpt-schools-teachers.html

Rudolph, J., Tan, S., & Tan, S. (2023). ChatGPT: Bullshit spewer or the end of traditional assessments in higher education? *Journal of Applied Learning & Teaching*, *6*(1). Advance online publication. doi:10.37074/jalt.2023.6.1.9

Sircar, N. (2023). *UAE: AI enters the classroom, but experts say role of the teacher is safe.* Khaleej Times. https://www.zawya.com/en/business/technology-and-telecom/uae-ai-enters-the-classroom-but-experts-say-role-of-the-teacher-is-safe-m783vwgr

Sitter, P. (2023). *Iowa school districts, universities work on policies for AI tools that could be used to cheat.* Ames Tribune.

Southworth, J. (2023). Rethinking university writing pedagogy in a world of ChatGPT. *University Affairs.*

Steinberg, E. (2023). Faculty split on using ChatGPT as university prepares to confront AI boom. *The Tufts Daily.* https://tuftsdaily.com/news/2023/02/16/faculty-split-on-using-chatgpt-as-university-prepares-to-confront-ai-boom/

UNESCO. (2023). *ChatGPT and Artificial Intelligence in Higher Education.* https://unesdoc.unesco.org/ark:/48223/pf0000385146

UNICEF. (2022). *Safer Chatbots Implementation Guide.* UNICEF.

Victor, V. (2023). *AI challenges pedagogy, learning assessments*. Deccan Herald. https://www.deccanherald.com/opinion/panorama/ai-challenges-pedagogy-learning-assessments-1177049.html

Villasenor, J. (2023). *How ChatGPT Can Improve Education, Not Threaten it*. Scientific American. https://www.scientificamerican.com/article/how-chatgpt-can-improve-education-not-threaten-it/

Voigt, A. (2023). *Schools right now face a choice - fight the wave of ChatGPT, or surf it*. The Sydney Morning Herald. https://www.smh.com.au/national/schools-right-now-face-a-choice-fight-the-wave-of-chatgpt-or-surf-it-20230118-p5cdle.html

Zygomatic. (2003). *Free online word cloud generator and tag cloud creator*. Zygomatic. https://www.wordclouds.com/

Chapter 3
ChatGPT Acceptance and Use Among Undergraduate Students:
A Pilot Study

ABSTRACT

In this chapter, the authors use a adapted technology acceptance model (ATAM) to examined the extent to which undergraduate students perceived ChatGPT to be a resource that is useful and easy to use. A pilot study was performed from different discipline of undergraduate students exploring their perceptions of ChatGPT as part of their research process. A statistical analysis was performed using Smart-PLS 4.0. The current study confirmed the use of adapted technology acceptance model for predicting undergraduate student use of ChatGPT.

BACKGROUND

The potential of information and communication technology (ICT) to improve the learning and teaching process is widely recognized. It is crucial to address the critical aspect of acceptance or rejection of learning technologies. Considering that the research field of educational technology has reached a level of maturity where it stands as a distinct subject of study, it becomes

DOI: 10.4018/978-1-6684-9300-7.ch003

necessary to identify and evaluate existing studies to gain insights into the current state of the field (Davis, 2011; Hrastinski & Keller, 2007).

ChatGPT is recently launched by OpenAI, a tool that is trained to follow an instruction in a prompt and provide a detailed response. It is currently an important source of information among undergraduate students and there is lot of discussion on its uses and it applications in academic and research. However, there is no current information on what factors that can influence the students to use the ChatGPT. To explore the factors, the study has inspired from Tanya Cothran research on Google scholar and modified the technology acceptance model to study ChatGPT acceptance and use among undergraduate student.

The objective of current study includes:

1. How often undergraduate students use ChatGPT?
2. What factors contribute to undergraduate students' adoption of ChatGPT? Is the technology acceptance model applicable to ChatGPT acceptance by undergraduate students?

Figure 1. The proposed adapted technology acceptance model (ATAM) based on Tanya Cothran (2011) and Davis (1989) technology acceptance model

Based on the model described above, the following associations are hypothesized adapted from Tanya Cothran (2011) technology acceptance model.

H1. Perceived usefulness is positively associated with intended use of ChatGPT.
H2. Perceived ease of use is positively associated with intended use of ChatGPT.
H3. Perceived ease of use is positively associated with perceived usefulness of ChatGPT.
H4. Comprehensiveness is positively associated with perceived usefulness of ChatGPT.
H5. System quality is positively associated with perceived ease of use of ChatGPT
H6. Accessibility is positively associated with perceived ease of use of ChatGPT.
H7. Perceived ease of use is positively associated with satisfaction of ChatGPT.
H8. Satisfaction is positively associated with loyalty to ChatGPT.
H9. Loyalty is positively associated with intended use of ChatGPT.

METHODOLOGY

The current study was conducted in 2023, with the survey population consisting of undergraduate students. The A total of 330 undergraduate students received an initial and follow-up e-mail, requesting that they participate in the study by completing an online survey about their perceptions of ChatGPT using survey monkey. A total of fifty-six response has received. Five response were removed as they disagree with the informed consent and one response were deleted due to incomplete information. The measurements of the study were developed or modified based on the TAM (Davis, 1989, 1993; Cothran, 2011). Reliability of the constructs was established by Cronbach's alpha (see Table 4), with all variables reporting alpha calculations above the 0.70 accepted limit for social science research.

RESULTS AND DISCUSSION

The survey had a response rate of 16.96%. The rate is slightly higher compare to similar experiment in understanding technology acceptance model on scholar google (11.4%) (Cothran, 2011). The study has lower response rate compare with norm of 60% plus or minus 20 established by (Baruch, 1999). The item descriptive statistics has been presented in Table 1, whereas demographic statistics were given in Table 2. The results are positive towards many factors such as PEOU, System quality, PU and IU of ChatGPT. The study suggests strong satisfaction with the use of ChatGPT. However, some factors such as comprehensiveness and loyalty were indicated as more neutral. It is understandable as ChatGPT has recently launched and every new technology need time to develop loyalty and comprehensiveness.

Table 1. Item descriptive statistics

Variable	Survey Item	(%)				
		Strongly Agree	**Agree**	**Neither Agree or Disagree**	**Disagree**	**Strongly Disagree**
Perceived ease of use (PEOU)	PEOU1: I find ChatGPT easy to use.	38.8	42.9	16.3	2.0	0.0
	PEOU2: Learning to use ChatGPT is easy for me.	36.7	46.9	10.2	6.1	0.0
	PEOU3: Interacting with ChatGPT does not require a lot of mental effort.	36.7	42.9	18.4	0.0	2.0
	PEOU4: I find it easy to get ChatGPT to do what I want it to do.	22.4	49.0	24.5	2.0	2.0
	PEOU5: I understand most of the functions used throughout ChatGPT.	14.3	42.9	28.6	12.2	2.0
	PEOU6: I find my answer easy to receive using ChatGPT.	24.5	38.8	28.6	6.1	2.0
Accessibility	A1: I can find answer of any question when asked using ChatGPT.	24.5	28.6	32.7	6.1	8.2
	A2: ChatGPT helps to makes information easy to access.	28.6	51.0	18.4	0.0	2.0
	A3: ChatGPT allows information to be readily accessible to me.	34.7	42.9	20.4	0.0	2.0
System quality	SQ1: The user interface design of ChatGPT is friendly.	28.6	49.0	22.4	0.0	0.0
	SQ2: It is easy to navigate ChatGPT.	34.7	49.0	14.3	2.0	0.0

continues on following page

Table 1. Continued

Variable	Survey Item	(%)				
		Strongly Agree	Agree	Neither Agree or Disagree	Disagree	Strongly Disagree
Perceived usefulness (PU)	PU1: Using ChatGPT in my education or academic enables me to accomplish tasks more quickly.	26.5	36.7	24.5	8.2	4.1
	PU2: Using ChatGPT in my research enables me to accomplish tasks more quickly.	18.4	42.9	32.7	2.0	4.1
	PU3: Using ChatGPT makes it easier to do my education such as assignments.	24.5	42.9	24.5	6.1	2.0
	PU4: Using ChatGPT makes it easier to do my research.	24.5	32.7	32.7	8.2	2.0
	PU5: I find ChatGPT useful in my education in preparing my assignments.	22.4	38.8	28.6	8.2	2.0
	PU6: I find ChatGPT useful in my research.	22.4	42.9	30.6	2.0	2.0
	PU7: Using ChatGPT enhances my searching effectiveness.	32.7	38.8	28.6	0.0	0.0
	PU8: I can find my answer with one search in ChatGPT.	24.5	34.7	24.5	14.3	2.0
Comprehensiveness	C1: The resources in ChatGPT relate well to my academic.	20.4	34.7	38.8	4.1	2.0
	C2: The resources in ChatGPT relate well to my research.	10.2	44.9	34.7	10.2	0.0
	C3: ChatGPT has enough resources for my study	16.3	28.6	40.8	8.2	6.1
	C4: ChatGPT covers a wide range of topics in my particular interest.	16.3	57.1	22.4	2.0	2.0
	C5: I often find exactly what I am looking for while using ChatGPT.	16.3	46.9	28.6	6.1	2.0

continues on following page

Table 1. Continued

Variable	Survey Item	(%)				
		Strongly Agree	Agree	Neither Agree or Disagree	Disagree	Strongly Disagree
Satisfaction	S1: I think I made the correction decision to use ChatGPT.	20.4	40.8	36.7	2.0	0.0
	S2: In general, I am satisfied with the results I have received from ChatGPT.	20.4	40.8	28.6	10.2	0.0
	S3: I am happy with using ChatGPT.	26.5	51.0	18.4	4.1	0.0
	S4: I am very satisfied with ChatGPT.	22.4	38.8	34.7	4.1	0.0
Loyalty	L1: I trust ChatGPT.	8.2	28.6	51.0	4.1	8.2
	L2: I consider myself to be loyal to ChatGPT in future.	4.1	22.4	59.2	6.1	8.2
	L3: ChatGPT will be my favorite place to search for scholarly articles in future.	6.1	28.6	44.9	14.3	6.1
	L4: ChatGPT will be my favorite place to search for my assignments in future.	10.2	26.5	44.9	10.2	6.1
	L5: ChatGPT will be the first place I go to start my academic work in future.	6.1	28.6	44.9	14.3	6.1
Intended use	IU1: I intend to use ChatGPT as often as needed.	14.3	34.7	36.7	8.2	6.1
	IU2: I intend to continue using ChatGPT in the future.	16.3	44.9	34.7	0.0	4.1
	IU3: I would use ChatGPT for any research question.	6.1	38.8	44.9	2.0	8.2
	IU4: I would use ChatGPT for any education/academic related question.	14.3	44.9	30.6	2.0	8.2

Table 2. Demographic statistics

Variable	Survey Item	(%)
Age	18	4.1
	19	8.2
	20	26.5
	21	32.7
	22	12.2
	23	14.3
	24	0.0
	25	2.0
Gender	Male	28.6
	Female	71.4
Academic discipline	Business and Management	10.2
	Computer Science	4.1
	Health Science	49.0
	Humanities	4.1
	Physical science, biological science	4.1
	Other (please specify)	28.6
Degree status	Final year project or internship completed	4.1
	Still taking courses	83.7
	Working on Final year project or internship	12.2

The results on Partial least squares structural equation modeling (PLS-SEM) on adapted technology acceptance model (ATAM) have been presented in Figure 1. R-square (R^2) is a statistical measure used in SmartPLS to indicate the proportion of variance in the dependent variable that can be explained by the independent variables in the model. It is also known as the coefficient of determination. In SmartPLS, R-square is calculated for each endogenous construct in the model. It provides an indication of how well the independent variables in the model explain the variation in the dependent variable. R-square values range from 0 to 1, where 0 indicates that none of the variance in the dependent variable is explained by the independent variables, and 1 indicates that all of the variance in the dependent variable is explained by the independent variables. Table 3 has presented the R-squared value.

Figure 2. Partial least squares structural equation modeling (PLS-SEM) on adapted technology acceptance model (ATAM)

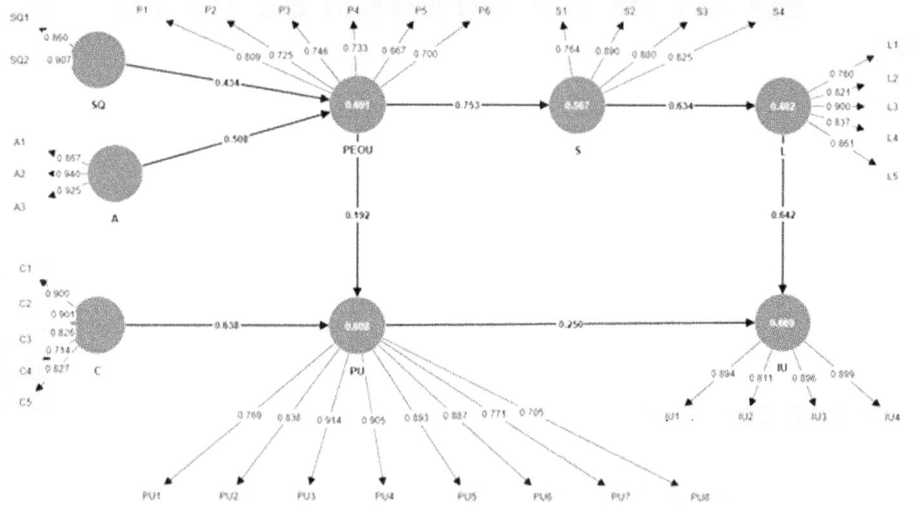

Table 3. R-square (R^2)

Dependent Variable	R^2
Intended use	0.669
Perceived usefulness	0.608
Perceived ease of use	0.691
Satisfaction	0.567
Loyalty	0.402

Table 4. Construct reliability and validity

Independent Variable	Cronbach's Alpha
Accessibility	0.897
Comprehensiveness	0.893
Intended use	0.898
Loyalty	0.894
PEOU	0.828
PU	0.938
Satisfaction	0.861
System quality	0.721

The results are significant in path coefficient when testing the hypothesis (p>0.05) except (H3) perceived ease of use is positively associated with perceived usefulness of ChatGPT. The results have been presented in Table 5. Total Indirect effect on model is significant among most of the relationships except with Accessibility and system quality towards perceived use. The results have been given in Table 6. Specific Indirect effect on model have been illustrated in Table 7. The results were consisted when observed in total effects on model given in Table 8.

Table 5. Path coefficient on model

	Original Sample (O)	Sample Mean (M)	Standard Deviation (STDEV)	T statistics (|O/ STDEV|)	P Values
A -> PEOU	0.512	0.580	0.122	4.179	0.000
C -> PU	0.638	0.644	0.114	5.596	0.000
L -> IU	0.644	0.641	0.102	6.336	0.000
PEOU -> PU	0.192	0.198	0.115	1.672	0.095
PEOU -> S	0.756	0.765	0.052	14.509	0.000
PU -> IU	0.246	0.248	0.106	2.319	0.020
S -> L	0.634	0.632	0.075	8.494	0.000
SQ -> PEOU	0.432	0.371	0.168	2.571	0.010

Table 6. Total indirect effect on model

	Original Sample (O)	Sample Mean (M)	Standard Deviation (STDEV)	T Statistics (|O/ STDEV|)	P Values
A -> IU	0.182	0.211	0.073	2.480	0.013
A -> L	0.245	0.282	0.078	3.156	0.002
A -> PU	0.098	0.119	0.083	1.180	0.238
A -> S	0.387	0.444	0.102	3.794	0.000
C -> IU	0.157	0.160	0.076	2.065	0.039
PEOU -> IU	0.356	0.360	0.079	4.509	0.000
PEOU -> L	0.479	0.485	0.071	6.793	0.000
S -> IU	0.408	0.407	0.088	4.647	0.000
SQ -> IU	0.154	0.131	0.064	2.397	0.017
SQ -> L	0.207	0.178	0.085	2.443	0.015
SQ -> PU	0.083	0.067	0.049	1.710	0.087
SQ -> S	0.327	0.283	0.130	2.522	0.012

Table 7. Specific indirect effect on model

	Original Sample (O)	Sample Mean (M)	Standard Deviation (STDEV)	T Statistics (|O/STDEV|)	P Values
PEOU -> S -> L -> IU	0.308	0.311	0.067	4.633	0.000
A -> PEOU -> S -> L -> IU	0.158	0.182	0.061	2.597	0.009
PEOU -> PU -> IU	0.047	0.050	0.037	1.273	0.203
A -> PEOU -> PU	0.098	0.119	0.083	1.180	0.238
SQ -> PEOU -> PU	0.083	0.067	0.049	1.710	0.087
SQ -> PEOU -> S -> L -> IU	0.133	0.113	0.056	2.383	0.017
PEOU -> S -> L	0.479	0.485	0.071	6.793	0.000
C -> PU -> IU	0.157	0.160	0.076	2.065	0.039
A -> PEOU -> S -> L	0.245	0.282	0.078	3.156	0.002
A -> PEOU -> S	0.387	0.444	0.102	3.794	0.000
A -> PEOU -> PU -> IU	0.024	0.030	0.025	0.974	0.330
SQ -> PEOU -> PU -> IU	0.020	0.017	0.016	1.312	0.190
SQ -> PEOU -> S	0.327	0.283	0.130	2.522	0.012
SQ -> PEOU -> S -> L	0.207	0.178	0.085	2.443	0.015
S -> L -> IU	0.408	0.407	0.088	4.647	0.000

For the approximate fit indices such as SRMR and NFI, the threshold level is (e.g., SRMR < 0.08 and NFI > 0.90). The researchers have suggested that a HTMT ratio below 0.85 is generally considered acceptable, while a ratio above 0.90 may indicate a lack of discriminant validity. Collinearity statistics (VIF) must between 1 to 5. The current study liable to measurement error as the sample collected on a small scale. The current study is a pilot trial. It is suggested to collect the large sample to observe the fit indices.

The results of the regression analysis demonstrate the relative influence of the independent variables on the dependent variables, and establish relationships between the variables. The independent variables affecting PU (R2=0.610), PEOU (R2=0.694), and intended use (R2=0.682) shown in Table 4 explain 61%, 69%, and 68% of the variance in each factor. Overall, this data set confirms the ATAM proposed relationships between these variables. The study suggest that PEOU (β=0.638, $p<0.001$), and comprehensiveness (β=0.19 $p<0.001$) were significant determinants of PU (supporting H3, H4). As hypothesized, accessibility (β=0. 0.432, $p<0.001$) and system quality (β=0.512, $p<0.001$) were positively associated with PEOU (supporting H5 and H6, respectively). In other words, a student's perceptions of the system quality of ChatGPT affected his or her feelings about the ease of using the resource. PEOU was also a significant determinant of a student's satisfaction with ChatGPT (R2=0.756, which supports H7). Less than half of the variance in student loyalty was contributed by their satisfaction (R2=0.401, which supports H9). When exploring the factors that influence a student's intention to use ChatGPT, PU (β=0.147, p=0.127) does not support whereas, loyalty (β=0.651, p=0.000), and PEOU (β=0.151, p=0.084) were positively associated with intended use, supporting H2, and H9. The results are consistent with previous studies by Cothran on google scholar. There is need to take cautions when compare with Cothran results as our study is a trial on a small scale. A full length study in process to endorse the results.

Table 8. Total effects on model

	Original Sample (O)	Sample Mean (M)	Standard Deviation (STDEV)	T Statistics (|O/STDEV|)	P Values
A -> IU	0.182	0.211	0.073	2.480	0.013
A -> L	0.245	0.282	0.078	3.156	0.002
A -> PEOU	0.512	0.580	0.122	4.179	0.000
A -> PU	0.098	0.119	0.083	1.180	0.238
A -> S	0.387	0.444	0.102	3.794	0.000
C -> IU	0.157	0.160	0.076	2.065	0.039
C -> PU	0.638	0.644	0.114	5.596	0.000
L -> IU	0.644	0.641	0.102	6.336	0.000
PEOU -> IU	0.356	0.360	0.079	4.509	0.000
PEOU -> L	0.479	0.485	0.071	6.793	0.000
PEOU -> PU	0.192	0.198	0.115	1.672	0.095
PEOU -> S	0.756	0.765	0.052	14.509	0.000
PU -> IU	0.246	0.248	0.106	2.319	0.020
S -> IU	0.408	0.407	0.088	4.647	0.000
S -> L	0.634	0.632	0.075	8.494	0.000
SQ -> IU	0.154	0.131	0.064	2.397	0.017
SQ -> L	0.207	0.178	0.085	2.443	0.015
SQ -> PEOU	0.432	0.371	0.168	2.571	0.010
SQ -> PU	0.083	0.067	0.049	1.710	0.087
SQ -> S	0.327	0.283	0.130	2.522	0.012

Table 9. Path coefficient

	Path Coefficients
A -> PEOU	0.512
C -> PU	0.638
L -> IU	0.644
PEOU -> PU	0.192
PEOU -> S	0.756
PU -> IU	0.246
S -> L	0.634
SQ -> PEOU	0.432

Table 10. Model fit summary

	Saturated Model	Estimated Model
SRMR	0.124	0.170
d_ULS	10.776	20.430
d_G	10.835	11.545
Chi-square	1608.592	1659.205
NFI	0.441	0.423

Table 11. Heterotrait-monotrait ratio (HTMT)

	Heterotrait-Monotrait Ratio (HTMT)
C <-> A	0.825
IU <-> A	0.647
IU <-> C	0.675
L <-> A	0.510
L <-> C	0.643
L <-> IU	0.860
PEOU <-> A	0.836
PEOU <-> C	0.752
PEOU <-> IU	0.486
PEOU <-> L	0.356
PU <-> A	0.835
PU <-> C	0.799
PU <-> IU	0.689
PU <-> L	0.628

continues on following page

Table 11. Continued

	Heterotrait-Monotrait Ratio (HTMT)
PU <-> PEOU	0.662
S <-> A	0.842
S <-> C	0.917
S <-> IU	0.825
S <-> L	0.706
S <-> PEOU	0.842
S <-> PU	0.845
SQ <-> A	0.688
SQ <-> C	0.460
SQ <-> IU	0.479
SQ <-> L	0.360
SQ <-> PEOU	0.905
SQ <-> PU	0.566
SQ <-> S	0.595

Table 12. Collinearity statistics (VIF)

	VIF
A1	1.960
A2	5.133
A3	4.652
C1	3.492
C2	3.423
C3	2.341
C4	1.790
C5	2.358
IU1	3.092
IU2	2.182
IU3	5.189
IU4	5.650
L1	2.237
L2	3.214
L3	3.537
L4	2.680
L5	2.655

continues on following page

Table 12. Continued

	VIF
P1	4.157
P2	3.611
P3	2.278
P4	1.774
P5	1.915
P6	1.698
PU1	3.386
PU2	7.133
PU3	8.616
PU4	5.991
PU5	6.546
PU6	6.758
PU7	2.514
PU8	1.923
S1	1.866
S2	2.732
S3	2.418
S4	2.381
SQ1	1.466
SQ2	1.466

Another study on the perception of AI were conducted among health care workers. The results are presented in table 14.

A study by Cross et al., indicated that ChatGPT has been expeditiously embraced by a faction of the collegiate faculty Caribbean medical school, American University of Antigua College of Medicine (AUA), thereby illustrating the progressive acknowledgment of its utility illustrated in Figure 3 (Cross et al., 2023).

FUTURE RESEARCH DIRECTIONS

After a successful pilot testing, the researchers are in-process of collecting the data for full length study on the large population. The researcher has planned to performed multi-national study and compare the findings between different countries.

Table 13. Summary of regression models for hypothesis testing (n=49, p £0.10)

Dependent Variable	R^2	Independent Variable	β	p-Value	Hypothesis Results
Intended use	0.682	PU	0.147	0.127	**Not Supported**
		PEOU	0.151	0.084	**Supported**
		Loyalty	0.651	0.000	**Supported**
PU	0.610	PEOU	0.638	0.000	**Supported**
		Comprehensiveness	0.192	0.065	**Supported**
PEOU	0.694	SQ	0.512	0.000	**Supported**
		Accessibility	0.432	0.000	**Supported**
Satisfaction	0.572	PEOU	0.756	0.000	**Supported**
Loyalty	0.401	Satisfaction	0.634	0.000	**Supported**

Table 14: Health care workers perceived obstacles to using AI (Artificial Intelligence) in healthcare practice currently (Temsah et al., 2023)

Independent Variable	Percentage (%)
Lack of credibility/Unknown source of information of data in the AI Model	46.9
Worry of harmful or wrong medical decisions recommendations	40.2
Not available in my setting	38.1
AI Chatbots are not yet well-developed	37.6
Medicolegal implications of using AI for patients' care	30.8
I do not know which AI model can be used in healthcare	29.4
Unfamiliarity with using AI Chatbots	28
Worry about patient's confidentiality	25.8
Resistance to adopt AI Chatbot in medical decisions	23.6
Worry of AI taking over human role in healthcare practice	20.6
Others (lack of personalized care and inability to adapt to prognostic factors)	4.1

CONCLUSION

The current study involves adapted technology acceptance model (ATAM) to provides a clearer understanding of different factors that affect undergraduate students in adopting the use of ChatGPT in academic and research. The pilot study found a positive perception and attitude towards the use of ChatGPT in academic and research. The results support the use ATAM to proceed it for full-length study.

Figure 3. ChatGPT adaptation by a American University of Antigua College of Medicine
Source: Cross et al. (2023)

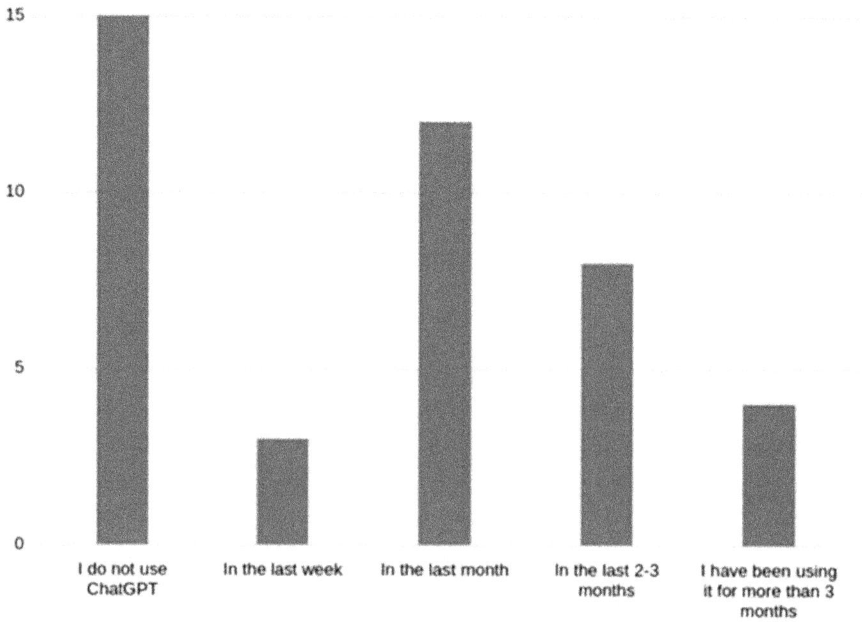

REFERENCES

Baruch, Y. (1999). Response Rate in Academic Studies-A Comparative Analysis. *Human Relations*, *52*(4), 421–438. doi:10.1177/001872679905200401

Cothran, T. (2011). Google Scholar acceptance and use among graduate students: A quantitative study. *Library & Information Science Research*, *33*(4), 293–301. doi:10.1016/j.lisr.2011.02.001

Cross, J., Robinson, R., Devaraju, S., Vaughans, A., Hood, R., Kayalackakom, T., Honnavar, P., Naik, S., & Sebastian, R. (2023). Transforming Medical Education: Assessing the Integration of ChatGPT Into Faculty Workflows at a Caribbean Medical School. *Cureus*, *15*(7). Advance online publication. doi:10.7759/cureus.41399 PMID:37426402

Davis, F. D. (1989). Perceived Usefulness, Perceived Ease of Use, and User Acceptance of Information Technology. *Management Information Systems Quarterly*, *13*(3), 319. doi:10.2307/249008

Davis, F. D. (1993). User acceptance of information technology: System characteristics, user perceptions and behavioral impacts. *International Journal of Man-Machine Studies, 38*(3), 475–487. doi:10.1006/imms.1993.1022

Davis, F. D. (2011). *Foreword in Technology Acceptance in Education: Research and Issues. Rotterdam.* Sense Publishers. https://www.scirp.org/(S(351jmbntvnsjt1aadkozje))/reference/referencespapers.aspx?referenceid=2967483

Hrastinski, S., & Keller, C. (2007). An Examination of Research Approaches that Underlie Research on Educational Technology: A Review From 2000 to 2004. *Journal of Educational Computing Research, 36*(2), 175–190. doi:10.2190/H16L-4662-6000-0446

Temsah, M.-H., Aljamaan, F., Malki, K. H., Alhasan, K., Altamimi, I., Aljarbou, R., Bazuhair, F., Alsubaihin, A., Abdulmajeed, N., Alshahrani, F. S., Temsah, R., Alshahrani, T., Al-Eyadhy, L., Alkhateeb, S. M., Saddik, B., Halwani, R., Jamal, A., Al-Tawfiq, J. A., & Al-Eyadhy, A. (2023). ChatGPT and the Future of Digital Health: A Study on Healthcare Workers' Perceptions and Expectations. *Health Care, 11*(13), 1812. doi:10.3390/healthcare11131812 PMID:37444647

Chapter 4
ChatGPT or Google Scholar?
Which Tool Is Trending?

ABSTRACT

In this chapter, the authors have compared two applications (ChatGPT and Google Scholar) used among the students and scholars. The researchers have collected the data from Google trends from the past 90 days to compare ChatGPT and Google Scholar. The search criteria were focused on education, from the website and YouTube. ChatGPT was launched on November 30, 2022 by San Francisco–based OpenAI. The results have found an increasing web search trend of ChatGPT from 19th December 2022 till 15th March 2023 with an average percentage of 27.71%. Google Scholar is a well-known tool among scholars, academician, and students. The study found a fluctuating result between the same timeline for web search with an average percentage of 71.71%. The study has found a surprising decreasing YouTube search trends of Google Scholar (10.45%) compared with ChatGPT (35.74%).

BACKGROUND

Internet data are increasingly being integrated into health informatics research and are proving to be an effective tool for studying human behavior (Mavragani & Ochoa, 2019). Google trends data is a useful tool to analyze online health information-seeking behavior (Dreher et al., 2018) and providing valuable information (Tijerina et al., 2019).

DOI: 10.4018/978-1-6684-9300-7.ch004

With an increasing advancement of the technology, there is an increase in availability of several artificial intelligence (AI) tools. ChatGPT is a major breakthrough in AI which include its unique generative pretrained transformer model. It possess capability to perform several language-based tasks and function it as a sophisticated chatbot (Lund & Wang, 2023). There are several papers that confirm the use of ChatGPT in writing the literature review such as the applications of digital twin in the health field (Aydın & Karaarslan, 2022). ChatGPT can formulate and refine Boolean queries for systematic reviews in recent paper by (Wang et al., 2023). Climate research can benefit from the usage of ChatGPT in a number of areas, such as model parameterization, data analysis and interpretation, scenario creation, and model evaluation (Biswas, 2023). The application of ChatGPT is useful in healthcare where it is useful in exploring the literature and generating new research hypotheses (Cascella et al., 2023).

METHODOLOGY

The current study will use the mix method to explore the comparison of search between ChatGPT and Google scholar using Google Trends. The sample data will be drawn from Google trends between 19th December 2022 till 15th March 2023. The keywords used to compare the results have been presented in table 1. The study involves the locations worldwide and focus on education as category.

Table 1. Data collection

Items	Search
Keywords	ChatGPT AND Google Scholar
Time	90 days
Categories	Education
Location to search	Worldwide
Search category	Web search, YouTube Search

RESULTS AND DISCUSSION

The results indicate an increase in web search for ChatGPT from 19th December 2022 with 7% percentage to 55% on 15th March 2023. The results for Scholar google was fluctuating from 72% on 19th December 2022 to 99% on 15th March 2023. The average web search for ChatGPT was 27.71%, whereas, the average search for google scholar was 71,71%. Figure 1 is the visualization comparison between two applications and found and increasing trend in search of ChatGPT. However, the results were surprising on YouTube search with ChatGPT has gained more attention compared with Google scholar with an average of 35.74% and 10.45% respectively. Figure 2 represents the visualization of Google trends results between ChatGPT and Google Scholar for YouTube search.

Figure 1. Visualization of Google trends results between ChatGPT and Google Scholar for web search

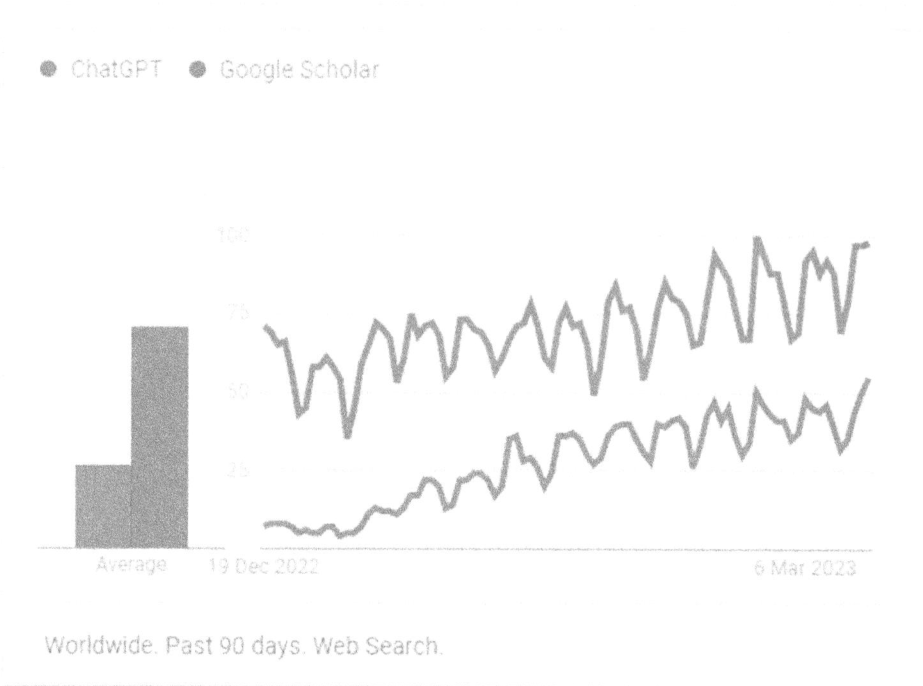

Figure 2. Visualization of Google trends results between ChatGPT and Google Scholar for YouTube search

The study observes an increasing web search trends of ChatGPT in cities such as Mississauga (77%), Brampton (71%), Richmond Hill (77%), Songshan District in Taiwan (87%), Ilford (81%), Bloomington (62%), Boston (59%), Windsor (57%), Greater Noida (58%), Kathmandu (57%), Toronto (59%), Surrey (57%) and Markham (65%).

According to OpenAI, ChatGPT acquired 1 million users just 5 days after launching in November 2022. By comparison, it took Instagram approximately 2.5 months to reach 1 million downloads. Whereas Netflix had to wait around 3.5 years to reach 1 million users (Duarte, 2023).

A working paper of Cotton et al., represent an increase in global search interest for ChatGPT as measured by Google Trends (Cotton et al., 2023). The tentative title of their work is "Chatting and Cheating: Ensuring academic integrity in the era of ChatGPT".

Figure 3. City wise comparison between ChatGPT and Google Scholar

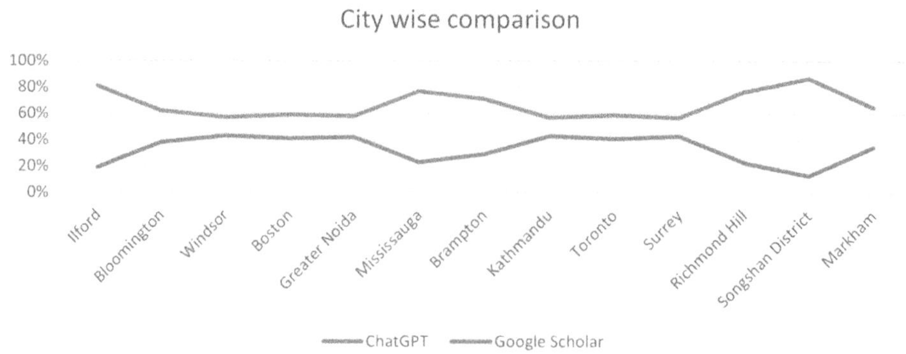

Figure 4. Time taken to reached one million users by comparison
Source: Duarte (2023)

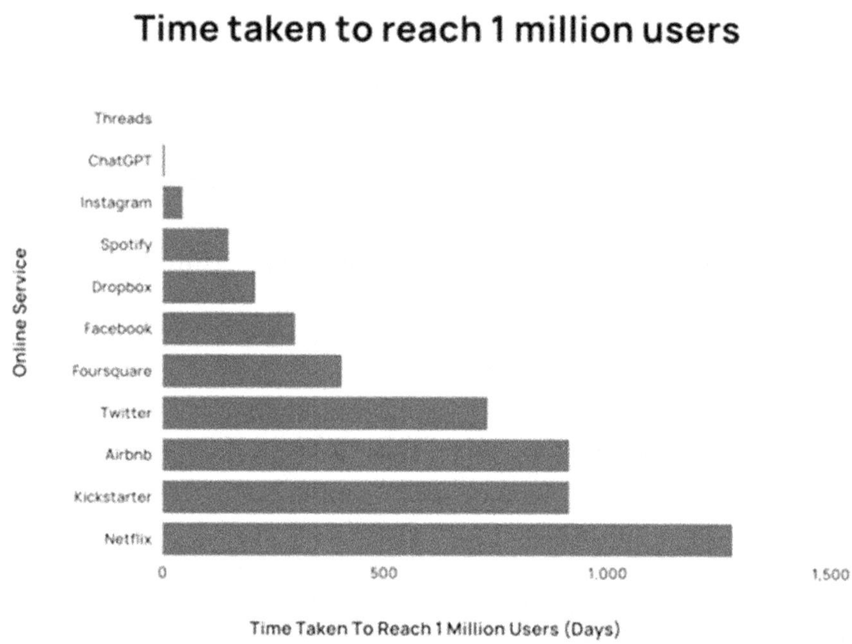

Figure 5. Global search interest for ChatGPT as measured by Google Trends
Source: Cotton et al. (2023)

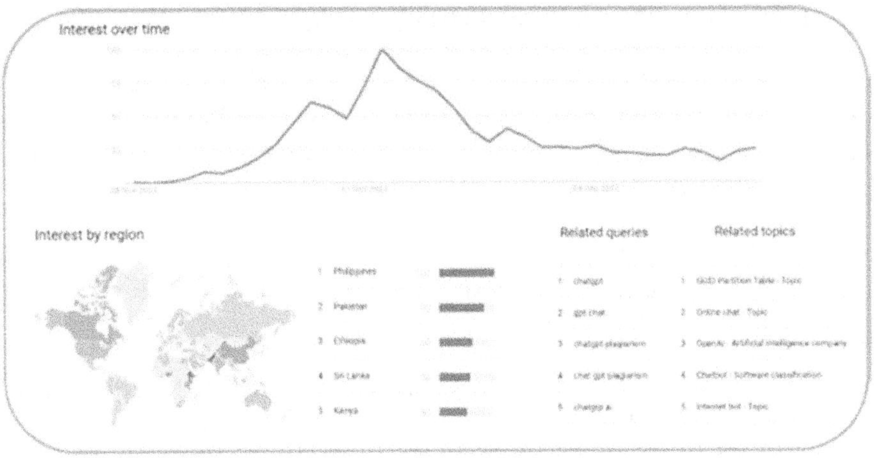

CONCLUSION

This chapter has addressed the increasing search trend of ChatGPT in website and YouTube. The authors use google trends to compare the visibility between two applications. It is concluded that the general populations including students, scholars and academician are interested to explore the potential of AI such as ChatGPT. Although it's a new tool yet, there is an increase curiosity of understanding the tool among several categories of populations such as students, researchers, scholars, working professionals, and others. With an extensive increase in search trend of ChatGPT brings some major health concern such as mental health issues. There is a need of future studies to explore how an increasing use of ChatGPT could affect the health of adolescents and among various age group? It is important to investigate the psychological issues with ChatGPT on human personality traits.

REFERENCES

Aydın, Ö., & Karaarslan, E. (2022). OpenAI ChatGPT Generated Literature Review: Digital Twin in Healthcare. SSRN *Electronic Journal*. doi:10.2139/ssrn.4308687

Biswas, S. S. (2023). Potential Use of Chat GPT in Global Warming. *Annals of Biomedical Engineering*, *1–2*(6), 1126–1127. Advance online publication. doi:10.100710439-023-03171-8 PMID:36856927

Cascella, M., Montomoli, J., Bellini, V., & Bignami, E. (2023). Evaluating the Feasibility of ChatGPT in Healthcare: An Analysis of Multiple Clinical and Research Scenarios. *Journal of Medical Systems*, *47*(1), 33. doi:10.100710916-023-01925-4 PMID:36869927

Cotton, D. R. E., Cottonm P. A., & Shipway, J. R. (2023). *Chatting and cheating: Ensuring academic integrity in the era of ChatGPT* (Issue February). https://doi.org/ doi:10.35542/osf.io/mrz8h

Dreher, P. C., Tong, C., Ghiraldi, E., & Friedlander, J. I. (2018). Use of Google Trends to Track Online Behavior and Interest in Kidney Stone Surgery. *Urology*, *121*, 74–78. doi:10.1016/j.urology.2018.05.040 PMID:30076945

Duarte, F. (2023). *Number of ChatGPT Users*. Exploding Topics. https://explodingtopics.com/blog/chatgpt-users

Lund, B. D., & Wang, T. (2023). Chatting about ChatGPT: How may AI and GPT impact academia and libraries? *Library Hi Tech News*, *40*(3), 26–29. doi:10.1108/LHTN-01-2023-0009

Mavragani, A., & Ochoa, G. (2019). Google Trends in Infodemiology and Infoveillance: Methodology Framework. *JMIR Public Health and Surveillance*, *5*(2), e13439. doi:10.2196/13439 PMID:31144671

Tijerina, J. D., Morrison, S. D., Nolan, I. T., Vail, D. G., Nazerali, R., & Lee, G. K. (2019). Google Trends as a Tool for Evaluating Public Interest in Facial Cosmetic Procedures. *Aesthetic Surgery Journal*, *39*(8), 908–918. doi:10.1093/asjjy267 PMID:30304356

Wang, S., Scells, H., Koopman, B., & Zuccon, G. (2023). *Can ChatGPT Write a Good Boolean Query for Systematic Review Literature Search?* https://doi.org/ doi:10.1145/nnnnnnn.nnnnnnn

Chapter 5
How to Use Prompt Engineering for ChatGPT in Medical Education

ABSTRACT

In this chapter, the authors present an appropriate use of prompt engineering in ChatGPT in developing a hypothetical case study for students in understanding basic medical science. In artificial intelligence, particularly in natural language processing, the idea of prompt engineering is used. In prompt engineering, the task description that the AI is expected to complete is incorporated into the input, for example, as a question. Students and teachers can develop hypothetical case studies for their learning of the subjects such as pathology, pharmacology, Western medical diagnostic, and internal medicine. The chapter provided the structure of composing the prompt with a hypothetical case study of peptic ulcer disease of a 45 year of women that underwent endoscopy for H. pylori detection.

BACKGROUND

Prompt engineering (PE) is an increasingly important skill set needed to converse effectively with large language models (LLMs) (White et al., 2023). Language models have a history dating back to the 1950s; however, it was not until the emergence of the BERT and GPT models in 2018 that language models truly gained widespread acceptance and became the dominant approach

DOI: 10.4018/978-1-6684-9300-7.ch005

in the field (Wang et al., 2023). It is known as prompt engineering, prompt design, or prompt programming.

PE used to design, enhance, and optimizing input prompts in order to effectively convey the user's purpose to a language model like ChatGPT is known as prompt engineering. To get the model to respond in a way that is accurate, pertinent, and cohesive, this practice is necessary. Proper prompt engineering is now a crucial skill for users who want to fully utilize ChatGPT and obtain the best results in a variety of applications as language models continue to improve.

Table 1. The iterative process of composing prompts

Purpose	Prompt
Subject	Subject terms Keywords
Modifier	Question Refinement Alternative Approaches Cognitive Verifier Refusal Breaker
Solidifier	Pattern recognition Error analysis Fine-tuning Citation/Reference
Variation	Alternative terms Synonyms
Weightage	Priority terms Exclusion terms Mixing inclusion and exclusion terms

Case Study: A Hypothetical Case Study of Peptic Ulcer Disease of a 45-Year-Old Woman Who Underwent Endoscopy for *H. pylori* Detection

Conditioning the model on specific keywords: We can provide the model with specific keywords related to peptic ulcer disease, such as "gastric pain," "stomach discomfort," and "endoscopy for H. pylori detection," so that it knows what the patient's symptoms and diagnosis are. Providing example outputs to guide the model's responses: We can provide the model with sample explanations of peptic ulcer disease and endoscopy that are written in patient-friendly language and that avoid technical jargon. For example: "Peptic ulcer disease is a condition where painful sores develop in the lining

Figure 1. Visualization of items for prompt engineering in developing the hypothetical case study

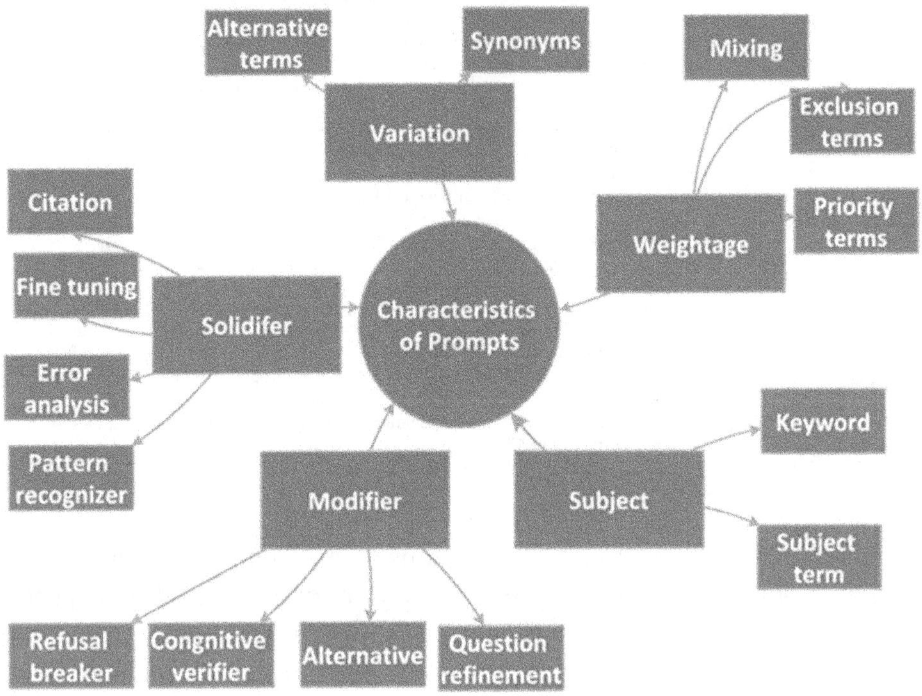

of the stomach or the duodenum. Endoscopy is a procedure where a flexible tube with a camera is inserted into your stomach and duodenum to check for signs of ulcers and to detect H. pylori bacteria."

Using a combination of multiple prompts to achieve the desired result: We can use a combination of prompts that consider the patient's individual circumstances, such as: Patient's age and gender: "As a 45-year-old woman, you are at higher risk for developing peptic ulcer disease than younger individuals or men." Medical history: "Your symptoms of stomach discomfort and pain suggest that you may have peptic ulcer disease. Your endoscopy results will help confirm the diagnosis and detect any H. pylori bacteria that may be causing your symptoms." The inclusion of Solidifier is a term used in prompt writing to refer to a tool or technique that is used to refine and optimize prompts for use with language models. The goal of a solidifier is to make prompts more effective at eliciting high-quality outputs from the model, while also minimizing errors and improving overall performance.

Table 2. The solidifier of composing prompts

Analyzing successful prompts	We can analyze the prompts that have successfully elicited accurate and informative responses from the language model. For example, we might find that prompts that provide additional context or explanation of the risk factors for peptic ulcer disease are more successful. Based on this analysis, we might modify the prompt to include additional information, such as *"Peptic ulcer disease is more common in women over the age of 45 and those with a history of smoking, alcohol use, or non-steroidal anti-inflammatory drugs (NSAIDs)."*
Error analysis	We can analyze the errors made by the language model in response to the prompt to identify areas where the model may struggle to generate accurate or informative outputs. For example, we might find that the model sometimes provides inaccurate or incomplete information about the risk factors for peptic ulcer disease. Based on this analysis, we might modify the prompt to provide more specific information, such as *"As a postmenopausal woman, you are at higher risk for developing peptic ulcer disease due to changes in hormones and a decrease in protective mucus in the stomach lining."*
Fine-tuning	We can fine-tune the language model on a specific set of prompts related to peptic ulcer disease and risk factors. By training the model on this specific task, we can improve its ability to generate accurate and informative outputs in response to prompts related to the case study. For example, we might fine-tune the model on a dataset of patient charts or medical articles that contain information about risk factors for peptic ulcer disease in women over the age of 45.

Variation in prompt writing refers to the use of different prompts or variations of a prompt to elicit different types of responses or explore different aspects of a given topic or problem. By using variations of a prompt, we can obtain a wider range of outputs and gain a more comprehensive understanding of the subject matter. Here's an example of how variation in prompt writing could be applied to the case study of the 45-year-old woman with peptic ulcer disease: The prompt "As a 45-year-old woman, you are at higher risk for developing peptic ulcer disease than younger individuals or men" can be varied in multiple ways to elicit different types of responses or explore different aspects of the patient's condition. For example: "What are the risk factors for peptic ulcer disease in women over the age of 45?" - This prompt encourages the language model to generate a list of risk factors that are specific to women in this age group, which can provide more detailed information about the patient's condition and potential causes of her peptic ulcer disease. "How does smoking increase the risk of peptic ulcer disease in postmenopausal women?" - This prompt focuses specifically on the role of smoking in increasing the patient's risk of developing peptic ulcer disease, which can help to identify potential lifestyle factors that may be contributing to her condition. "What are some common symptoms of peptic ulcer disease in women over the age of 45?" - This prompt encourages the language model to generate a list of symptoms that are specific to the patient's demographic group, which can provide more targeted information about her condition and potential treatment options. Weightage in prompt writing refers to the process of assigning relative importance or priority to different elements or keywords in a prompt. By assigning weights to different words or phrases, we can guide the language model to focus on specific aspects of the prompt and generate more accurate or informative responses. Here's an example of how weightage could be applied to the prompt "As a 45-year-old woman, you are at higher risk for developing peptic ulcer disease than younger individuals or men" in the case study of the 45-year-old woman with peptic ulcer disease: We might assign higher weights to specific keywords or phrases that are particularly relevant or informative for the patient's condition. For example: "peptic ulcer disease" - This keyword is highly relevant to the patient's condition and should be given a high weight to ensure that the language model generates accurate and informative responses related to this topic. "45-year-old woman" - This phrase provides important demographic information about the patient and should be given a moderate weight to ensure that the language model generates responses that are tailored to her specific age and gender. "higher risk" - This phrase highlights the patient's increased risk for peptic ulcer disease and should be given a moderate weight to ensure that the language model generates responses that address this specific aspect of her condition. By assigning weights to these keywords and phrases, we can guide the language model to focus on the most relevant and informative aspects of the prompt and generate responses that are tailored to the patient's specific condition and risk factors. This can help to improve the accuracy and effectiveness of the model's outputs and provide more targeted information to inform the patient's diagnosis and treatment plan.

CONCLUSION

By using prompt engineering techniques, ChatGPT can generate personalized explanations of peptic ulcer disease and endoscopy that are tailored to the patient's individual circumstances and that are easy for the patient to understand.

REFERENCES

Wang, J., Shi, E., Yu, S., Wu, Z., Ma, C., Dai, H., Yang, Q., Kang, Y., Wu, J., Hu, H., Yue, C., Zhang, H., Liu, Y., Li, X., Ge, B., Zhu, D., Yuan, Y., Shen, D., Liu, T., & Zhang, S. (2023). *Prompt Engineering for Healthcare: Methodologies and Applications*. https://arxiv.org/abs/2304.14670

White, J., Fu, Q., Hays, S., Sandborn, M., Olea, C., Gilbert, H., Elnashar, A., Spencer-Smith, J., & Schmidt, D. C. (2023). *A Prompt Pattern Catalog to Enhance Prompt Engineering with ChatGPT*. https://arxiv.org/abs/2302.11382v1

Chapter 6
Bring Your Own Paper (BYOP) Involving ChatGPT to Enhance Traditional Chinese Medicine (TCM) Student Engagement in Pharmacology and Pathology

ABSTRACT

In this chapter, the authors present a practical application of ChatGPT in teaching pedagogy to improve traditional Chinese medicine student engagement in the subjects pharmacology and pathology. ChatGPT is a conversational AI model developed by OpenAI. It is based on the GPT (generative pre-trained transformer) architecture, specifically GPT-3.5, which is the third iteration of the GPT series. GPT-3.5 is a state-of-the-art language model that has been trained on a vast amount of text data from the internet. The authors presented a teaching plan that involve the use of ChatGPT. The authors bring the idea of "bring your own paper" (BYOP) that could help students and teachers to improve student critical thinking and does allow the use with student's own device (BYOD).

DOI: 10.4018/978-1-6684-9300-7.ch006

BACKGROUND

Up to this point, ChatGPT and AI have been able to create texts that, at least on the surface, appear to be well-written and creative. However, due to the nature of generation and synthesis, the process relies on templates that might not be flexible enough or contain references to sources that can be verified (Naumova, 2023). Moreover, several articles did raised ethical issues and asked for all stakeholder to develop set of code of ethics (Sallam, 2023; Ali & Djalilian, 2023).

In a relatively short period of time, ChatGPT has gained impressive interest from academics, research, and industry (Ray, 2023). An artificial intelligence-based chatbot, ChatGPT, was launched in November 2022 (Lo, 2023) and has been used to generate accurate differential medical diagnosis (Liu et al., 2023), research (Zhu et al., 2023) and teaching (Wardat et al., 2023). In The public and easy availability of knowledge will bring benefits to teachers and students. Students who are reluctant to ask question from their teachers can get help from ChatGPT. However, the beginning of ChatGPT era bring an enormous challenge to teachers. The teachers may worry that excessive use of ChatGPT may decrease the critical thinking of students. Therefore, teachers need to revisit their assessment methodology and innovate in their teaching and assessment pedagogy.

The current study involved mixed teaching pedagogy (Flipped teaching and Passive teaching). Flip teaching, also known as flipped learning or the flipped classroom model, is an instructional approach that reverses the traditional order of content delivery and homework assignments in a classroom setting. In flip teaching, students are introduced to new content or concepts outside of the classroom through pre-recorded lectures, videos, readings, or other resources, which they can access independently before attending the class. Passive teaching refers to a learning approach where individuals acquire knowledge or skills in a relatively passive manner, typically through observation or exposure to information without actively engaging in active participation or interaction. In passive learning, the learner is a recipient of information rather than an active participant in the learning process.

You may hear about the policy or practice "bring your own device" in different setting. Bring Your Own Device (BYOD) refers to a policy or practice where employees or individuals are allowed or encouraged to use their personal computing devices, such as smartphones, laptops, or tablets, for work-related tasks or accessing company resources. This has getting the popularity since the easy availability of computing device. It has already implemented in education setting. However, bring your own device can bring decline in student's handwriting skills and cognitive ability. Excessive use of device is always a controversial issue and it could easily argue that such habits are dangerous for our mental health. Several papers publish on the highlighted issue.

The objective of current book chapter is to introduce the concept called "Bring Your Own Paper" (BYOP) as a teaching method along with the application of BYOD "Bring Your Own Device".

METHODOLOGY

The teaching pedagogy involve a mixed approach of passive learning and flipped learning. Background Knowledge in the form of videos will be provided before the class. The lecturer will expect that student take notes on the video and be prepared to use the notes in class. The students can use ChatGPT to compare their notes prepared from the Video. The comparison will help students for better understanding of the content. The notes can be used a tool for discussion inside the classroom among peers. However, the lecturer is aware that traditional Chinese Medicine students (TCM) may find flip teaching as difficult due to their language barrier. Therefore, the lecturer keeps passive learning as well a teaching module in class. Passive learning involves Case-based learning (CBL) as sub pedagogy in each topic. The lecture tried to maintain a balance between both pedagogies. ChatGPT will used as a tool in flipped teaching so that students understand the content of the videos. Moreover, the lecturer made several engaging class activities involving the use of ChatGPT that are given at the end of session, to help students in developing their critical thinking.

Table 1. Lesson plan: Introduction to pharmacology and pharmacokinetics

<table>
<tr><td>Learning Objective(s):
1. Explain the principles and mechanisms of drug action.
2. Describe pharmacokinetics and pharmacodynamics properties of drugs.
3. Discuss the key concept in Pharmacokinetics.</td><td>Lesson Objective(s):
· Students will classify various receptor and its functions in human body.
· Students will demonstrate their understanding of the function of receptor through applications to various scenarios.</td></tr>
<tr><td>Background/Previous Knowledge:
· Students will have previously learned about the physiology of human body, specifically, how cells, tissues, and organisms' function, how your digestive system works, what is the functions of liver and how your body process the medicine.
· As a Mixed pedagogy methodology (Passive learning & flipped learning), students watched the videos (See Multimedia support) to develop their background knowledge.
· The expectation is that student take notes on the video and be prepared to use the notes in class. The students can use ChatGPT to compare their notes prepared from the Video. The comparison will help students for better understanding of the content.</td><td>[Class Room] Day 1: The objective of today's lesson is to introduce the subject Pharmacology. Before we start our slides. The students were presented a video on what is pharmacology.
Multimedia support: What is Pharmacology?
Watch the video and write down notes on what did you understand it?
The students will use Pingo tool to get the access and write down their notes. Students will use the code (874133) to get the access. (20 Minutes)
The slides were presented as a part of passive learning (40 minutes).
Discussion: (10 minutes) (3 students in one group)
· Identify TWO (2) drugs each used in prevention and diagnosis of disease through ChatGPT or literature search.
Humanistic perspective. (20 Minutes).
Amy Greenwood story
Why Do I Need a Pulmonary Function Test?
1. Discuss the relationship between lung disease and pulmonary function test.
2. What step UK government did to control the asthma?</td></tr>
<tr><td>Multimedia Support:
The following videos to develop students background knowledge and basic knowledge
1. What Are The Levels Of Organization In The Body - Organization Of The Human Body.
2. How your digestive system works
3. What does the liver do?
4. How does your body process medicine?
5. How the Body Absorbs and Uses Medicine
6. Body Fluid Compartments-Physiology
7. Formation of Urine - Nephron Function.</td><td rowspan="2">[Class Room] Day 2: The objective of today's lesson is to discuss some key basic concept of pharmacokinetics as a part of passive learning (60 minutes).
Discussion: (20 minutes) (3 students in one group)
· Identify two (2) examples each of drug which absorb in intracellular fluid and blood plasma?
· Find two drugs cannot given orally? Justify why these drugs cannot give orally?
Humanistic perspective. (20 Minutes).
Read Meth-related ER visits on the rise in Ontario, following western Canada trend: study
· How drug clearance could be a useful tool in treating the patient with drug over dose?</td></tr>
<tr><td>Materials need:
· White sheet(s)
· Color pen or pencil
· Notes prepared from Multimedia support.
· Use only paper and pen to complete the questions given and write down your name and student id.</td></tr>
</table>

Table 2. Lesson plan: Drug receptors and pharmacodynamics

<table>
<tr>
<td>Learning Objective(s):
· Define receptors and classification of receptors.
· Describe Signaling mechanism.</td>
<td>Lesson Objective(s):
· Students will classify various receptor and its functions in human body.
· Students will demonstrate their understanding of the function of receptor through applications to various scenarios.</td>
</tr>
<tr>
<td>Background/Previous Knowledge:
· Students will have previously learned about the cellular communication.
· As a Mixed pedagogy methodology (Passive learning & flipped learning), students watched the videos (See Multimedia support) to develop their background knowledge on cellular communication and receptors.
· The expectation is that student take notes on the video and be prepared to use the notes in class. The students can use ChatGPT to compare their notes prepared from the Video. The comparison will help students for better understanding of the content.</td>
<td>[Classroom]Day 1: The objective of today's lesson is to introduce the receptors, and its classifications.
The slides were presented as a part of passive learning (60 minutes).
Discussion: (20 minutes) (3 students in one group)
· Identify TWO (2) drugs each that act on M2 Receptor, Nicotinic receptor and B1-receptor.
· Find out the clinical uses of drugs identified from previous question. Student can search through ChatGPT.
Humanistic perspective. (20 Minutes).
Read Jillian Currie story
3. Write a short summary of your understanding in Jillian Currie story.
4. Brief about the relationship between receptor and Sjögren's Syndrome.</td>
</tr>
<tr>
<td>Multimedia Support:
The following videos to develop students background knowledge and basic knowledge
· Intro to Cell Signaling
· 3 Stages of Cell Signaling
· The Difference Between Agonists vs. Antagonists
· Types of Drug Receptors
· Receptors: Types & Functions</td>
<td rowspan="2">[Class room]Day 2: The objective of today's lesson is to discuss signaling mechanism as a part of passive learning (60 minutes).
Discussion: (20 minutes) (3 students in one group)
· Identify TWO (2) examples of drugs at act through nuclear receptor.
· Identify One (1) examples of drugs at act through Cytokine receptor.
· Search out the mechanism of any one example using ChatGPT.
Humanistic perspective. (20 Minutes).
Read Benzodiazepines and their links to UK youth culture
· Give a brief summary Harmful side effects of Benzodiazepines.
· Describe Benzodiazepine involve which Signaling mechanism?</td>
</tr>
<tr>
<td>Materials need:
· White sheet(s)
· Color pen or pencil
· Notes prepared from Multimedia support.
· Use only paper and pen to complete the questions given and write down your name and student id.</td>
</tr>
</table>

Table 3. Lesson plan: Cholinomimetics and cholinoceptor-activating and cholinesterase-inhibiting drugs

<table>
<tr><td>Learning Objective(s):
· Describe Classification of cholinergic agonists with examples.</td><td>Lesson Objective(s):
· Students will learn case studies to understand different therapeutic uses and adverse effect of cholinergic drugs.</td></tr>
<tr><td>Background/Previous Knowledge:
· Students will have previously learned about sympathetic and parasympathetic outflow and its functions.
· Student must learn autonomic nervous system neurotransmitter and its receptor.
· As a Mixed pedagogy methodology (Passive learning & flipped learning), students watched the videos (See Multimedia support) to develop their background knowledge on the difference between sympathetic and parasympathetic nervous system; autonomic nervous system and somatic nervous system.
· The expectation is that student take notes on the video and be prepared to use the notes in class. The students can use ChatGPT to compare their notes prepared from the Video. The comparison will help students for better understanding of the content.</td><td>[Classroom]Day 1: The objective of today's lesson is to discuss the therapeutic actions and adverse effect of Bethanechol and Carbachol
The slides were presented as a part of passive learning (30 minutes).
Discussion: (20 minutes) (3 students in one group)
· Find out the clinical uses of Bethanechol and Carbachol through ChatGPT.
· Students need to find the clinical uses as many as they could able to find using ChatGPT. In case of technical error (ChatGPT does not working), the students will search it from scholar google or textbook.
Humanistic perspective. (20 Minutes).
Case report: Acute unintentional carbachol intoxication
5. List down the symptoms that results in Carbachol intoxications.</td></tr>
<tr><td>Multimedia Support:
The following videos to develop students background knowledge and basic knowledge
· Nervous System
· The Autonomic Nervous System: Sympathetic and Parasympathetic Divisions
· Autonomic nervous system</td><td rowspan="2">[Class room] Day 2: The objective of today's lesson is to discuss the therapeutic actions and adverse effect of Pilocarpine, Physostigmine and Neostigmine (40 minutes).
Discussion: (20 minutes) (3 students in one group)
· Find out the clinical uses Pilocarpine, Physostigmine and Neostigmine through ChatGPT.
· Students need to find the clinical uses as many as they could able to find using ChatGPT. In case of technical error (ChatGPT does not working), the students will search it from scholar google or textbook.
Humanistic perspective. (40 Minutes).
Read Cheap Nasal Spray May Save Snakebite Victims
Understand the content in the report and ask the question given below from ChatGPT. The answer from ChatGPT verify with Scholar google with appropriate citation (APA format).
· How Neostigmine could be helpful in treating snakebite victims?</td></tr>
<tr><td>Materials need:
· White sheet(s)
· Color pen or pencil
· Notes prepared from Multimedia support.
· Use only paper and pen to complete the questions given and write down your name and student id.</td></tr>
</table>

Table 4. Lesson plan: Adrenergic agonists and adrenergic antagonists

Learning Objective(s): · Discuss some of drugs as adrenergic agonists and adrenergic antagonist.	Lesson Objective(s): · Discuss the actions of Dopamine. · Describe the relationship between ma huang and Ephedrine. · Discuss the adverse effects observed with adrenergic agonists. · Discuss therapeutic actions and adverse effects of Prazosin. · Discuss the actions of Yohimbine. · Discuss the therapeutics and adverse effects of Propranolol and atenolol.
Background/Previous Knowledge: · Students will have previously learned about sympathetic and parasympathetic outflow, the difference between vasodilation and vasoconstrictions, differentiate between Chronotropic, Inotropic, Dromotropic, Bathmotropic Action. Moreover, students must know the anatomy and physiology of mesenteric artery and renal blood flow. · As a Mixed pedagogy methodology (Passive learning & flipped learning), students watched the videos (See Multimedia support) to develop their background knowledge. · The expectation is that student take notes on the video and be prepared to use the notes in class. The students can use ChatGPT to compare their notes prepared from the Video. The comparison will help students for better understanding of the content.	[Classroom]Day 1: The objective of today's lesson is to discuss the therapeutic actions and adverse effect of adrenergic agonist. The slides were presented as a part of passive learning (45 minutes). Humanistic perspective. (20 Minutes). [REMOVED HYPERLINK FIELD] Understanding prehospital vasopressors: Dopamine, epinephrine or norepinephrine? Read the report and answer the question. · Do you think dopamine is the first drug of choice in treating the shock? If your answer is no then give rational and suggest the alternative drugs. · Read the literature, list different types of shock states and explain in brief.
Multimedia Support: The following videos to develop students background knowledge and basic knowledge · Superior Mesenteric Artery Anatomy: Animated Gross anatomy of Abdomen · Regulation of Renal Blood Flow · Chronotropic, Inotropic, Dromotropic, Bathmotropic Actions Explained || Cardiac Tropism · The Autonomic Nervous System: Sympathetic and Parasympathetic Divisions · Vasodilation & Vasoconstriction · Male Hypogonadism, Causes, Signs and Symptoms, Diagnosis and Treatment.	[Class room] Day 2: The objective of today's lesson is to discuss the therapeutic actions and adverse effect of adrenergic antagonist (45 minutes). Humanistic perspective. (40 Minutes). USDA reports yohimbe bark supplements fail to meet label claims Health Ministry bans erectile dysfunction medicine, issues stiff warning to sellers Read these two reports and answer the question. · Discuss the adverse effect of yohimbine. Identify it from the given report. · Selling the banned product will results in which kind of penalty in Malaysia?
Materials need: · White sheet(s) · Color pen or pencil · Notes prepared from Multimedia support. · Use only paper and pen to complete the questions given and write down your name and student id.	

Table 5. Lesson plan: Pharmacology of drugs used in asthma

<table>
<tr>
<td>Learning Objective(s):
· Discuss some of drugs used in the treatment of asthma</td>
<td>Lesson Objective(s):
· To understand the clinical uses of drugs used in the treatment of asthma.
· Discuss the adverse effects, contraindications and precautions of drugs used in treatment of asthma.
· Discuss the motivation story from humanistic perspective of patient suffering from asthma.</td>
</tr>
<tr>
<td>Background/Previous Knowledge:
· Students will have previously learned about asthma and its various types.
· As a Mixed pedagogy methodology (Passive learning & flipped learning), students watched the videos (See Multimedia support) to develop their background knowledge.
· The expectation is that student take notes on the video and be prepared to use the notes in class. The students can use ChatGPT to compare their notes prepared from the Video. The comparison will help students for better understanding of the content.</td>
<td rowspan="3">[Classroom]Day 1: The objective of today's lesson is to discuss the pharmacology of various drugs used in the treatment of asthma.
The slides were presented as a part of passive learning (60 minutes).
Humanistic perspective. (20 Minutes).
Asthmatic child and super mum who became fastest women in Southeast Asia
It's getting harder to breathe in Malaysia
Read the report and answer the question.
· What did you learn from reports?
· Can you provide any TCM herbal prescription that could treat asthma? Search it from literature/scientific articles. One example.</td>
</tr>
<tr>
<td>Multimedia Support:
The following videos to develop students background knowledge and basic knowledge
· Understanding Asthma: Mild, Moderate, and Severe
· Understanding Asthma
· Asthma - causes, symptoms, diagnosis, treatment, pathology</td>
</tr>
<tr>
<td>Materials need:
· White sheet(s)
· Color pen or pencil
· Notes prepared from Multimedia support.
· Use only paper and pen to complete the questions given and write down your name and student id.</td>
</tr>
</table>

Table 6. Lesson plan: Drugs used in the treatment of gastrointestinal diseases

<table>
<tr><td>Learning Objective(s):
· Understand various treatment strategies in several types of gastrointestinal tract (GIT) disorders.</td><td>Lesson Objective(s):
· Describe different therapeutic approach of acid-peptic disease.
· Understand the Adverse effects of H2-receptor antagonists.
· Discuss classification of acid-peptic disease.
· Describe different drugs used in the treatment of Diarrhea.
· Compare the efficacy of lopramide and Diphenoxylate
· Classify antidiarrheal drugs.
· Understand drugs used in the treatment of constipation.
· Discuss drugs classes used as laxatives in the treatment of constipation.</td></tr>
<tr><td>Background/Previous Knowledge:
· Students will have previously learned about the physiology of the digestive system.
· As a Mixed pedagogy methodology (Passive learning & flipped learning), students watched the videos (See Multimedia support) to develop their background knowledge.
· The expectation is that student take notes on the video and be prepared to use the notes in class. The students can use ChatGPT to compare their notes prepared from the Video. The comparison will help students for better understanding of the content.</td><td rowspan="3">[Classroom]Day 1: The objective of today's lesson is to discuss the pharmacology of various drugs used in the treatment of several kind of GIT disorders.
The slides were presented as a part of passive learning (80 minutes).
Humanistic perspective. (20 Minutes).
[REMOVED HYPERLINK FIELD] FDA Cracks Down On Imodium Abuse
Another Overdose Of An Anti-Diarrhea Drug: This Time A Death From Loperamide
Questions:
How lopramide is become an abuse or misuse by consumer? Discuss the rational behind its abuse or misuse.
Describe the adverse effect of loperamide over-dosage.</td></tr>
<tr><td>Multimedia Support:
The following videos to develop students background knowledge and basic knowledge
· Digestive System, Part 1: Crash Course Anatomy & Physiology #33
· Digestive System, Part 2: Crash Course Anatomy & Physiology #34
· Digestive System, Part 3: Crash Course Anatomy & Physiology #35</td></tr>
<tr><td>Materials need:
· White sheet(s)
· Color pen or pencil
· Notes prepared from Multimedia support.
· Use only paper and pen to complete the questions given and write down your name and student id.</td></tr>
</table>

Table 7. Lesson plan: Introduction to pathology

Learning Objective(s): · Understand the common term use in Pathology · Describe some important personality in the field of Pathology.	Lesson Objective(s): · Students will understand some basic definition and concept of pathology. · Students will learn evolution of pathology from the beginning till today.
Background/Previous Knowledge: · Students will have previously learned about the physiology of muscle tissue, types of tissues human body, composition of white blood cells · As a Mixed pedagogy methodology (Passive learning & flipped learning), students watched the videos (See Multimedia support) to develop their background knowledge. · The expectation is that student take notes on the video and be prepared to use the notes in class. The students can use ChatGPT to compare their notes prepared from the Video. The comparison will help students for better understanding of the content.	[Class Room] Day 1: The objective of today's lesson is to introduce the subject pathology. The slides were presented as a part of passive learning (40 minutes). Discussion: (20 minutes) (3 students in one group) Read the article. Leishmaniasis · Identify the etiology of disease. · Search the pathogenesis of disease. Use ChatGPT. Answer Hunt: · Can you find out 10 blood related disorder? Use textbook only.
Multimedia Support: The following videos to develop students background knowledge and basic knowledge · Tissues · Types of Tissue · Types of Connective Tissues Materials need: · White sheet(s) · Color pen or pencil · Notes prepared from Multimedia support. · Use only paper and pen to complete the questions given and write down your name and student id.	[Class Room] Day 2: The objective of today's lesson is to understand the history of pathology (40 minutes). Discussion: (3 students in one group) · Read the manuscript Thiery, M. Gabriele Fallopio (1523–1562) and the Fallopian tube. Answer the question in a white paper · Discuss the scientific contribution and importance of contribution in the manuscript given above. (20 Minutes) · Read the article: Percivall Pott And The Chimney Sweeps' Cancer Answer the question in white sheet of paper · What is the contribution of Sir. Percivall pot in medical science? · What is the impact of his contribution in the society. (20 Minutes) · Read the story of "The Directed Steps of Hans Christian Gram" Answer the question in white sheet of paper · How Gram stain is helpful in the field of pathology? · Which disease could be identified easily using gram stain? Give Three examples. (20 minutes)

Table 8. Lesson plan: Cellular adaptation

Learning Objective(s): · Understand and differentiate various etiology of Cell injury. · Define pathogenesis of cellular injury and discuss different factors. · Discuss the Morphology of reversible cell injury. · Understand different kinds of cellular accumulation. · Understand the pathogenesis and morphology of fatty liver. · Discuss types of Pigmentation. · Understand necrosis and apoptosis with some examples. · Brief about the pathologic role of calcification and understand its different types. · Understand the physiological and pathological differences among different adaptive disorder.	Lesson Objective(s): · Students will understand types of cell injury, pathogenesis of cellular injury, morphology of reversible cell injury, necrosis, cellular accumulation and different types of adaptive disorders.
Background/Previous Knowledge: · Students will have previously learned the following topic to understand this lecture. (a)Types of cells in the human body. (b) Cell cycles: Mitosis (c) Epithelium and glands · As a Mixed pedagogy methodology (Passive learning & flipped learning), students watched the videos (See Multimedia support) to develop their background knowledge. · The expectation is that student take notes on the video and be prepared to use the notes in class. The students can use ChatGPT to compare their notes prepared from the Video. The comparison will help students for better understanding of the content.	[Class Room] Day 1: The objective of today's lesson (a) Cell injury, factors (b) Etiology of cellular injury The slides were presented as a part of passive learning (30 minutes). Discussion: Read following news reports. 1) Three Malaysians die in suspected carbon monoxide poisoning in their vehicle 2) Kids Almost Die From Carbon Monoxide Poisoning On Roadtrip To Selangor, Even Mom Affected [Situation Room] If you are policy makers how you prevent carbon monoxide poisoning in Malaysia and China. Write minimum six guidelines or suggestion. (3 students in one group) (3×2=6 guidelines). If you search with ChatGPT then find out the literature source such as scientific article (TAKE HELP GOOGLE SCHOLAR) (20minutes) [Video time] (3 students in one group) Watch the following videos Chernobyl Disaster 1986: What really happened? What fact did you find from the video? (20 minutes) [Story time] (3 students in one group) Twitter user Ayuizany Story What did you learn from the story? 30-50 words (10 Minutes) [Policy report] (3 students in one group) China's aging population threatens a Japan-style lost decade - Nikkei Asia Answer the following question? · What problems could results in increase in ageing? · What did you learn from the report. Give three statement? · What policies must be implemented in Malaysia after reading the report. Give one statement.

continues on following page

Table 8. Continued

<table>
<tr>
<td>Multimedia Support:
The following videos to develop students background knowledge and basic knowledge
· Levels of Organisation
· Tissues, Part 2 - Epithelial Tissue
· Types of Epithelial Tissue
· Mitosis vs. Meiosis: Side by Side Comparison
· The Cell Cycle</td>
<td rowspan="3">[Class Room] Day 2:
The objective of today's lesson
(a) Pathogenesis of Cellular injury
(b) Types of reversible injury
(c) Morphology
(d) Examples
The slides were presented as a part of passive learning (60 minutes).
[Class participation] (3 students in one group)

Identify different part of Kidney and label them.
You can use search engine such as Google or ChatGPT (30-40 Minutes)
[Class Activity] Do you know FIVE (5) pigments in our body? (10 Minutes)
• Write down five pigments in our body and search their functions through ChatGPT
• Write it in a white paper by handwriting (3 member in one group)
• A random group will be called to explain it.</td>
</tr>
<tr>
<td>Literature support:
· What are the most common patterns of tissue organization? https://histology.siu.edu/layerslumps.htm
· Read histology of fallopian tube https://v15.proteinatlas.org/learn/dictionary/normal/fallopian+tube</td>
</tr>
<tr>
<td>Materials need:
· White sheet(s)
· Color pen or pencil
· Notes prepared from Multimedia support.
· Use only paper and pen to complete the questions given and write down your name and student id.</td>
</tr>
<tr>
<td>[Class Room] Day 3:
The objective of today's lesson
(a) Necrosis
(b) Classification
(c) Changes after cell death
The slides were presented as a part of passive learning (60 minutes).
[Class Activity] (3 members in one group)
Do you like Cheese? (30 Minutes) Can you search Five (5) disease that showed Caseous necrosis?
· Use ChatGPT to search it or any appropriate search engine.
· Give me the etiology of disease identified.
· A random group will be called for question and answer session.</td>
<td>[Class Room] Day 4:
The objective of today's lesson
(a) Gangrene
(b) Calcification
(c) Cellular Adaptation
The slides were presented as a part of passive learning (40 minutes).
[Class Activity] (3 members in one group)
Read it
Autoamputation of diabetic toe with dry gangrene: a myth or a fact?
Read the article and write down a 50 words summary to justify dry gangrene is a myth or fact. (10 minutes)
[Find out] (3 members in group) (10-15 minutes).
Find Six (6) Disease in which excessive absorption of calcium from the gut will result in Metastatic calcification using ChatGPT.
In case unable to from ChatGPT, then use textbook.
Write it in a white sheet of paper.
[Make a padlet] (6-7 members in one group)
· Visit https://padlet.com/dashboard
· Make your own poster
· Question: Illustrate examples of Physiological atrophy.
· Search disease using search engine, literature or ChatGPT.
· Each student will search two disease.
· Search the image related to disease and upload into their respective poster group.
· The Poster will develop by each group (3 groups)
· Each member will participate in each group by searching two disease and related image and upload.</td>
</tr>
</table>

Table 9. Lesson plan: Repair the damage

<table>
<tr><td>Learning Objective(s):
· Discuss how tissue damage can be repaired?
· Outline the mechanism of action of tissue repair
· Discuss different steps in repair by scarring formation
· Understand the factors that impair tissue repair
· Describe some of defects in healing chronic wound.</td><td>Lesson Objective(s):
· Students will understand the process of repair in humans.</td></tr>
<tr><td>Background/Previous Knowledge:
· Students will have previously learned about connective tissues. Proliferation, progenitor cells, macrophages and difference between acute and chronic disease.
· As a Mixed pedagogy methodology (Passive learning & flipped learning), students watched the videos (See Multimedia support) to develop their background knowledge.
· The expectation is that student take notes on the video and be prepared to use the notes in class. The students can use ChatGPT to compare their notes prepared from the Video. The comparison will help students for better understanding of the content.</td><td rowspan="3">[Class Room] Day 1: The objective of today's lesson is to introduce the subject pathology. The slides were presented as a part of passive learning (80 minutes).
Discussion: (20 minutes) (3 students in one group)
Read the article.
<u>Stem Cells Could Help Diabetics Produce Their Own Insulin</u>
· Which type of diabetes is discussed in the article?
· Write a small summary of report in own words.
· [20-30 words]
· Who is Eelco de Koning? and can you find his contribution in research in diabetes? Search using Google</td></tr>
<tr><td>Multimedia Support:
The following videos to develop students background knowledge and basic knowledge
· <u>Connective tissue introduction</u>
· <u>What are stem cells?</u></td></tr>
<tr><td>Materials need:
· White sheet(s)
· Color pen or pencil
· Notes prepared from Multimedia support.
· Use only paper and pen to complete the questions given and write down your name and student id.</td></tr>
</table>

Table 10. Lesson plan: Thrombosis and embolism

Learning Objective(s): · Define and differentiate thrombosis and thrombus. · Discuss the difference between blood clot and thrombus. · Discuss the factors that predispose to thrombus formation. · Describe the Clinical correlation of venous thrombi. · Define embolism. · Discuss the different types of embolism.	Lesson Objective(s): · Students will understand how to differentiate between thrombosis and embolism.
Background/Previous Knowledge: · Students will have previously learned about the overview of the circulation; pressure, flow, and resistance of blood. Knowledge about the function of each component of the blood vessel wall. Student can Distinguish among arteries, arterioles, capillaries, and veins in terms of their anatomical characteristics and their functions · Moreover, students understand the coagulation system. · Common term used in the lesson plan include platelets, coagulation cascade, clotting factors. Please see footnotes given in lecture slides if you want to revise your background knowledge. · As a Mixed pedagogy methodology (Passive learning & flipped learning), students watched the videos (See Multimedia support) to develop their background knowledge. · The expectation is that student take notes on the video and be prepared to use the notes in class. The students can use ChatGPT to compare their notes prepared from the Video. The comparison will help students for better understanding of the content.	[Class Room] Day 1: The objective of today's lesson is to discuss the difference between thrombosis and thrombus. The student will learn the relationship between homeostasis and thrombosis. The second objective of today's lecture is understanding the pathophysiology of thrombosis and discuss some situation of altered blood flow. The slides were presented as a part of passive learning (60 minutes). [Task]: (30 minutes) (3 students in one group) Can you search FIVE situations that can cause Turbulence? · Can you search FIVE situations that can cause Turbulence in our body? · Write it on a white sheet of paper · 30 minutes have been given · Try to think, write in own words and avoid to use ChatGPT.
· Multimedia Support: · The following videos to develop students background knowledge and basic knowledge · Blood, Part 1 - True Blood: Crash Course Anatomy & Physiology #29 · Blood, Part 2 - There Will Be Blood: Crash Course Anatomy & Physiology #30 · Platelets & Blood Clotting | Biology | FuseSchool · Circulatory System and Pathway of Blood Through the Heart · Coagulation Cascade Animation - Physiology of Hemostasis	[Class Room] Day 2: The objective of second day lesson plan is to discuss about Hypercoagulability, causes of Hypercoagulability, morphology of thrombi, clinical aspect of deep thrombi, classification of thrombi, embolism and its types. The slides were presented as a part of passive learning (80 minutes). [Search Activity] Can you search illustration of pathophysiology of non-traumatic cause of fat embolism? · You can search it from scholar google or text-book. · This is a group assignment and the class is subdivided into groups (A,B,C,D,E,F) · Each group will search it as a team, One illustration from each group. The group will present their illustration at the end of the session and explain briefly according to their understanding. · Time: 30 minutes
Materials need: · White sheet(s) · Color pen or pencil · Notes prepared from Multimedia support. · Use only paper and pen to complete the questions given and write down your name and student id.	

Table 11. Lesson plan: Inflammation

<table>
<tr><td>Learning Objective(s):
· Understand key definition of oedema.
· Describe different pattern of oedema.
· Differentiate between transudate and exudate.
· Discuss the pathogenesis of oedema.
· Describe water and sodium retention mechanism.
· Discuss the mechanism of action of cardiac oedema.</td><td>Lesson Objective(s):
· Students will understand edema, causes and mechanism of action.</td></tr>
<tr><td>Background/Previous Knowledge:
· Students will have previously learned about intracellular cell, extracellular cell, interstitial cell and cavities in human body. Moreover, student must understand the role of pressure in vascular system.
· As a Mixed pedagogy methodology (Passive learning & flipped learning), students watched the videos (See Multimedia support) to develop their background knowledge.
· The expectation is that student take notes on the video and be prepared to use the notes in class. The students can use ChatGPT to compare their notes prepared from the Video. The comparison will help students for better understanding of the content.</td><td rowspan="3">[Class Room] Day 1: Student will learn on how to define edema? what are the pattern found in edema? How to differentiate between transudate and exudates? The students will learn few mechanism of edema.
The slides were presented as a part of passive learning (60 minutes).
[Class activity]
● How traditional Chinese Philosophy explain Edema?
● Discuss the theory of TCM that explain edema.
● Search traditional herbal medicine that solve edema problem. (Provide minimum two herbs name)(Chinese name and English name)
● Discuss the herbs identified and explain their TCM mechanism in brief.
● Do not use CHATGPT.
● Search answer using scientific literature and provide reference.
● Time for the activity is 30 minutes.</td></tr>
<tr><td>Multimedia Support:
The following videos to develop students background knowledge and basic knowledge
· Extracellular Matrix And Interstitial Fluid - What Is The Extracellular Matrix
· Capillary Exchange and Edema, Animation
· Oncotic and Hydrostatic Pressure in the Capillaries</td></tr>
<tr><td>Materials need:
· White sheet(s)
· Color pen or pencil
· Notes prepared from Multimedia support.
· Use only paper and pen to complete the questions given and write down your name and student id.</td></tr>
</table>

Table 12. Lesson plan: Oedema

<table>
<tr><td>Learning Objective(s):
· Define inflammation and highlight the various inflammation processes.
· Outline the role of biological mediators in the inflammation process.
· Discuss the regulation of inflammation
· Understand the role of different inflammatory cells</td><td>Lesson Objective(s):
· Students will understand the basic definition of inflammation, inflammation processes, role of biological mediators in the inflammation process and role of various inflammatory cells.</td></tr>
<tr><td>Background/Previous Knowledge:
· To understand inflammation, it is helpful to have a basic understanding of biology and anatomy. Specifically, it would be beneficial to have knowledge of: Cells: Understanding the types and functions of immune cells such as white blood cells (leukocytes), which are involved in the inflammatory response, as well as other cells such as tissue cells, endothelial cells, and platelets. Immune System: A basic understanding of the immune system, including the innate and adaptive immune responses, which are involved in inflammation. Pathogens and Damaged Tissue: Understanding the different types of pathogens and how they can trigger inflammation, as well as the different types of tissue damage that can lead to inflammation.
· As a Mixed pedagogy methodology (Passive learning & flipped learning), students watched the videos (See Multimedia support) to develop their background knowledge.
· The expectation is that student take notes on the video and be prepared to use the notes in class. The students can use ChatGPT to compare their notes prepared from the Video. The comparison will help students for better understanding of the content.</td><td rowspan="3">[Class Room] Day 1: Student will learn on how to define inflammation? what process involve in inflammation? Then we will discuss different mediators of inflammation and last will see some inflammatory cells.
The slides were presented as a part of passive learning (60-70 minutes).
[Class activity] (20 minutes)
● List down 10 chronic diseases that involve inflammation.
● Identify their inflammatory mediators in each chronic disease (10 diseases).
● The study will divide it into six group (A,B,C,D,E,F).
[Installation of Biolucida Software] (10 Minutes)

· Mandatory to bring your laptop
· https://biolucida.net/login
· Click the link above.
· Follow the instructions given in the slides available in Moodle.</td></tr>
<tr><td>Multimedia Support:
The following videos to develop students background knowledge and basic knowledge
· Types of Immune Cells Part 1: Immune Cell Function
· Types of Immune Cells Part 2: Myeloid and Lymphoid Lineages</td></tr>
<tr><td>Materials need:
· White sheet(s)
· Color pen or pencil
· Notes prepared from Multimedia support.
· Use only paper and pen to complete the questions given and write down your name and student id.</td></tr>
</table>

CONCLUSION

Fusing "Bring Your Own Paper" (BYOP) and "Bring Your Own Device" (BYOD) as teaching methods along with permission to use ChatGPT is an excellent and engaging methods, that can solve teachers' problems. It is not possible to ban the technology as currently several virtual AI assistances available. Some researcher suggests to ban the technology or institution provide controlled device (BYOD) that allow only specific application. However, it will increase the financial Burdon to institution, moreover, students still can access the technology by purchasing their own device or getting the access of technology using virtual private networks (VPN). I suggest to teachers and institution to change the teaching pedagogies with mixed methodology, bring back paper and hand writing activities and develop complex and robust assessments. Allow the students to use ChatGPT in their learning and develop game-based education environment where, student's engagement is encouraged along with passive case-based learning. The given approach will help all kind of students (introvert and extrovert).

REFERENCES

Ali, M. J., & Djalilian, A. (2023). Readership Awareness Series – Paper 4: Chatbots and ChatGPT - Ethical Considerations in Scientific Publications. *Seminars in Ophthalmology*, *38*(5), 403–404. doi:10.1080/08820538.2023.2193444 PMID:36945119

Liu, J., Wang, C., & Liu, S. (2023). Utility of ChatGPT in Clinical Practice. *Journal of Medical Internet Research*, *25*, e48568. doi:10.2196/48568 PMID:37379067

Lo, C. K. (2023). What Is the Impact of ChatGPT on Education? A Rapid Review of the Literature. *Education Sciences*, *13*(4), 410. doi:10.3390/educsci13040410

Naumova, E. N. (2023). A mistake-find exercise: A teacher's tool to engage with information innovations, ChatGPT, and their analogs. *Journal of Public Health Policy*, *44*(2), 173–178. doi:10.105741271-023-00400-1 PMID:36914712

Ray, P. P. (2023). ChatGPT: A comprehensive review on background, applications, key challenges, bias, ethics, limitations and future scope. *Internet of Things and Cyber-Physical Systems*, *3*(April), 121–154. doi:10.1016/j.iotcps.2023.04.003

Sallam, M. (2023). Practice : Systematic Review on the Promising Perspectives and Valid Concerns. *Health Care*, *11*(6), 887. PMID:36981544

Wardat, Y., Tashtoush, M. A., AlAli, R., & Jarrah, A. M. (2023). ChatGPT: A revolutionary tool for teaching and learning mathematics. *Eurasia Journal of Mathematics, Science and Technology Education*, *19*(7), em2286. Advance online publication. doi:10.29333/ejmste/13272

Zhu, J.-J., Jiang, J., Yang, M., & Ren, Z. J. (2023). ChatGPT and Environmental Research. *Environmental Science & Technology*, *1–4*, acs.est.3c01818. Advance online publication. doi:10.1021/acs.est.3c01818 PMID:36943179

Chapter 7
The Epistemology of ChatGPT

ABSTRACT

It is true that our beliefs are formed through personal experiences, upbringing, cultural influences, education, and other external factors, and we do not have direct control over our beliefs. Our belief is not entirely under our conscious control. Let's put questions on the ethical use of ChatGPT in education. Why are people fearful of adopting the new technology such as artificial intelligence? The recent launch of ChatGPT, an AI tool, led to banned in several institutions after hearing about its potential as creating content and generating a wide range of textual output. So, how, or can, we inspire the institutions to change their beliefs by not banning the tool? How can we morally use ChatGPT with values, principles, and norms that govern ethical behavior?

BACKGROUND

In the technological advancement, I find students are fearful that artificial intelligence will take their jobs. The institutions are concerned that ChatGPT may increase the prevalence of academic misconducts. I would like to point out on the plagiarism issues before ChatGPT. Some students known how to play with plagiarism software such as Turnitin. The student adjusts the structure of the content, change the vocabulary of the content or using paraphrasing tool such as Quillbot. There are several questions I ask from myself. Why student cheat their lecturer or institutions? Even though, the

DOI: 10.4018/978-1-6684-9300-7.ch007

students understand the academic misconduct, yet some students do. Why? The new technology may bring some challenges but why some students use them which are morally wrong?

Our moral beliefs affect our behaviors and choices. I do not belief that every student will cheat their lecturer or institution. Only immoral students will do. There is a famous idiom "*Where there's a will, there's a way*". Morally good people will not use tool or applications to do immoral act such as cheating or academic misconduct against institutions policies.

Let discuss the epistemological approach to understand on why students who have read institution policy against cheating or plagiarism will commit the offence. I think we do not have a direct control over our belief and it is indirectly controlled by various factors such as biases, social conditioning, or unconscious attitudes. Yinxia Zhang et al., research explain moral attitude and integrity engagement were the major predictors, that subjective norm accounted for marginal variations of academic dishonesty, and that the influence of penalty enforcement was insignificant (Zhang et al., 2018). I think the subjective norm affect our moral beliefs and behaviors can depend on individual factors and social contexts.

ANTI-CHATGPT ARGUMENTS

Those who oppose to use ChatGPT, on moral grounds

P1) ChatGPT can cause academic dishonesty.
P2) Academic dishonesty is morally wrong.
P3) ChatGPT is morally wrong.

I agree that we are imperfect being and we tend to act several morally wrong acts in our daily life such as procrastination on completing a task. Yet, these are not morally disastrous and we do not change our life style. People will not belief in using ChatGPT use as morally wrong as it does not have sufficient argument to belief.

THE NATURE OF BELIEFS

The key point in the current study is that typical ChatGPT user refuse to avoid the use of Artificial intelligence (AI) in their academic and research because they do not believe that ChatGPT and other AI is seriously wrong and may decline their cognitive skills and creative thinking. There is no study till now publish that confirm the loss of cognitive skill or decline in critical thinking. ChatGPT and other new AI tool are still new and need research and evidence to proof the claim and justify to students and lecturer. It is important to understand the rational use of ChatGPT in academic and research. It is important that lecturer must know on how they incorporate ChatGPT tool in their assessment in a rational manner so that students will use their understanding, knowledge and thinking in their study. Moreover, students need education on the ethical use of ChatGPT.

LITERATURE AVAILABLE

Let discuss the current available literature on the ethical implication of ChatGPT. ChatGPT has attracted remarkable attentions from academia, research, and industries in a very short span of time (Ray, 2023). By creating deceptive or erroneous content, ChatGPT has the potential to do harm said by Emma Bowman (Bowman, 2022) . Michael Liebrenz et al has raised the issues in increasing the research output by using ChatGPT (Liebrenz et al., 2023). A recent study published by Zhuo et al., showing the evidence of ethical risks using ChatGPT (Zhuo et al., 2023). Another study emphasis on the privacy, fairness, non-discrimination, transparency in the use of ChatGPT in education (Mhlanga, 2023). There are several pre-print available that stress on the responsible use of ChatGPT (Krügel et al., 2023).

ROBUST ANTI-CHATGPT ARGUMENT

P1) Causing serious academic dishonesty by using ChatGPT.
P2) Academic dishonesty is seriously morally wrong.
P3) ChatGPT is seriously morally wrong.

However robust anti-ChatGPT argument are still not strong enough to refrain people on not to use such tool. It is possible that user can potentially involve multiple AI tool to generate the content in order to avoid the academic dishonesty and plagiarism detecting software such as turnitin. In order to refrain people on not to use ChatGPT, there must be strong argument that motivate students and teachers to avoid AI tool. For example, the available literature points out the deceptive and erroneous content produced by ChatGPT (Bowman, 2022). Therefore, the argument will be given below as

1) The belief that ChatGPT use can produce seriously deceptive, and erroneous content.
2) The belief that producing deceptive, and erroneous content by ChatGPT seriously morally wrong.

However,

(1) Many consumers do not believe that ChatGPT can produce deceptive and erroneous content.
(2) Of those consumers who believe that ChatGPT content can be verified through literature and scientific content.
(3) And perhaps some consumers do not believe that it is seriously morally wrong to use ChatGPT.

CONCLUSION

However, I still belief that the future AI tool are more powerful and can produce the content that is error free and avoid of deceptive content. Therefore, avoiding such tool cannot never help users in long run. Therefore, rational and ethical use of ChatGPT argument is necessary to bring awareness among users. It is necessary that the lecturer will develop robust assessment that minimize the risk of producing error-based content by ChatGPT and incorporate ChatGPT as an effective active teaching method that can check and verify the content if produced by ChatGPT.

REFERENCES

Bowman,E.(2022). *ChatGPTcouldtransformacademia.Butit'snotanA+student yet.* NPR. https://www.npr.org/2022/12/19/1143912956/chatgpt-ai-chatbot-homework-academia

KrügelS.OstermaierA.UhlM. (2023). *The moral authority of ChatGPT.* https://arxiv.org/abs/2301.07098v1

Liebrenz, M., Schleifer, R., Buadze, A., Bhugra, D., & Smith, A. (2023). Generating scholarly content with ChatGPT: Ethical challenges for medical publishing. *The Lancet. Digital Health*, *5*(3), e105–e106. doi:10.1016/S2589-7500(23)00019-5 PMID:36754725

Mhlanga, D. (2023). Open AI in Education, the Responsible and Ethical Use of ChatGPT Towards Lifelong Learning. SSRN *Electronic Journal*. doi:10.2139/ssrn.4354422

Ray, P. P. (2023). ChatGPT: A comprehensive review on background, applications, key challenges, bias, ethics, limitations and future scope. *Internet of Things and Cyber-Physical Systems*, *3*, 121–154. doi:10.1016/j.iotcps.2023.04.003

Zhang, Y., Yin, H., & Zheng, L. (2018). Investigating academic dishonesty among Chinese undergraduate students: Does gender matter? *Assessment & Evaluation in Higher Education*, *43*(5), 812–826. doi:10.1080/02602938.2017.1411467

ZhuoT. Y.HuangY.ChenC.XingZ. (2023). *Exploring AI Ethics of ChatGPT: A Diagnostic Analysis*. https://arxiv.org/abs/2301.12867v3

Chapter 8
Unleashing the Potential of ChatGPT:
A Personal Perspective

ABSTRACT

ChatGPT's extensive and strong capabilities make it useful for various applications, such as scholarly research, content creation, and language translation. Natural language processing is revolutionized by its capacity to produce human-like writing and deliver pertinent information quickly and accurately. Artificial intelligence aids in class material preparation can improve the efficiency, accessibility, engagement, personalization, and collaboration of the teaching and learning process. As technology evolves, it will likely become an even more essential academic tool. Academics can benefit greatly from ChatGPT's ability to provide content suited to particular subject matter or writing styles. It enables individuals to provide instructional materials that are more precise, pertinent, and consistent with their own preferred writing style. The accessibility of ChatGPT is a major advantage for academics, as it allows them to create class materials quickly and conveniently from anywhere with an internet connection.

DOI: 10.4018/978-1-6684-9300-7.ch008

BACKGROUND

The modern language model ChatGPT was created by OpenAI and is based on the GPT (Generative Pre-trained Transformer) architecture. It is a deep learning model that can produce language that resembles a human's by responding to cues after being trained on a sizable text dataset. The capacity of ChatGPT to produce cohesive, grammatically correct, and semantically meaningful text is one of its key features. The model can capture long-range dependencies and context in the input text by combining several cutting-edge approaches, including positional encoding, multi-head attention, and self-attention processes. ChatGPT can be adjusted for various language tasks, including text completion, summarization, translation, and question-answering. As a result, the model can be trained using certain datasets. The ability of ChatGPT to produce original, diversified material is another important feature. The process is accomplished using a method known as "sampling," which enables the model to produce several potential outputs for a given prompt instead of just one predetermined output. ChatGPT is helpful for inspiring creative writing, stimulating thoughts, or investigating other options.

Additionally, ChatGPT can be adjusted to produce content suited to a topic, writing style, or personal preferences by adjusting the model on individual datasets and training it to produce pertinent and particular content to a given area. ChatGPT is a potent language model that can produce text that resembles human speech and is coherent and semantically significant. It is a useful tool for various language-related tasks and applications due to its versatility and capacity to produce various original outputs.

ChatGPT can produce text on various topics because it was trained on a large corpus of text data, including books, papers, and web pages. ChatGPT can generate text generation, question-answering, language translation, text summarization, text completion, sentimental analysis, and statistical interpretation. Using supplied prompts, ChatGPT may produce text that appears human. It may produce sentences, paragraphs, or entire grammatically sound and coherent papers. ChatGPT can respond to queries based on the context that is provided. It might, for instance, respond to straightforward factual queries or explain complex ideas. Text can be translated from one language to another using ChatGPT. It has been trained on a sizable amount of multilingual data and can translate across many different languages. Using supplied cues, ChatGPT can finish sentences or paragraphs with ideas or finish statements that are not full. ChatGPT can determine whether a text's sentiment is good, negative, or neutral by doing a sentiment analysis on it.

Several manuscripts have inquired about the destiny of humanity with the involvement of CHATGPT, seeking readers' perspectives on the matter. For example, Is ChatGPT a blessing or blight in disguise? (Arif et al., 2023) the future of discharge summaries? (Patel & Lam, 2023) or How may AI and GPT impact academia and libraries? (Lund & Wang, 2023)

Technology in Education

In today's digital world, using technology to help with class content preparation is becoming increasingly crucial. Improved efficiency, better accessibility, enhanced engagement, personalization, and collaboration are just a few advantages that technology offers that might assist academics in producing more valuable and interesting course materials. Many of the time-consuming procedures involved in creating course materials, like formatting, organizing, and proofreading, can be automated thanks to technology. Academics can gain significant time savings and boost the caliber of their work by using the technology.

Thanks to technology, academics can now produce content that a larger audience can read. For instance, students with visual impairments or learning problems can access digital textbooks. More interesting and dynamic course materials can be produced using technology. For instance, simulations, films, and animations can help students comprehend complex concepts by bringing them to life. Technology can be utilized to adapt instructional materials for each student. For instance, based on a student's progress and performance, adaptive learning platforms might change the difficulty level of the questions and exercises. Academics may collaborate easily thanks to technology, sharing ideas, and receiving feedback while they work on course materials.

ChatGPT has been tested in various medical licensing examinations such as the United States Medical Licensing Examination (USMLE) (Gilson et al., 2023), American Heart Association (AHA) Basic Life Support (BLS) and Advanced Cardiovascular Life Support (ACLS) exams (Fijačko et al., 2023). These results suggest that large language models may potentially assist with medical education and clinical decision-making (Kung et al., 2023; Liu et al., 2023).

Advantage of ChatGPT

One of its main benefits is the ability to save time when creating class materials with ChatGPT. A language model called ChatGPT, which has been trained on many data, can produce text quickly in response to input or prompts. As a result, academics can produce lecture notes, tests, assignments and even complete courses using ChatGPT in a fraction of the time it would take to do so manually. For instance, an academic may enter a query relating to the topic into ChatGPT, and the tool would output text that could be used to develop lecture notes in seconds rather than spending hours researching and creating lecture notes for a particular topic. Similarly, academics can utilize ChatGPT to produce questions and prompts tailored to the course or topic being taught rather than manually producing quizzes or assignments.

Academics can save much time by automating the content generation process using ChatGPT so they can concentrate on other important tasks like teaching, research, or student involvement. This time-saving benefit can also help academics operate more productively and efficiently, ultimately benefiting the teacher and the pupils. For instance, an academic can utilize ChatGPT to quickly produce a first draught of lecture notes for a class based on a specific prompt. The academics can concentrate on honing the material rather than beginning from scratch using the model, which can offer ideas and suggestions. The ability to tailor ChatGPT's output to certain topics or writing styles is another benefit for educational use. ChatGPT can be adjusted to produce content specific to a certain subject of study or writing style because it can learn from the input data it receives.

For instance, an academic with expertise in pharmacy may modify ChatGPT to produce content pertinent to that area of study by putting the model through training on a particular corpus of pharmaceutical-relevant material, such as books, articles, or research papers. As a result, ChatGPT will be more likely to produce pertinent and correct content in response to a cue about pharmaceuticals. Similarly, ChatGPT can be customized to generate content in a specific writing style. For example, an academic who prefers a more formal writing style can train ChatGPT on data that reflects that style, such as academic journals or textbooks in the model, generating content more consistent with the academic's preferred writing style.

ChatGPT is easily accessible from any location with an internet connection, making it a practical tool, which is another significant benefit of using it for academic purposes. Creating lecture notes, course content, or exams are traditional techniques of producing class materials that often take a lot of time and effort and frequently ask for access to particular tools or resources. With ChatGPT, academics can use any internet-connected device to access the model without requiring specialized hardware or software. For academics who travel frequently, work remotely, or have restricted access to resources, this accessibility can be beneficial. Additionally, it implies that academics may produce information fast while on the go, maximizing their time.

On a variety of subjects, ChatGPT can be used to rapidly and effectively write lecture notes. Here are several methods for using ChatGPT to create lecture notes, topic suggestions, key ideas, literature reviews, and summaries. A prompt that outlines the subject they intend to discuss in their lecture notes might be sent by academics to ChatGPT. After that, ChatGPT will produce a manuscript on that subject that is logically organized and can serve as the foundation for teaching notes. Academics can give ChatGPT a list of the important terms or concepts they want to cover in their lesson notes. The description or definition of each topic produced by ChatGPT can subsequently be utilized as the foundation for teaching notes.

Academics may find ChatGPT useful for creating quiz questions and assignment ideas. Here are some strategies for using questions, essay prompts, and case study questions in ChatGPT to make tests and assignments. Academics can send ChatGPT a prompt describing the subject they intend to cover in their exam or assignment. Based on the prompt, ChatGPT will produce a set of questions that might be quite helpful when developing multiple-choice or short-answer questions. The user can use ChatGPT to generate essay questions on various subjects. A topic or theme can be given to ChatGPT by academics, and it will provide an organized and cogent essay prompt that students can utilize as a starting point. Writing prompts for creative writing projects can be generated using ChatGPT. A genre or theme can be given to ChatGPT by academics, and it will then produce several writing prompts that students can use to improve their writing abilities. To create case studies on a certain subject, use ChatGPT. A real-world scenario can be given to ChatGPT as a prompt by academics, and it will produce a case study that students can utilize to analyze and hone their problem-solving abilities. The user can create syllabi for a course on a certain subject using ChatGPT. Academics can submit a course description, learning objectives, and other pertinent data to ChatGPT, creating a well-structured syllabus including the course material, assignments, and grading standards.

BEST PRACTICES FOR USING CHATGPT IN ACADEMIA

Even though ChatGPT can produce information quickly, checking the output for accuracy and relevance to the subject under discussion is crucial. ChatGPT's content can contain mistakes or inconsistencies because it is imperfect. It is crucial to check the output for errors and inaccuracies and fix them. Although ChatGPT can provide content on various subjects, it might not necessarily be pertinent to the discussed subject. Examining the results to ensure they support the course's learning objectives and aims is crucial. ChatGPT can produce content that is identical to or similar to already published works, which can raise concerns about plagiarism. It is crucial to check the output to ensure it is original and plagiarism-free. Academics can check that the generated content adheres to their criteria for quality and correctness by reviewing ChatGPT's output, making it more likely that students will obtain comprehensive, high-quality resources to help them succeed in the course.

CAUTION IN USING CHATGPT

Although ChatGPT can be a helpful tool for academics to create material, it should not be used in place of critical thinking and subject-matter knowledge. While ChatGPT can produce articles quickly, it lacks a seasoned professor's subject-matter skills and knowledge. Academics should add to the generated content using their knowledge and experience to ensure that it is accurate, thorough, and appropriate for the course's particular context and target audience. While ChatGPT generates content by recognizing patterns from extensive text data, it may not always critically analyze the information it provides. This could lead to the dissemination of incorrect information, posing potential health risks (Choudhury & Shamszare, 2023).

In order to assess the generated information, find any gaps or contradictions, and ensure that it satisfies the course's learning objectives and aims, academics should employ their critical thinking skills. Even though ChatGPT can develop content rapidly and effectively, original content might not always result. In order to engage students and make sure that the course stands out, academics must employ their creativity and originality when creating the course materials. ChatGPT's content may not always be relevant to the individual needs and interests of the students taking a given course because it is based on patterns discovered from massive volumes of text data. Academics should personalize the course materials and ensure they are interesting based on their understanding of their pupils and learning preferences.

ETHICAL CONSIDERATION

Based on the observation, ChatGPT may produce information that displays bias that can lead to offensive or discriminatory information. It is crucial to be conscious of potential biases and take precautions to guarantee that the created content is impartial and inclusive. As we previously noted, it is crucial to check the generated content's correctness to make sure that it is factually accurate and pertinent to the subject being discussed. Giving kids false information can be immoral and detrimental to their learning.

It is crucial to ensure proper credit is given to the tool if ChatGPT is used to create content that is subsequently used in academic work. Employing ChatGPT in academic work can be unethical without acknowledging its use. It is crucial to be open and honest about how ChatGPT was utilized and how much it contributed to creating the course materials; when creating content using it will ensure that the students are aware of the tool's purpose in the class and are not misled about the extent of the instructor's involvement in creating the materials.

CONCLUSION

In conclusion, using ChatGPT to make quizzes and assignments can help academics save time and effort while guaranteeing that the questions and prompts are thorough and well-structured. It is crucial to remember that academics should check the automatically generated questions and prompts to ensure they adhere to the course's learning objectives and aims. Academics can save time and produce better materials by using ChatGPT to create lecture notes. It enables academics to ensure that their lecture notes are thorough and precise while focusing on other facets of teaching, like interacting with students and offering feedback. ChatGPT can be an effective tool for creating content, but it is crucial to remember that proper planning is still required. Academics should always examine the generated content to ensure it is correct, pertinent, and suitable for the course's particular context and target audience. Academics can use ChatGPT and other tools to improve their teaching and offer top-notch course materials to their students by being aware of ethical aspects and taking action to prevent any problems.

REFERENCES

Arif, T., Munaf, U., & Ul-Haque, I. (2023). The future of medical education and research: Is ChatGPT a blessing or blight in disguise? *Medical Education Online*, *28*(1), 2181052. Advance online publication. doi:10.1080/10872981.2023.2181052 PMID:36809073

Choudhury, A., & Shamszare, H. (2023). Investigating the Impact of User Trust on the Adoption and Use of ChatGPT: Survey Analysis. *Journal of Medical Internet Research*, *25*, e47184. doi:10.2196/47184 PMID:37314848

Fijačko, N., Gosak, L., Štiglic, G., Picard, C. T., & John Douma, M. (2023). Can ChatGPT pass the life support exams without entering the American heart association course? *Resuscitation*, *185*, 109732. doi:10.1016/j.resuscitation.2023.109732 PMID:36775020

Gilson, A., Safranek, C. W., Huang, T., Socrates, V., Chi, L., Taylor, R. A., & Chartash, D. (2023). How Does ChatGPT Perform on the United States Medical Licensing Examination? The Implications of Large Language Models for Medical Education and Knowledge Assessment. *JMIR Medical Education*, *9*, e45312. doi:10.2196/45312 PMID:36753318

Kung, T. H., Cheatham, M., Medenilla, A., Sillos, C., De Leon, L., Elepaño, C., Madriaga, M., Aggabao, R., Diaz-Candido, G., Maningo, J., & Tseng, V. (2023). Performance of ChatGPT on USMLE: Potential for AI-assisted medical education using large language models. *PLOS Digital Health*, *2*(2), e0000198. doi:10.1371/journal.pdig.0000198 PMID:36812645

Liu, S., Wright, A. P., Patterson, B. L., Wanderer, J. P., Turer, R. W., Nelson, S. D., McCoy, A. B., Sittig, D. F., & Wright, A. (2023). Using AI-generated suggestions from ChatGPT to optimize clinical decision support. *Journal of the American Medical Informatics Association : JAMIA*, *30*(7), 1237–1245. doi:10.1093/jamia/ocad072 PMID:37087108

Lund, B. D., & Wang, T. (2023). Chatting about ChatGPT: How may AI and GPT impact academia and libraries? *Library Hi Tech News*, *40*(3), 26–29. doi:10.1108/LHTN-01-2023-0009

Patel, S. B., & Lam, K. (2023). ChatGPT: The future of discharge summaries? *The Lancet. Digital Health*, *5*(3), e107–e108. doi:10.1016/S2589-7500(23)00021-3 PMID:36754724

Chapter 9
A PubMed Scoping Review:
Advancing the Role of ChatGPT in Medical Education

ABSTRACT

The current study reviews the challenges of using ChatGPT within medical education to address challenges and proposed solutions given by experts in the medical field. The scoping review uses PubMED using Levac, Colquhoun, and O'Brien's Framework as a reference. A total of 13 studies, out of 102 communication, viewpoints, comments, editorials, brief reports, and letters were included and reviewed. Two reviewers independently conducted the selection process, and the decision was consensually made. The study excluded the review, original, and irrelevant articles. The scoping review did identify concerns about the ethical and rational use of ChatGPT. Several experts have raised questions on how to use ChatGPT so that it does not violate the epistemological methods, which generally involve the critical examination of the sources, methods, and justifications for knowledge claims.

BACKGROUND

Several important potentials for improving medical education are presented by artificial intelligence (AI) and generative language models (GLMs), including the availability of realistic simulations, digital patients, tailored feedback, evaluation techniques, and the removal of language barriers (Karabacak et

DOI: 10.4018/978-1-6684-9300-7.ch009

al., 2023). AI chatbots, like ChatGPT, examine previous AI applications in healthcare and preview some potential AI chatbot-assisted in-basket assistance, such as communicating test results with patients, providing patient education, and supporting clinical decision-making during history-taking, reviewing the characteristics of previous diagnostic tests, and common management scenarios (Matulis & McCoy, 2023).

OpenAI's ChatGPT large language model (LLM), made available to the public in November 2022, quickly passed the milestone of having more than 100 million users. Since the start of the ChatGPT revolution, AI tools have become accessible, and this study considers how they can alter physicians' opinions of this ground-breaking technology (Mesko, 2023).

Figure 1. Benefits and challenges of ChatGPT Use in medical education

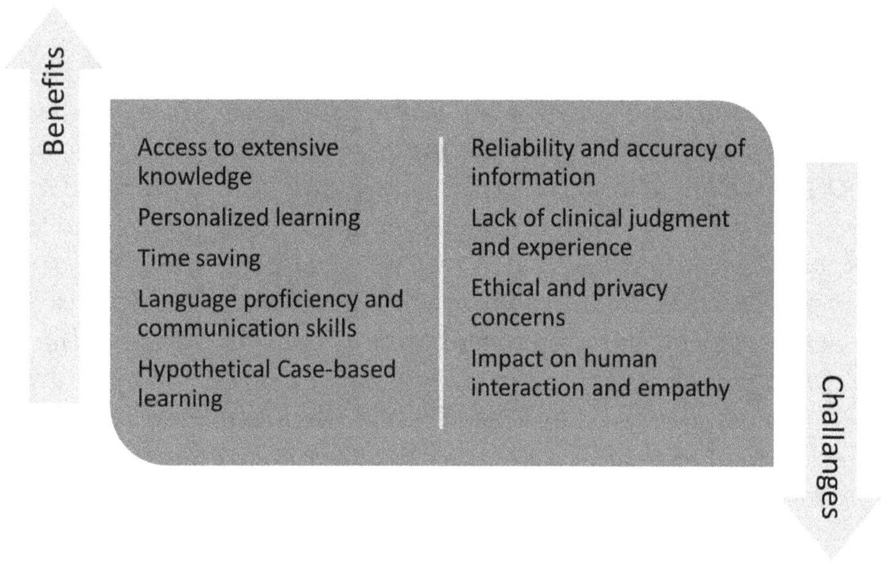

METHODOLOGY

Levac, Colquhoun, and O'Brien's Framework: The current study has adapted the Levac, Colquhoun, and O'Brien proposed framework (Levac et al., 2010). In order to better understand how ChatGPT (a language model) will be used in education in 2023, this research topic will examine the points of view shared in communication, viewpoints, comments, editorials, brief reports, and letters. It attempts to discover what different academic and educational community stakeholders believe are the challenges of incorporating ChatGPT in educational situations.

The study has systematically searched PubMed for Communication, Viewpoints, Comments, editorials, brief reports and letters published in 2023 that focus on integrating ChatGPT in educational settings. The key search terms consist of ChatGPT and education to identify communication, viewpoints, comments, editorials, brief reports, and letters to narrow the search results. The research screening identified studies based on their relevance to the research question, ensuring they address the perceived benefits of integrating ChatGPT in educational contexts. Include studies that present authors' opinions, viewpoints, or experiences regarding the challenges of using ChatGPT in educational settings. Exclude studies that do not directly discuss the challenges of ChatGPT integration or those that focus on other topics unrelated to the research question. The study on the rational use of ChatGPT focuses on the main theme, such as "*What challenges are raised by researchers?* Moreover, *What will be the possible solution to solve the challenges?*

The current scoping review will focus on the publication year (2023), the focus on ChatGPT integration in education, and discussions on perceived challenges. One hundred and two articles were screened, and only thirteen articles were included in the study. Irrelevant articles that do not have clear challenges or solutions were excluded. The selected articles will be evaluated based on the given theme in Table 1. The content extracted from Table 1 was used to develop the word cloud (https://www.wordclouds.com/).

Table 1. List of questions prepared to test ChatGPT

Framework Stage	
Research question	What challenges are associated with integrating ChatGPT in educational settings, as discussed in communication, viewpoints, comments, editorials, brief reports, and letters?
Relevant studies using a search strategy	(ChatGPT[Title/Abstract]) AND (Education[Title/Abstract]) "ChatGPT"[Title/Abstract] AND "Education"[Title/Abstract]
Study selection	Communication, Viewpoints, Comments, editorials, brief reports, and letters available for open access and published in a research journal in 2023. The time stamp starts from 1st January 2023 till 1st July 2023. The research article, review articles, case studies, or preprint is excluded. The grey literature is excluded and will discuss in another book chapter. Closed-access articles are excluded.
Charting the data	The study involves the qualitative content analysis approach.
Collating, summarizing, and reporting the results	What are the challenges raised by researchers? What will be the possible solution to solve the challenges?

RESULTS AND DISCUSSION

In teaching and learning using ChatGPT, a crucial question arises (van de Ridder et al., 2023): How can we effectively leverage the advantages offered by ChatGPT while upholding principles of integrity, ethics, and professionalism? It is important to consider the potential implications of outsourcing critical thinking to an AI-powered system without compromising the essential ethos of both faculty and learners. Striking a balance between harnessing the benefits of ChatGPT and preserving the core values of education requires careful deliberation and proactive measures. This entails establishing clear guidelines, ensuring transparency, and fostering an environment that promotes critical thinking, engagement, and active participation. By integrating ChatGPT thoughtfully into educational settings, we can maximize its potential while safeguarding the fundamental principles and goals of teaching and learning.

Ken Masters raised the issue of referencing and citation within ChatGPT. Firstly, examining whether ChatGPT genuinely comprehends referencing and citation is necessary. While ChatGPT may generate text that appears to include citations, it is essential to consider whether it truly grasps the concept or mimics the structure, which raises concerns about the potential creation of a false perception that ChatGPT understands citing and referencing when, in reality, it may not possess true comprehension. Another challenge arises when all references provided by ChatGPT appear to be correct. In such cases, it becomes crucial to determine whether every citation genuinely supports the statement it claims to support. Unthinkingly accepting citations without verifying their accuracy or relevance could lead to the propagation of misinformation or faulty claims (Masters, 2023b).

The details list of challenges raised by various researchers has been presented in Table 2.

Table 2. Challenges, comments, and solutions reported in the Scoping review

Questions Raised in the Manuscript	Comments	Solution	Reference
How can we harness the benefits of ChatGPT in teaching and learning while maintaining integrity, ethics, and professionalism? Can critical thinking be outsourced without compromising the ethos of faculty and learners?	The user must not ignore ChatGPT in medical education.	Development of Consensus-based guidelines for Generative Artificial Intelligence (GAI). Implementation of transparency in utilizing ChatGPT and acknowledgment given to ChatGPT. Faculty should advocate responsible and ethical use of Generative Artificial Intelligence (GAI). GAI's inherent risks include biased content infringing copyright or plagiarizing from another source. In the future, a critical human review of GAI content is required.	(van de Ridder et al., 2023)
Does ChatGPT understand referencing and citation? Does ChatGPT create a false perception that ChatGPT understands citing and referencing? What do we do when all the references are correct? Should we verify that every citation supports the statement it claims to support?	ChatGPT does not understand the reference and may create an inappropriate reference.	The journal staff and reviewers must be able to detect inappropriate use of AI tools.	(Masters, 2023b)
May Artificial Intelligence (AI) influence future Pediatric research?	Although AI is still developing, it is important to be aware of its potential drawbacks and risks and to think about the implications of its application in medicine.	Ethical and social implications must be considered to ensure that AI is used responsibly and beneficially.	(Corsello & Santangelo, 2023)
Should AI systems with reasoned consciousness and decision-making abilities be granted AI rights, and if so, which basic human rights should be extended to them? How would granting AI rights affect Health Professions Education (HPE)?	HPE must take necessary actions now to address ethical issues in the future.	Education Institutions should establish Education Ethics Boards with similar authority to Research Ethics Boards. These boards would specifically address AI-related issues, focusing on using student data in AI-enhanced Health Professional Education (HPE). The appointment of Chief AI Ethics Officers suggests that HPE institutions should have a similar position dedicated to AI Ethics.	(Masters, 2023a)
Is passing a medical exam enough?	Chat Generative Pre-trained Transformer correctly answered most questions and showed consistency across all different MCQ sources exceeding 60% in most analyses. ChatGPT achieves a score above or near the pass mark.	ChatGPT is currently not a substitute for critical thinking, innovation, and creativity, some of the key attributes doctors are expected to showcase.	(Skalidis et al., 2023)

continues on following page

Table 2. Continued

Questions Raised in the Manuscript	Comments	Solution	Reference
What is the role of ChatGPT, Generative Language Models, and Artificial Intelligence (AI) in Medical Education?	The well-known disturbing tendency of large language models to hallucinate became evident when ChatGPT fabricated references.	JMIR Medical Education has launched a call for papers for a new e-collection and theme issue to understand the challenges faced with AI's advent.	(Eysenbach, 2023)
How is ChatGPT changing nursing and healthcare education? If AI technology becomes the biggest determining factor in research, how should we evaluate human researchers' contributions? Will it become more difficult for junior researchers to establish independent research programs? How should we train the next generation of multidisciplinary researchers and scientists?	ChatGPT, trained on vast amounts of data, possesses extensive knowledge across various disciplines, potentially surpassing many human instructors in basic to moderate-level subjects.	Our educators and policymakers may need to rethink and reshape our education system by allowing students to use ChatGPT as a learning assistant.	(Miao & Ahn, 2023)
What is ChatGPT, and what do we do with it?	Assessment methods that rely solely or largely on text-based responses prepared and uploaded individually by the student may compound academic integrity concerns. Beyond claims of plagiarism, a student or novice nurse could compromise patient safety if ChatGPT was inappropriately utilized within clinical practice without knowledge of the limitations, such as producing unverified or misleading information.	Expanding the curriculum and updating it with the moral and ethical use of Artificial intelligence is necessary.	(Irwin et al., 2023)
Academia needs creative, competent teachers and students. Do we want them to be automated as robots?	Some faculty feel these tools might destroy the art and craft of writing if all students in a class start using ChatGPT for the same assignments, which can lead to plagiarism, copyright problems, and the authenticity of the information.	The faculty should clarify in their syllabi that using generative AI tools such as ChatGPT is prohibited. If students try to use it, it can lead to administrative actions against them. They were updating the assessment methods using adaptive learning methods. The faculty can use ChatGPT for controversial topics with pros and cons. ChatGPT. The student can use ChatGPT and summarise it in their own words in a group discussion.	(Khurana & Vaddi, 2023)

continues on following page

Table 2. Continued

Questions Raised in the Manuscript	Comments	Solution	Reference
Should applicants use ChatGPT to write their personal statements?	Increased awareness and use of ChatGPT requires an urgent review for appropriate management of program procedures, iteration of policies, and a meaningful national discussion.	Program directors and other stakeholders to increase their awareness and explore considerations for AI in training program application materials, processes, and policy needs, starting with this application cycle.	(Zumsteg & Junn, 2023)
The integration of ChatGPT in medical education raises a significant question: Is it a paradigm shift or a dangerous tool?	ChatGPT succinctly and accurately provided a coherent response.	Large language models, such as ChatGPT, represent an enormous opportunity to provide even more efficient and accessible information to learners. As such, we should lean into these discussions, not away from them.	(Grabb, 2023)
Will ChatGPT undermine ethical values in nursing education, research, and practice?	Using ChatGPT in nursing poses ethical challenges that could undermine nursing's core values, while integrating AI in nursing research, education, and practice offers potential advancement.	Scholars and educators must engage in critically reflective dialogues and philosophical analyses of the implications, ethics, and potential drawbacks of using AI in nursing contexts.	(Abdulai & Hung, 2023)
Does ChatGPT provide information is reliable similar to PubMed or MEDLINE?	ChatGPT produces artificial hallucinations or delusions, and the information is not reliable.	There is a need for open debate and discussion on addressing AI-generated content.	(Shaw et al., 2023)

Furthermore, the question analysis asks about the challenges of using ChatGPT in medical education and revealed key concepts and research focus areas by generating a word cloud based on questions extracted from relevant studies using a search strategy. The word cloud prominently displayed terms such as 'chatgpt,' 'referencing,' 'education,' 'citation,' and 'artificial,' indicating issues related to the validation of content produced by ChatGPT. Citation or Bibliography is the most important aspect of data integrity. Figure 2 indicates the word cloud on challenges of ChatGPT use identified in medical education. The analysis of viewpoints, comments, editorials, and communications regarding the solutions to use ChatGPT rationally encompassed a comprehensive examination of various terms. Notably, the word cloud prominently featured terms like 'responsible,' 'policy,' and 'ethics,' signaling the importance of developing policies that promote the rational utilization of ChatGPT. Moreover, the word cloud identified sub-themes such as 'guideline,' 'transparency,' and 'acknowledgment,' which highlight the need for stakeholders to establish guidelines that outline how to appropriately acknowledge the contributions of ChatGPT and enhance transparency in its usage, thereby facilitating its rational application. Figure 3 represents the word cloud on the solutions to address the challenges of using ChatGPT.

Figure 2. Word cloud on challenges of ChatGPT use identified in medical education

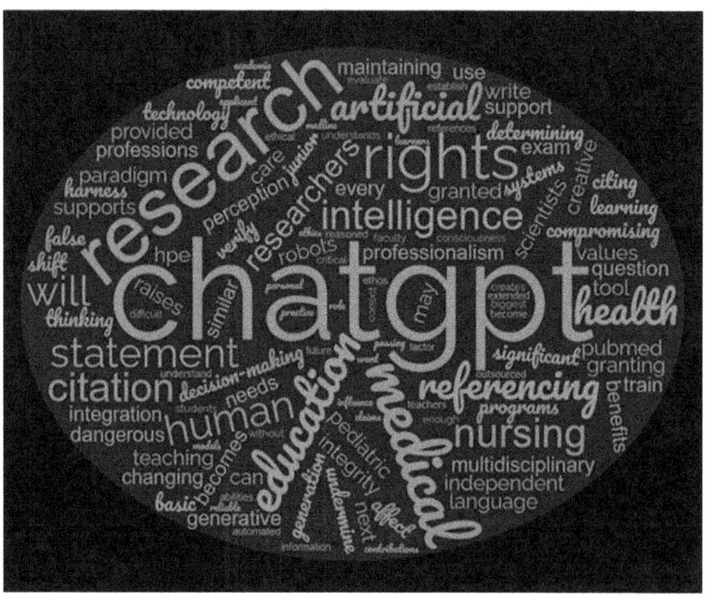

Figure 3. Word cloud on the solutions to address the challenges faces in using ChatGPT

Meo et al conducted a research to evaluate the knowledge of ChatGPT in basic and clinical Medical Sciences. The results revealed that out of 100 MCQs in various disciplines of basic and clinical medical sciences, ChatGPT attempted all the MCQs and obtained 37/50 (74%) marks in basic medical sciences and 35/50 (70%) marks in clinical medical sciences, with an overall score of 72/100 (72%) in both basic and clinical medical sciences (Meo et al., 2023).

Moreover, a recent paper published by Malik Sallam has address the same risks/concerns using ChatGPT such as misinformation, ethical concern, outdated information and copyright complication (Sallam, 2023).

Omar Temsah and his team studied the overview of early ChatGPT's presence in medical literature using Pubmed and Pubmed central where they examined the influence of ChatGPT on various aspects, including medical education, scientific investigation, medical authorship, ethical deliberations, diagnostic decision-making, potential for automation, and critiques. The results underscore a burgeoning collection of literature centered around ChatGPT's role and ramifications in the realm of healthcare, underscoring the necessity for continued exploration to gauge its efficacy and address ethical considerations. The theme identied were depicted in Table 3.

Figure 4. Marks obtained by ChatGPT in various basic and clinical medical science subjects
Source: Meo et al. (2023)

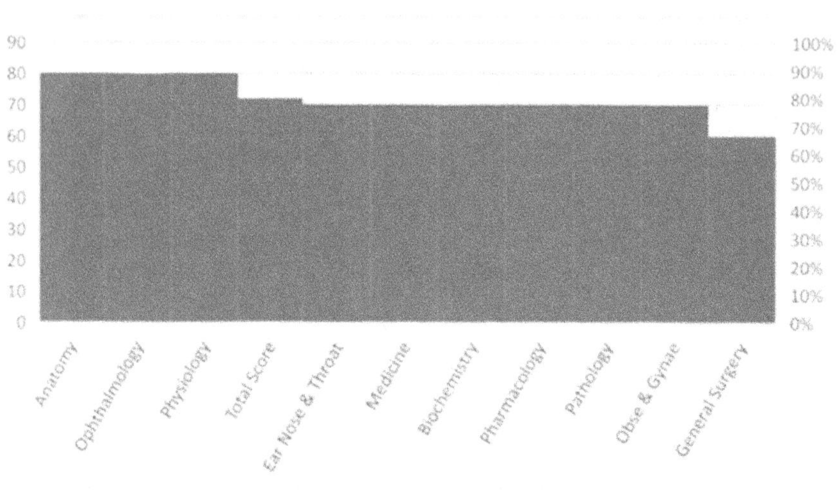

Figure 5. Summary of risks/concerns of ChatGPT use in health care education, research, and practice based on the included records
Source: Sallam (2023)

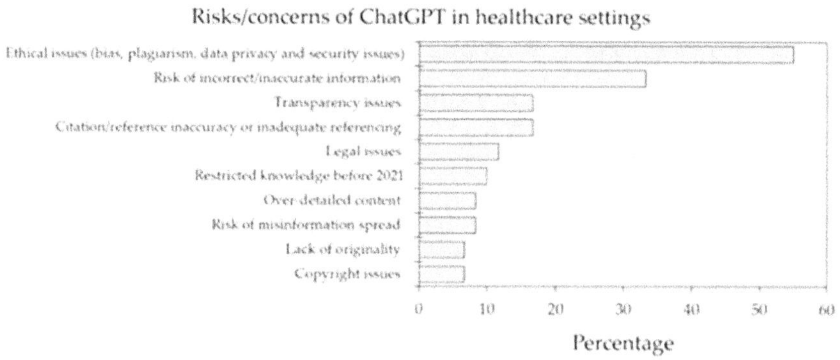

CONCLUSION

In conclusion, all stakeholders must consider the rational and ethical utilization of ChatGPT actively. As artificial intelligence advances, tools like ChatGPT are poised to become more commonplace soon. These tools function as language calculators, enabling the rapid exchange of information and knowledge.

Table 3. Summary of keyfinding retrived from (Temsah et al., 2023)

Theme	Key Findings
ChatGPT's impact on medical education	Improves comprehension, interpretation, and retention of medical knowledge. Offers dependable insights within distinct medical domains. Raises apprehensions about potentially weakening clinical decision-making.
Use in scientific research	Produces consistent and comprehensible material. Elicits ethical considerations concerning authorship, transparency, and responsibility. Raises alarms regarding precision and the propagation of conspiratorial ideas.
Use in medical writing	Widely used instrument for producing medical material. Disrupts conventional authorship norms. Raises considerations regarding precision and ethical ramifications.
Ethical considerations	Elicits worries regarding attribution, responsibility, and openness. Capacity to create deceptive or imprecise content and endorse detrimental beliefs. Underscores the significance of human supervision and clarity in its application.
Role in diagnostic decision-making	Enhances effectiveness and minimizes mistakes in decision-making processes. Raises considerations about precision, reinforcing prejudices, and the necessity of human supervision.
Role in public health	Furnishes dependable approximations in public health studies. Raises worries about the potential dissemination of misleading data and the amplification of detrimental convictions.
Potential for automating medical tasks	Apprehensions regarding devaluing human expertise. Emphasis on the necessity of human supervision.
Criticisms of use	Raising doubts concerning accuracy and the potential to foster conspiracy theories. Disrupting conventional notions of authorship and transparency. Giving rise to ethical concerns and the possibility of bias in influencing decision-making.

Source: Adapted from Temsah et al. (2023)

However, it is crucial to establish comprehensive policies among stakeholders regarding handling AI-generated content. This entails addressing issues such as transparency in using ChatGPT and ensuring appropriate acknowledgment of its role. By fostering transparency and adopting responsible practices, we can navigate the evolving landscape of AI tools effectively and promote their responsible and ethical use.

REFERENCES

Abdulai, A., & Hung, L. (2023). Will ChatGPT undermine ethical values in nursing education, research, and practice? *Nursing Inquiry*, *3–5*(3), e12556. Advance online publication. doi:10.1111/nin.12556 PMID:37101311

Corsello, A., & Santangelo, A. (2023). May Artificial Intelligence Influence Future Pediatric Research?—The Case of ChatGPT. *Children (Basel, Switzerland), 10*(4), 757. doi:10.3390/children10040757 PMID:37190006

Eysenbach, G. (2023). The Role of ChatGPT, Generative Language Models, and Artificial Intelligence in Medical Education: A Conversation With ChatGPT and a Call for Papers. *JMIR Medical Education, 9*, e46885. doi:10.2196/46885 PMID:36863937

Grabb, D. (2023). ChatGPT in Medical Education: A Paradigm Shift or a Dangerous Tool? *Academic Psychiatry, 0123456789*, 2–3. doi:10.100740596-023-01791-9 PMID:37160840

Irwin, P., Jones, D., & Fealy, S. (2023). What is ChatGPT and what do we do with it? Implications of the age of AI for nursing and midwifery practice and education: An editorial. *Nurse Education Today, 127*(May), 105835. doi:10.1016/j.nedt.2023.105835 PMID:37267643

Karabacak, M., Ozkara, B. B., Margetis, K., Wintermark, M., & Bisdas, S. (2023). The Advent of Generative Language Models in Medical Education. *JMIR Medical Education, 9*, e48163. doi:10.2196/48163 PMID:37279048

Khurana, S., & Vaddi, A. (2023). ChatGPT From the Perspective of an Academic Oral and Maxillofacial Radiologist. *Cureus, 15*(6). Advance online publication. doi:10.7759/cureus.40053 PMID:37425514

Levac, D., Colquhoun, H., & O'Brien, K. K. (2010). Scoping studies: Advancing the methodology. *Implementation Science : IS, 5*(1), 69. doi:10.1186/1748-5908-5-69 PMID:20854677

Masters, K. (2023a). Ethical use of Artificial Intelligence in Health Professions Education: AMEE Guide No. 158. *Medical Teacher, 45*(6), 574–584. doi:10.1080/0142159X.2023.2186203 PMID:36912253

Masters, K. (2023b). Medical Teacher 's first ChatGPT's referencing hallucinations: Lessons for editors, reviewers, and teachers. *Medical Teacher, 45*(7), 673–675. doi:10.1080/0142159X.2023.2208731 PMID:37183932

Matulis, J., & McCoy, R. (2023). Relief in Sight? Chatbots, In-baskets, and the Overwhelmed Primary Care Clinician. *Journal of General Internal Medicine, 1*. Advance online publication. doi:10.100711606-023-08271-8 PMID:37369892

Meo, S. A., Al-Masri, A. A., Alotaibi, M., Meo, M. Z. S., & Meo, M. O. S. (2023). ChatGPT Knowledge Evaluation in Basic and Clinical Medical Sciences: Multiple Choice Question Examination-Based Performance. *Healthcare (Basel), 11*(14), 1–11. doi:10.3390/healthcare11142046 PMID:37510487

Mesko, B. (2023). The ChatGPT (Generative Artificial Intelligence) Revolution Has Made Artificial Intelligence Approachable for Medical Professionals. *Journal of Medical Internet Research, 25*, e48392. doi:10.2196/48392 PMID:37347508

Miao, H., & Ahn, H. (2023). Impact of ChatGPT on Interdisciplinary Nursing Education and Research. *Asian/Pacific Island Nursing Journal, 7*, e48136. doi:10.2196/48136 PMID:37093625

Sallam, M. (2023). ChatGPT Utility in Healthcare Education, Research, and Practice: Systematic Review on the Promising Perspectives and Valid Concerns. *Health Care, 11*(6), 887. doi:10.3390/healthcare11060887 PMID:36981544

Shaw, D., Morfeld, P., & Erren, T. (2023). The (mis)use of ChatGPT in science and education. *EMBO Reports, 24*(7), e57501. Advance online publication. doi:10.15252/embr.202357501 PMID:37259767

Skalidis, I., Cagnina, A., Luangphiphat, W., Mahendiran, T., Muller, O., Abbe, E., & Fournier, S. (2023). ChatGPT takes on the European Exam in Core Cardiology: An artificial intelligence success story? *European Heart Journal. Digital Health, 4*(3), 279–281. doi:10.1093/ehjdh/ztad029 PMID:37265864

Temsah, O., Khan, S. A., Chaiah, Y., Senjab, A., Alhasan, K., Jamal, A., Aljamaan, F., Malki, K. H., Halwani, R., Al-Tawfiq, J. A., Temsah, M.-H., & Al-Eyadhy, A. (2023). Overview of Early ChatGPT's Presence in Medical Literature: Insights From a Hybrid Literature Review by ChatGPT and Human Experts. *Cureus, 15*(4). Advance online publication. doi:10.7759/cureus.37281 PMID:37038381

van de Ridder, J. M. M., Shoja, M. M., & Rajput, V. (2023). *Finding the Place of ChatGPT in Medical Education*. Academic Medicine, Publish Ah. doi:10.1097/ACM.0000000000005254

Zumsteg, J. M., & Junn, C. (2023). Will ChatGPT Match to Your Program? *American Journal of Physical Medicine & Rehabilitation, 102*(6), 545–547. doi:10.1097/PHM.0000000000002238 PMID:36912286

Chapter 10
ChatGPT and Its Impact on Education:
A Qualitative Narrative Study of a General Population's Experiences

ABSTRACT

ChatGPT has emerged as a ubiquitous tool across various age groups in contemporary times. Its widespread adoption is evident as individuals continually engage with it throughout the day, employing diverse prompts and pushing the boundaries of its capabilities. This current research seeks to investigate the perceptions and attitudes of the general populace concerning their usage of ChatGPT in their daily lives. The researcher obtained secondary data from prominent social question-and-answer platforms, predominantly from Quora and Reddit, to achieve this objective. The research centred on three key research questions (RQ), using them as a foundation to uncover pertinent themes and corresponding quotes from users. Employing a convenient method, the researcher efficiently identified noteworthy user quotes, enriching the study with valuable insights.

DOI: 10.4018/978-1-6684-9300-7.ch010

BACKGROUND

Social question-and-answer websites can be a valuable resource in research, especially in fields such as sociology, linguistics, information retrieval, and human-computer interaction. Websites like Quora, Reddit, Stack Exchange, and Yahoo Answers can provide a wealth of data and insights into various topics, user behaviour, and opinions—Quora is one of the most frequently used community-driven knowledge sites (Jang et al., 2023). Reddit is one of the most widely embraced social networks, boasting an impressive user base of over 50 million individuals actively participating daily. Within this vibrant digital landscape, Reddit houses a vast array of dynamic and active topical communities known as "subreddits," numbering more than 100,000 (Klebanov, 2022). They are among the most frequently utilized community-driven knowledge platforms.

The current study will contribute to finding answers to questions by exploring the experiences of the general population worldwide on the impact of ChatGPT on education and their perceptions. The research questions include: RQ1: What are the perceptions and attitudes of the general population towards ChatGPT as a teaching tool in various educational contexts? RQ2: How does the use of ChatGPT affect student engagement and motivation in the learning process? RQ3: What are the methods to adopt to change the learning assessment with the advent of ChatGPT?

METHODOLOGY

The current study was a qualitative descriptive design using secondary data from the social question-and-answer website. Xiamen University Malaysia in Sepang, Malaysia. The secondary data from the general population used in the study were from Quora, Reddit, Stack Overflow, answers, wikiHow, and stack exchange. Yahoo Answers is not part of the data collection website as it has shut down since May 4, 2021 (Yahoo, 2021). The study uses convenient sampling to collect the responses from the questions available. The selection of the website is based on the free availability of data. The paid website was excluded from the current study. The main keywords used to search the questions are "ChatGPT AND education" The title of questions must contain keywords "ChatGPT" and "Education". The irrelevant questions were excluded. If no one has answered questions but contains, keywords were excluded. The selections of answers were based on the questions and theme identified. Irrelevant answer that has no relationship with questions or theme will be excluded. Repetitive answer with similar context is excluded in the study. The study does not require ethical approval as the data is available in the public domain.

RESULTS AND DISCUSSION

Professor and Chair Dr. William Beeman from the Department of Anthropology, University of Minnesota, commented in one question about the potential applications of ChatGPT in medical education and training of healthcare professionals. He said, "ChatGPT is like an automated Wikipedia search engine. It can pull up quick answers to questions and put the information in an acceptable narrative format. It is also unreliable, so it needs to be checked carefully if it is used at all. A lot of medical education involves memorization, so generating lists of bones in the foot might be reasonable. But if you ask ChatGPT "what are the best treatments for cancer? I wouldn't trust the results at all.". Several users are debating on Reddit: Why doesn't education want ChatGPT? Some users argue that ChatGPT can make a student dumb while other users have counter argument to use the tool to learn new things fast. Another interesting topic on Reddit title as"ChatGPT Is a Plague Upon Education", the users were discussing the use of paper and pen strategy by the professor in computer science. One of the users commented, "My final for a C programming class included writing out an entire program with pencil". Some users are against the argument in using paper and pen strategy inside the classroom. I think the use of paper and pen strategy in a classroom to counter ChatGPT is subjective and depends upon the assessment's nature. There is no fixed rule in determining the rational use of ChatGPT or bringing back paper and pen inside the classroom. It depends upon the nature of the subject and assessment. Marketlurker, one active user in Reddit, has pointed out several issues with ChatGPT use. He called ChatGPT as "hallucinate", "black box", "data poisoning or toxicity"(Alkaissi & McFarlane, 2023)(Chen et al., 2023)(Deshpande et al., 2023). Another interesting post inside Reddit titled "ChatGPT and Education" discusses the use of ChatGPT for writing Letters of recommendation and job references among users. Each research question has been addressed separately in Table 1, Table 2, and Table 3 respectively.

Table 1. Key themes and quotes related to research question 1

Key Theme	Quote Number	Illustrative Quotes
Challenges to Universities/colleges/ school in education settings	Quote 1	*"The use of AI tools like ChatGPT is challenging traditional methods of assessment in universities. These tools can generate text that is indistinguishable from human-written text, which raises questions about how to assess student learning when it is difficult to tell the difference between human-generated and AI-generated work" (Quora user)*
	Quote 2	*"ChatGPT has successfully passed the American judicial examination and business school examination, and has almost become a "self-taught" examination master. Experts believe that ChatGPT's description can be understood as what people usually say "serious nonsense". But ChatGPT has been eagerly adopted by students to rush through their course work. However, although ChatGPT has certain creative capabilities, it is still difficult to systematically put forward innovative ideas" (Quora user)*
Not a threat to education	Quote 3	*"ChatGPT is not a threat to education. Rather, it can be seen as a tool that can enhance and support education in various ways" (Quora user)*
	Quote 4	*"Chatgpt is an artificial intelligence language model designed to assist and provide information to individuals seeking knowledge and advice in a wide range of fields, including education" (Quora user)*
Unemployment in education field	Quote 5	*"Educators may worry that the use of language models like ChatGPT could lead to a decrease in the need for human teachers and tutors, potentially leading to job losses in the field of education" (Quora user)*
		"ChatGPT has educators worriedbecause it is capable of generating high-quality responses on a wide range of topics, including subjects typically taught in schools. This could lead to the development of AI-powered tutors or even fully automated educational systems, which might make traditional teaching methods less valuable. Additionally, the rapid development of AI in this area is likely to have significant implications for the job market, with some educators concerned that they could be replaced by machines in the future" (Quora user)
	Quote 6	*"One of the drawbacks of artificial intelligence (AI) in education is the increase in teacher unemployment because computers can instruct students without the need for human intervention and because using computers to grade exams reduces workloads compared to using multiple instructors for each student" (Quora user)*
Plagariarsm and misinformation	Quote 7	*"Some educators may be worried about the potential impact of language models like ChatGPT on the field of education. For example, they may be concerned that the model's ability to generate human-like text could make it easier for students to cheat on written assignments, or that it could be used to create fake news or misinformation" (Quora user)*
	Quote 8	*"If the training data contains harmful stereotypes or biased information, this can be reflected in the answers generated by ChatGPT. This can reinforce harmful stereotypes and contribute to the spread of misinformation" (Quora user)*
Lack of context	Quote 9	*"ChatGPT was trained on a large corpus of text, but it does not have the ability to understand the context in which it is being used. This can lead to answers that are technically correct but not applicable to the specific situation or question being asked" (Quora user)*
Potential Bias	Quote 10	*"ChatGPT was trained on a large corpus of text that was scraped from the internet. This text may contain biases and inaccuracies, which can be reflected in the answers generated by the model" (Quora user)*

continues on following page

Table 1. Continued

Key Theme	Quote Number	Illustrative Quotes
Limited Creativity	Quote 11	*"ChatGPT is a language model that generates answers based on patterns it has learned from the text it was trained on. While it can provide helpful information, it may not be able to generate truly creative or original ideas" (Quora user)*
Lack of Critical Thinking	Quote 12	*"Relying on ChatGPT to answer questions can discourage students from developing critical thinking skills. By relying on a machine to provide answers, students may not learn to analyze and evaluate information, formulate arguments, or think creatively" (Quora user)*
	Quote 13	*The entire point of education is to teach students to think critically, to hold specialized knowledge in their brains, and communicate all this back to another human being in a clear, coherent way. What is the point of any of that if students are just learning to be a "meat vehicle" for AI? Where they're just typing questions into AI, then sending the AI's response back to the teacher? Is that where we're at now? Outsourcing our entire thought process to machines? (Reddit user)*
Concerns over AI and chatbots like ChatGPT are exaggerated.	Quote 14	*"These are very simple research tools, but they do not turn out original work. They are a shortcut to pulling up reference material. The one thing they can do is write comprehensive, largely grammatically correct prose, which may help non-native speakers of languages, but the content produced by these chatbots is very elementary and not very original. The concern over these tools reminds me of the time when hand-held calculators became widely available. People got all upset thinking that students couldn't think for themselves or do mathematics themselves if they were using calculators. Of course that concern was overblown. AI tools will be incorporated into our learning and knowledge production just as calculators were" (Quora user)*
Accepting the technology	Quote 15	*"As all new "technologies" educators have faced throughout history, it's part of the lifetime we are living, starting with the rebellion against changing from quills to slates and chalk and from that to pencils and paper, and pencils to pens, etc. It's incumbent upon us to learn everything we can about this new tool, integrate it where appropriate, and outlaw it where inappropriate be that age-appropriate, situationally appropriate, or contextually appropriate. Denying it; saying our students won't have it available; or attempting to create barriers, is counterproductive and not in the best interest of anyone, most of all our students" (Quora user)*
ChatGPT Hallucination	Quote 16	*"ChatGPT is known to hallucinate. That is the euphemism for when it gets things wrong. Unfortunately, it is built in such a way that the false information sounds correct" (Reddit user)*
Supervisory role of teachers in future.	Quote 17	*"Instead, the act of teaching may be turned upside down. Instead of relying on teachers with varying degrees of interpersonal skills, education may end up relying on AI teaching with directed studies. The teachers role then becomes one more of supervisor and of guidance, rather than over worked instructor and suspecting grader" (Reddit user)*

Table 2. Key themes and quotes related to research question 2

Key Theme	Quote Number	Illustrative Quotes
ChatGPT enhance learning experience	Quote 1	*"While Chatgpt may not replace the role of human teachers, mentors, or advisors, it can complement and enhance the learning experience by providing access to information and resources that may not be readily available or accessible otherwise. Overall, Chatgpt is a tool that can support and facilitate education, rather than a threat to it" (Quora user)*
	Quote 2	*"Chatgpt is an AI-powered chatbot designed to improve the quality of online learning experiences. By providing students with more personalized help, it helps improve their experience and learning outcomes" (Quora user)*
	Quote 3	*"Chatgpt can help with education by providing students with access to a virtual tutor. Chatgpt can provide students with personalized, on-demand help with their studies, allowing them to ask questions and receive answers in real-time. This can help students stay on top of their studies and get the help they need when they need it" (Quora user)*
		"ChatGPT can be a learning companion. It can provide explanations, examples, and guidance on various subjects. Whether math, science, history, or creative writing, ChatGPT can offer insights and help kids understand things better. It's like having a patient and knowledgeable tutor right at your fingertips" (Quora user)
		"ChatGPT can also inspire kids with its vast knowledge and creativity. It can share interesting facts, stories, and ideas that ignite their imagination. It can suggest books to read, movies to watch, and projects to try out. It's like having a mentor who encourages exploration and sparks curiosity" (Quora user)
	Quote 4	*"ChatGPT builds critical thinking, sort of an advanced version of searching Dr. Google. It provides personalized data to enhance work products with creativity and fun. I just finished helping my son with a final project before his graduation from college. He needed hypothetical characters to build a story around. ChatGPT gave him options galore that he could tweak and enjoy shaping into what fit the actual assignment. For language arts, reading, science, and social studies, I can see loads of fun ways it will enhance learning" (Quora user)*
	Quote 5	*"I started learning Japanese all by myself (with books of course) and gpt 4 does exactly that for me, also, it can create exercised and correct mistakes I make" (Reddit user)*
	Quote 6	*"ChatGPT taught me economics, bonds, REITs, fundamental analysis and trading futures in a week with all the corresponding formulas and wrote trading scripts. It also broke a lot of medical concepts pretty nicely. It's a tool" (Reddit user)*
	Quote 7	*"ChatGPT is a tool and users need to regard it as such. It has saved me time I would've spent tirelessly going through google results for help with a menial task. It has been especially helpful with producing code if what you want to accomplish is clearly defined. If the task is more difficult (like finding an appropriate empirical strategy for a research question), it's response will likely have errors that you will only catch if you already have knowledge of the subject. Often if you clarify your question, or point out the error in the response, it may produce a more correct solution, but not always. I think it is used best to save time on tedious tasks for which you are familiar. For example, I was quickly provided a list of publications in a subject matter that implemented a specific research method" (Reddit user)*
Real-time Feedback	Quote 8	*"ChatGPT can provide instant feedback to students, which can help them identify areas where they need to improve and adjust their learning accordingly" (Quora user)*
Collaborative learning	Quote 9	*"ChatGPT can facilitate collaborative learning by allowing students to work together on projects and assignments, even if they are not in the same physical location" (Quora user)*

Table 3. Key themes and quotes related to research question 3

Key Theme	Quote Number	Illustrative Quotes
Embedding AI tools into assessments	Quote 1	*"This involves using AI tools to generate questions or prompts for assessments, or to grade student work. For example, an AI tool could be used to generate a prompt that asks students to write a poem in the style of a famous poet. The AI tool could then be used to grade the student's poem based on its adherence to the style of the famous poet" (Quora user)*
Personalized assessments	Quote 2	*"AI tools can be used to create personalized assessments that are tailored to the individual needs of each student. For example, an AI tool could be used to assess a student's strengths and weaknesses in a particular subject. The AI tool could then be used to create an assessment that focuses on the student's weaknesses" (Quora user)*
Critical Thinking	Quote 3	*"I think we need to incorporate more critical thinking into education regardless of ChatGPT. AI cannot reason through the "why" very well. Asking students to solve problems, giving them bad solutions to correct, and asking them to relate the information to their own lives/ challenges in their own fields... will allow professors to evaluate both knowledge and understanding of that knowledge" (Quora user)*
	Quote 4	*"Consistently educate students on the importance of innovative thinking and deliberately raise the status of the importance of human writing (while simultaneously 'devalue' or raise awareness about the limitations and potential biases of AI generated content)" (Quora user)*
Modified assignments	Quote 5	*"Temporarily (and for the sake of experiment) substitute 'writing essays' assignments with in-class discussions or debates related to a subject being taught or a study of a book/research. This encourages critical thinking, collaboration and emphasizes on the importance of communication skills development" (Quora user)*
Promote research	Quote 6	*"Taking measure to make an educational habit of conducting research that requires social efforts like interviews, surveys and fieldwork. This helps maintain a solid foundation of knowledge and scientific inquiry while discouraging over-reliance on AI tools" (Quora user)*

CONCLUSION

The study investigates the impact of ChatGPT in education and observes user behaviour on social question-and-answer websites. The researcher identified mixed reactions to the impact of ChatGPT in education. ChatGPT may not be a threat to education. It may lead to plagiarism and misinformation. The perception of the population on ChatGPT use is subjective and depends upon user intentions and expectations. Moreover, different age groups may have different perceptions. It is necessary to perform further studies to investigate age-level perception and potential bias on an individual level.

REFERENCES

Alkaissi, H., & McFarlane, S. I. (2023). Artificial Hallucinations in ChatGPT: Implications in Scientific Writing. *Cureus*, *15*(2), 2–5. doi:10.7759/cureus.35179 PMID:36811129

ChenL.ChenJ.GoldsteinT.HuangH.ZhouT. (2023). *InstructZero: Efficient Instruction Optimization for Black-Box Large Language Models*. https://arxiv.org/abs/2306.03082v1

DeshpandeA.MurahariV.RajpurohitT.KalyanA.NarasimhanK. (2023). *Toxicity in ChatGPT: Analyzing Persona-assigned Language Models*. https://arxiv.org/abs/2304.05335v1

Jang, S. H., Youm, S., & Yi, Y. J. (2023). Anti-Asian Discourse in Quora: Comparison of Before and During the COVID-19 Pandemic with Machine- and Deep-Learning Approaches. *Race and Justice*, *13*(1), 55–79. doi:10.1177/21533687221134690

Klebanov, S. (2022). *Reddit's Journey to a Potential $15 Billion IPO. 2022*. https://www.businessofbusiness.com/articles/reddit-15-billion-ipo-cultural-force/

Yahoo. (2021). *Yahoo Answers has shut down*. https://help.yahoo.com/kb/SLN35642.html

Chapter 11
Analyzing the Future of ChatGPT in Medical Research:
A Pre-Print Investigation

ABSTRACT

ChatGPT, an advanced language model based on the GPT-3.5 architecture developed by OpenAI, has garnered significant attention and widespread discussions across various domains. Students, educators, professionals, and businesses alike are engaging in dialogues about the capabilities and potential applications of this cutting-edge technology. The objective of the study is to seek current research directions of ChatGPT by looking at various pre-print servers. The current research surrounding ChatGPT demonstrates a growing interest in its application within the context of medical examination boards. Researchers have observed the potential of ChatGPT as a beneficial tool in supporting medical assessments and evaluations. Other research directions include literature synthesis and clinical decision.

INTRODUCTION

The primary reasons supporting the sharing of work in its preliminary form are twofold. Firstly, expediting the availability of research results accelerates the progress of science, enabling timely dissemination of completed work. Secondly, by sharing work with a broader audience, articles benefit from valuable feedback from a diverse group of readers in addition to the formal

DOI: 10.4018/978-1-6684-9300-7.ch011

peer review conducted by a select panel of experts. This dual approach fosters continuous improvement and refinement of scientific publications (Rawlinson & Bloom, 2019). A preprint is a research article made publicly available prior to formal publication. A preprint server is a freely available archive and distribution medium for preprints, allowing rapid dissemination and use of multimedia and supporting files (Warr, 2003).

The current study will aim in the discovery of solutions that yet to be published in peer review journal and waiting in pre-print servers. The researcher examined the pre-print manuscript that are in process of peer review as it relates to ChatGPT's impact on medical education. Among the research inquiries are: RQ1: What forthcoming research can be anticipated on the utilization of ChatGPT in medical education?

METHODOLOGY

The current study investigates the pre-print manuscript that are yet to be peer reviewed. The researcher focused on manuscript published in 2023 based upon convenient narrative sampling. SSRN, Arxiv, Medrxiv, Biorxiv, and Authorea were the chosen preprint servers. Medrxiv possess the maximum number of relevant manuscript on ChatGPT. The identification of manuscript was based upon keywords such as "ChatGPT" and "Medical Education". Citations originating from the authored by the current authors are excluded in this document. Only external references to relevant works are included for a comprehensive and unbiased representation of the literature. Duplicate articles were removed in the given table inside the results. Incomplete manuscript, irrelevant article, abstract only articles were excluded. Given the timeline of this article's publication, it is conceivable that some of the peer-reviewed papers mentioned here might have been published before the release of this manuscript.

RESULTS AND DISCUSSION

The available pre-print encompasses a wide range of investigations exploring the application and performance of ChatGPT in various medical education and healthcare scenarios. These studies delve into areas such as medical examination boards, clinical decision support, radiology reporting, ophthalmological emergencies, treatment options for specific medical conditions, and more. Researchers assess the accuracy, reliability, and potential biases of ChatGPT's responses compared to human experts in medical knowledge and decision-making. Furthermore, the studies investigate the model's proficiency in different languages, such as Chinese and Arabic, and its ability to generate billing codes and predict cardiovascular disease risk. Some research focuses on identifying phenotypes of specific diseases using artificial intelligence, while others explore the implications of large language models on health equity and bias. Overall, these investigations shed light on the strengths, limitations, and promising applications of ChatGPT in the medical field, providing valuable insights for the advancement of healthcare and medical education.

The Table 1 depicts the expected research areas and themes concerning the integration of ChatGPT (Conversational AI language model) in medical education. The question seeks to explore the forthcoming investigations that aim to leverage ChatGPT technology to enhance and innovate medical

Figure 1. List of current pre-print topic on ChatGPT medical research

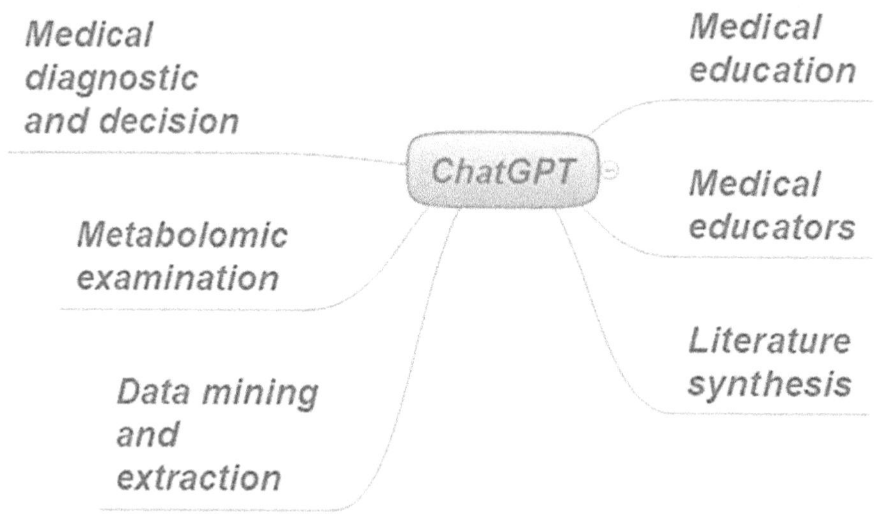

Table 1. Anticipated research on the utilization of ChatGPT in medical research

Research Themes/Topics	Research Objectives	Potential Research Methodologies	Outcomes	Relevant Literature
Medical education and clinical decision making	The current study evaluates the performance of ChatGPT-4 in the specialized field of radiation oncology using the 38th American College of Radiology (ACR) radiation oncology in-training (TXIT) exam and the 2022 Red Journal gray zone cases.	Benchmarking, giving all questions were entered into the ChatGPT website interface	ChatGPT-4 in medical education for the general public and cancer patients, as well as the potential to aid clinical decision-making.	(Huang et al., 2023)
Literature Synthesis	The present research highlight initial impact of ChatGPT in different fields of life that are evident in literature so far and integrated with relevant responses from ChatGPT.	Nil	ChatGPT helps in identification and demonstrate research gaps in the field of health and medical, education, knowledge management, library and information science, programming and organizations and organizational behavior.	(Amber, 2023)
Performance of ChatGPT on Clinical Medicine Entrance Examination for Chinese Postgraduate in Chinese	The objective of study aims to provide qualitative feedback on ChatGPT's problem-solving capabilities in medical education and clinical decision-making in Chinese.	A dataset of Clinical Medicine Entrance Examination for Chinese Postgraduate	ChatGPT's performance was suboptimal for medical education and clinical decision-making in Chinese compared with in English.	(Vera et al., 2023)
The Use of AI-Supported Chatbot in Psychology	The research aimed to discuss the use of AI chatbots in psychology in writing the essays.	A brief literature review article	ChatGPT can allow writing essays on various topics	(Uludag, 2023)
Analyzing the Performance of ChatGPT in Cardiology and Vascular Pathologies	The goal was to assess ChatGPT potential as a valuable tool in medical education compared to two well-ranked students of medicine.	The selected questions belong to the 6th year Medicine faculty program of Algiers, Algeria.	The results showcase how ChatGPT has the potential to be highly effective in the fields of cardiology and vascular pathologies by providing accurate answers to relevant questions.	(Hariri, 2023)
Performance of ChatGPT on USMLE	The study discuss the reliable of ChatGPT in answering complex medical and clinical questions.	United States Medical Licensing Examination (USMLE) questionnaire	The paper believes ChatGPT and other language learning models can be invaluable tools for e-learners; however, the study suggests that there is still room to improve their accuracy.	(Sharma et al., 2023)

continues on following page

Table 1. Continued

Research Themes/Topics	Research Objectives	Potential Research Methodologies	Outcomes	Relevant Literature
Opportunities and Challenges for ChatGPT and Large Language Models in Biomedicine and Health	The researcher examin the diverse applications of large language models (LLMs), such as ChatGPT, in biomedicine and health.	Literature review	Pros and cons of ChatGPT in biomedicine and health	(Tian et al., 2023)
Evaluating Large Language Models (LLMs) on a Highly-specialized Topic, Radiation Oncology Physics	The paper proposes evaluating LLMs on a highly-specialized topic, radiation oncology physics, which may be more pertinent to scientific and medical communities in addition to being a valuable benchmark of LLMs.	A multiple-choice examination on radiation oncology physics was created for this study by an experienced medical physicist.	The study demonstrated that LLMs, particularly ChatGPT (GPT-4), can excel in answering questions on a highly-specialized topic like radiation oncology physics as well as exhibit surprising capabilities in deductive reasoning.	(Holmes et al., 2023)
Large AI Models in Health Informatics	The manuscript discusses the applications, Challenges, and the future of large language AI.	Literature review	The researcher identifies seven key sectors that large AI models are applicable and might have substantial influence, including 1) molecular biology and drug discovery; 2) medical diagnosis and decision-making; 3) medical imaging and vision; 4) medical informatics; 5) medical education; 6) public health; and 7) medical robotics.	(Qiu et al., 2023)
Translating complex radiology reports into plain language.	The researcher investigates the feasibility of using ChatGPT in experiments on using ChatGPT to translate radiology reports into plain language for patients and healthcare providers so that they are educated for improved healthcare.	Chest CT screening reports and brain MRI screening reports from the Atrium Health Wake Forest Baptist clinical database.	ChatGPT can successfully translate radiology reports into plain language with an average score of 4.27 in the five-point system.	(Lyu et al., 2023)
ChatGPT vs. Bard: A Comparative Study	The aim of this study is to determine whether Bard has the potential to surpass ChatGPT as the most popular AI chatbot.	Literature review	The research highlight ChatGPT's exceptional performance, positioning it as a leading model.	(Ahmed et al., 2023)
ChatGPT-Enhanced ROC Analysis	The researcher are providing the ChatGPT-Enhanced ROC Analysis (CERA) tool which performs ROC curve analysis and optimal cutoff values with a shiny user-interface web tool.	ChatGPT-Enhanced ROC Analysis (CERA) web tool	A web-based shiny tool called CERA (ChatGPT-Enhanced ROC Analysis), designed to facilitate ROC curve analysis.	(Agraz & Karniadakis, 2023)

continues on following page

Table 1. Continued

Research Themes/Topics	Research Objectives	Potential Research Methodologies	Outcomes	Relevant Literature
Biomedical Text Generation and Mining with ChatGPT, benchmark study	The paper aims to contribute to the growing body of research in the field of biomedical NLP by providing a comprehensive evaluation of ChatGPT model on biomedical text generation and mining.	Benchmark data set for Biomedical NLP, the Biomedical Language Understanding & Reasoning Benchmark (BLURB)	ChatGPT built on the early version of GPT-3.5 performed poorly on several biomedical NLP benchmark data sets, the superior version can perform better,	(Chen et al., 2023)
GeneTuring tests GPT models in genomics	The aim of study is to developed GeneTuring, a comprehensive question-and-answer (Q&A) database, to evaluate the performance of GPT models in genomic.	GeneTuring to test GPT models.	It is essential to not only focus on improving the accuracy of the model but also to pay equal attention to enhancing its awareness of its own limitations or incapacity. This is particularly crucial to tackle a phenomenon called "AI hallucination,"	(Hou & Ji, 2023b)
LLMs used in NAPLEX	The study aims to evaluate the capabilities and limitations of three large language models (LLMs) – GPT-3, GPT-4, and Bard, in the field of pharmaceutical sciences by assessing their pharmaceutical reasoning abilities on a sample North American Pharmacist Licensure Examination (NAPLEX).	Multiple-choice questions was obtained from an online source.	GPT-4 exhibited superior performance compared to GPT-3 and Bard.	(Angel et al., 2023)
Automated cell type annotation with GPT-4 in single-cell RNA-seq analysis	The research demonstrate that GPT-4, a highly potent large language model, can automatically and accurately annotate cell types by utilizing marker gene information generated from standard single-cell RNA-seq analysis pipelines.	HuBMAP Azimuth project, manually annotated cell types and their marker genes were downloaded from the Azimuth website	Evaluated across hundreds of tissue types and cell types, GPT-4 generates cell type annotations exhibiting strong concordance with manual annotations, and has the potential to considerably reduce the effort and expertise needed in cell type annotation.	(Hou & Ji, 2023a)
Data mining and machine learning approach using GPT-4 in synthetic biology	Our study emphasizes the potential impact of Natural Language Processing (NLP) in synthetic biology research, enabling more streamlined data collection and swift consolidation of published case studies.	GPT-4 assisted database construction for *Yarrowia lipolytica* biomanufacturing	Generative AI to automate information extraction from research articles and advanced AI applications to facilitate design-build-test-learn (DBTL) for biomanufacturing as well as biotech commercial decisions.	(Xiao et al., 2023)

continues on following page

Table 1. Continued

Research Themes/Topics	Research Objectives	Potential Research Methodologies	Outcomes	Relevant Literature
Automated Extraction and Visualization of Metabolic Networks from Biomedical Literature Using a Large Language Model	The objective of the work contributes to the advancement of text mining techniques for extracting metabolic pathways from research literature.	Using GPT-3.5 Turbo model that is based on Instruction-Tuned LLM (Language Model) to extract bioentities and relationships from each abstract that is fetched from PubMed via Entrez API.	The researchers enable to gain insights into complex biological systems, advancing our understanding of metabolic pathways and their components	(Phongwattana & Chan, 2023)
Perceptions and Experiences of ChatGPT in Medical Education	The study aimed to explore the knowledge, perceived benefits, concerns, and limitations of using ChatGPT in medical education, among faculty and students at a leading Saudi Arabian university.	Qualitative study	Participants demonstrated good knowledge of ChatGPT and its functions. The main themes were knowledge, perception of ChatGPT, and roles of ChatGPT in research and medical education. The perceived benefits included collecting and summarizing information and saving time and effort.	(Abouammoh et al., 2023)
Explorative Assessment of ChatGPT as an Aid in Medical Education	To explore the use of ChatGPT by educators and students in a medical school setting. Method:	Prompts to create the contents.	ChatGPT can function as an aid to educators, but it is not yet suitable as a reliable information resource for educators and medical students.	(Wang et al., 2023)
Concise review of literature of ChatGPT using PubMed	A concise review combined with a SWOT (strengths, weaknesses, opportunities, threats) analysis on ChatGPT potentials in natural science including medicine	Literature review	ChatGPT has been used to write essays, pass exams, translate knowledge for various peer groups, or write comments on the most diverse topics.	(Gödde et al., 2023)
Comparative Analysis of GPT-4 and GPT-3.5 on Turkish Medical Specialization Exam Performance	The goal of this study was to compare the performance of the GPT-4 and GPT-3.5 AI models in answering questions on the Turkish Medical Specialty Examination (TUS), with an emphasis on the differences between the clinical and fundamental science parts.	Turkish Medical Specialties (TUS) examination records from the past three years.	GPT-4 demonstrated a better overall success rate (70.56%) than GPT-3.5 (40.17%) and physicians (38.14%) in this study examining the competency of GPT-4 and GPT-3.5 in answering questions from the Turkish Medical Specialization Exam (TUS).	(Kılıç, 2023)
Performance of ChatGPT on Chinese National Medical Licensing Examinations	This study aimed to quantitatively evaluate the performance of ChatGPT on three types of national medical examinations in China, including National Medical Licensing Examination (NMLE), National Pharmacist Licensing Examination (NPLE), and National Nurse Licensing Examination (NNLE).	Questions from Chinese NMLE, NPLE and NNLE	ChatGPT failed to pass the threshold score (0.6) in any of the three types of examinations over the five years.	(Zhi et al., 2023)

continues on following page

Table 1. Continued

Research Themes/Topics	Research Objectives	Potential Research Methodologies	Outcomes	Relevant Literature
Exploratory survey about using ChatGPT in education, healthcare, and research	A hybrid (virtual and in-person) panel discussion event, in examining various perspectives regarding the use of ChatGPT in education, research, and healthcare	Quantitatively analyzed received responses on questions about the use of ChatGPT.	Despite the growing interest, the acceptability of ChatGPT's usage remained uncertain, as a considerable number of respondents believed it was premature to form a definitive opinion. Nonetheless, they expressed ongoing interest in exploring the potential of ChatGPT.	(Hosseini et al., 2023)
ChatGPT in Dermatology	The goals of this study are to evaluate the literature concerning the applications of ChatGPT and its potential impact on various fields within dermatology.	Systematic review	There are advancements in interactive learning, integrations with image-based AI, and enhancing language models for dermatology applications.	(Gabashvili, 2023)
Diagnostic accuracy of ChatGPT	In the current study we tested the ability of ChatGPT to find the correct diagnoses for full-text clinical case vignettes of patients.	Clinical Case	ChatGPT might be a good tool to assist human medical doctors in diagnosing difficult cases, but despite the good diagnostic accuracy, ChatGPT should be used with caution by non-professionals	(Mehnen L., Gruarin, S., Vasileva, M., Knapp, 2023)
Appropriateness of ChatGPT in answering heart failure related questions	The study focuses on three key aspects of ChatGPT's performance. Firstly, it evaluates the accuracy of ChatGPT's responses to questions related to heart failure. Secondly, it examines the reproducibility of ChatGPT's answers across multiple attempts. Lastly, it assesses the improvement in performance between GPT-3.5 and the newer version, GPT-4.	The researchers curated a list of 125 frequently asked questions related to heart failure from medical societies, renowned medical institutions, and Facebook support groups.	The study compared the performance of GPT-4 and GPT-3.5 in generating responses to questions. GPT-4 demonstrated superiority over GPT-3.5, providing more comprehensive answers (83.2% vs. 78.5%) and avoiding any incorrect responses. Additionally, both models showed high reproducibility, but GPT-4 achieved a slightly higher score (100% vs. 94%) in delivering consistent responses to most questions.	(King et al., 2023)
Comparison of ChatGPT vs. Bard to Anesthesia-related Queries	The study aims to analyze the LLMs' response to patient's anesthesia- related queries.	Commonly asked anesthesia related questions during the pre-anesthesia consultation procedure prior to surgery in a hospital setting.	The study shows that LLMs can generate effective responses from patient queries. ChatGPT was technical, precise, and descriptive, whereas Bard was conversational, adequate and exhibited "hallucinations".	(Patnaik & Hoffmann, 2023)

education practices, highlighting the potential benefits and challenges in this evolving field.

CONCLUSION

In conclusion, ChatGPT, a state-of-the-art language model developed by OpenAI, has captured widespread attention and sparked discussions across diverse fields. The present study aimed to explore current research directions of ChatGPT by examining various pre-print servers. Notably, researchers have identified a burgeoning interest in utilizing ChatGPT in the context of medical examination boards, showcasing its potential as a valuable tool for medical assessments and evaluations. Additionally, other research directions encompass literature synthesis and clinical decision-making, underscoring the model's versatility and applicability in advancing various domains. As ChatGPT continues to evolve, its impact on education, industry, and scientific endeavors is poised to be profound, paving the way for new possibilities and innovations in natural language processing and beyond.

REFERENCES

AbouammohN.RainaR.SolimanM. (2023). *Original Research : Exploring Perceptions and Experiences of ChatGPT in Medical Education : A Qualitative Study Among Medical College Faculty and Students in Saudi ArabiaAcknowledgments : Declaration of.* doi:10.1101/2023.07.13.23292624

AgrazM.KarniadakisG. E. (2023). *ChatGPT-Enhanced ROC Analysis (CERA): A Shiny Web Tool for Finding Optimal Cutoff in Biomarker Analysis Authors summary.* doi:10.1101/2023.07.13.548794

AhmedI.KajolM.HasanU.DattaP. P. (2023). *ChatGPT vs. Bard: A Comparative Study.* doi:ndownloader.figshare.com/files/41277468

Amber, Q. (2023). *ChatGPT Revolution in Different Fields of Life : Literature Synthesis and Research Agenda ChatGPT Avenues : Integrated Evidence from Literature and ChatGPT.* https://papers.ssrn.com/sol3/papers.cfm?abstract_id=4451821

AngelM.PatelA.AlachkarA.BaldiP. F. (2023). Clinical Knowledge and Reasoning Abilities of AI Large Language Models in Pharmacy: A Comparative Study on the NAPLEX Exam. In bioRxiv. doi:10.1101/2023.06.07.544055

ChenQ.SunH.LiuH.JiangY.RanT.JinX.XiaoX.LinZ.NiuZ.ChenH. (2023). A Comprehensive Benchmark Study on Biomedical Text Generation and Mining with ChatGPT. BioRxiv, 2023.04.19.537463. doi:10.1101/2023.04.19.537463

GabashviliI. S. (2023). *ChatGPT in Dermatology: A Comprehensive Systematic Review*. doi:10.1101/2023.06.11.23291252

Gödde, D., Nöhl, S., Wolf, C., Rupert, Y., & Rimkus, L. (2023). *ChatGPT in medical literature – A concise review and SWOT analysis*. Academic Press.

HaririW. (2023). *Analyzing the Performance of ChatGPT in Cardiology and Vascular Pathologies*. doi:10.21203/rs.3.rs-2782768/v1www.researchsquare.com/article/rs-2782768/v1

HolmesJ.LiuZ.ZhangL.DingY.SioT. T.McGeeL. A.AshmanJ. B.LiX. LiuT.ShenJ.LiuW. (2023). *Evaluating Large Language Models on a Highly-specialized Topic, Radiation Oncology Physics*. https://arxiv.org/abs/2304.01938

Hosseini, M., Gao, C. A., Liebovitz, D., Carvalho, A., Ahmad, F. S., Luo, Y., MacDonald, N., Holmes, K., & Kho, A. (2023). *An exploratory survey about using ChatGPT in education, healthcare, and research Mohammad*. https://doi.org/https://doi.org/10.1101/2023.03.31.23287979

HouW.JiZ. (2023a). Reference-free and cost-effective automated cell type annotation with GPT-4 in single-cell RNA-seq analysis. In bioRxiv. doi:10.1101/2023.04.16.537094

Hou, W., & Ji, Z. (2023b). GeneTuring tests GPT models in genomics. BioRxiv *: The Preprint Server for Biology, 6*, 1–8. doi:10.1101/2023.03.11.532238

HuangY.GomaaA.SemrauS.HaderleinM.LettmaierS.WeissmannT.GrigoJ. Ben TkhayatH.FreyB.GaiplU.DistelL.MaierA.FietkauR.BertC.PutzF. (2023). *Benchmarking ChatGPT-4 on ACR Radiation Oncology In-Training (TXIT) Exam and Red Journal Gray Zone Cases: Potentials and Challenges for AI-Assisted Medical Education and Decision Making in Radiation Oncology*. doi:10.2139/ssrn.4457218

KılıçM. E. (2023). *AI in Medical Education: A Comparative Analysis of GPT-4 and GPT-3.5 on Turkish Medical Specialization Exam Performance*. https://doi.org/https://doi.org/10.1101/2023.07.12.23292564

King, R. C., Samaan, J. S., Yeo, Y. H., Mody, B., Lombardo, D. M., & Ghashghaei, R. (2023). *Appropriateness of ChatGPT in answering heart failure related questions*. Academic Press.

Lyu, Q., Tan, J., Zapadka, M. E., Ponnatapura, J., Niu, C., Myers, K. J., Wang, G., & Whitlow, C. T. (2023). Translating Radiology Reports into Plain Language using ChatGPT and GPT-4 with Prompt Learning: Promising Results, Limitations, and Potential. *Visual Computing for Industry, Biomedicine, and Art*, *6*(1), 9. Advance online publication. doi:10.118642492-023-00136-5 PMID:37198498

MehnenL.GruarinS.VasilevaM.KnappB. (2023). ChatGPT as a medical doctor? A diagnostic accuracy study on common and rare diseases. In medRxiv. doi:10.1101/2023.04.20.23288859

PatnaikS. S.HoffmannU. (2023). Comparison of ChatGPT vs. Bard to Anesthesia-related Queries. In MedRxiv. doi:10.1101/2023.06.29.23292057

PhongwattanaT.ChanJ. H. (2023). *Automated Extraction and Visualization of Metabolic Networks from Biomedical Literature Using a Large Language Model*. doi:10.1101/2023.06.27.546560

QiuJ.LiL.SunJ.PengJ.ShiP.ZhangR.DongY.LamK.LoF. P.-W.XiaoB.YuanW. XuD.LoB. (2023). *Large AI Models in Health Informatics: Applications, Challenges, and the Future*. https://arxiv.org/abs/2303.11568

Rawlinson, C., & Bloom, T. (2019). New preprint server for medical research. *BMJ (Clinical Research Ed.)*, *365*, l2301. doi:10.1136/bmj.l2301 PMID:31167753

SharmaP.ThapaK.ThapaD.DhakalP.UpadhayaM. D.AdhikariS.KhanalS. R. (2023). *Performance of ChatGPT on USMLE: Unlocking the Potential of Large Language Models for AI-Assisted Medical Education*. https://arxiv.org/abs/2307.00112

TianS.JinQ.YeganovaL.LaiP.-T.ZhuQ.ChenX.YangY.ChenQ.KimW. ComeauD. C.IslamajR.KapoorA.GaoX.LuZ. (2023). *Opportunities and Challenges for ChatGPT and Large Language Models in Biomedicine and Health*. https://arxiv.org/abs/2306.10070v1

UludagK. (2023). *The use of AI-supported Chatbot in Psychology*. doi:10.2139/ssrn.4331367

VeraP.MarieM.GaviriaJ. A.MiroslavT.PetrH.EstherB.TudorT.NinaM. ChawdheryR. A. (2023). *Performance of ChatGPT on Clinical Medicine Entrance Examination for Chinese Postgraduate in Chinese*. doi:10.2139/ssrn.4415697

Wang, Y., Sibaii, F., Lee, K., Gill, J. M., & Hatch, J. (2023). NOTE: This preprint reports new research that has not been certified by peer review and should not be used to guide clinical practice. medRxiv. https://doi.org/https://doi.org/10.1101/2023.02.13.23285879

Warr, W. A. (2003). Evaluation of an Experimental Chemistry Preprint Server. *Journal of Chemical Information and Computer Sciences*, *43*(2), 362–373. doi:10.1021/ci025627a PMID:12653498

XiaoZ.LiW.MoonH.RoellG. W.ChenY.TangY. J.RoellG.TangY. (2023). Generative artificial intelligence GPT-4 accelerates knowledge mining and machine learning for synthetic biology. In bioRxiv. doi:10.1101/2023.06.14.544984

ZhiT.LeiL.RenyuanW.SongG. (2023). *Performance of ChatGPT on Chinese National Medical Licensing Examinations: A Five-Year Examination Evaluation Study for Physicians, Pharmacists and Nurses*. https://doi.org/https://doi.org/10.1101/2023.07.09.23292415

Chapter 12
Analyzing the PESTEL Factors on ChatGPT and Its Impact on the Population

ABSTRACT

An AI application called ChatGPT has spurred discussions about how it can affect education. The researcher used the PESTEL analysis framework to understand the political, economic, social, technological, environmental, and legal aspects of ChatGPT in education and research. The political aspect observed leaned towards the left orientation. The economic aspect is loosely inclined towards increased productivity and efficiency. The social aspect is directed towards improved social services sectors. The environmental aspect raised concerns about carbon emissions and is yet not explored in detail by researchers, leading to a clear research gap. Last, the authors discuss the legal impact of ChatGPT on the population, and there is an unclear picture towards the AI laws and regulations. There is a need for research to differentiate traditional AI and generative AI. Moreover, generative AI must subclassify before developing the policy for all stakeholders. In conclusion, the responsible use of ChatGPT will benefit the productivity of the general population.

DOI: 10.4018/978-1-6684-9300-7.ch012

BACKGROUND

ChatGPT has been discussed extensively in every discipline. It has been stated as beneficial in every field, including education, medicine, science, and research. ChatGPT has been discussed widely in education with its pros and cons. However, it is essential to assess ChatGPT rationally. Therefore, it is necessary to discuss the tool with a framework that covers all aspects of a population's productivity. Therefore, the researcher uses PESTEL as a framework to observe the truthfulness of the argument that ChatGPT is productive in all dimensions and is unbiased, neutral and positively impacts society. The researcher did observe several positive and negative aspects of ChatGPT in various disciplines in a population and is somewhat sceptical. The current study discusses the impact of ChatGPT on the productivity of the general population using the PESTAL framework: RQ1: What will be the overall impact of ChatGPT on the productivity of a general population?

PESTEL ANLAYSIS FRAMEWORK

A political, economic, sociocultural, technological, environmental and legal (PESTEL) analysis is a framework or tool used to analyze and monitor the macro-environmental factors that impact an organization (Nurmi & Niemelä, 2018). It has been used to understand productivity research (Pan et al., 2019). PESTEL analysis of using ChatGPT in education was illustrated in Figure 1.

PESTEL ANALYSIS INTERPRETATION

Political

David Rozado, in his paper titled "The political bias of ChatGPT", has observed left-leaning political orientation when administering several political orientation tests to ChatGPT (Rozado, 2023). Jerome Rutinowski et al. have performed multiple tests to observe the political orientation of ChatGPT and found a similar orientation from an authoritarian left or libertarian left quadrant of the political compass. In addition, ChatGPT perceives itself to be highly open and agreeable, which are traits associated with progressive political views (Rutinowski et al., 2023). Martin, John Levi has expressed similar observation when testing ChatGPT and called its political views and beliefs align with the left side of the political spectrum (Martin, 2023).

Economical

Ali Zarifhonarvar from Indiana University has evaluated the economic impact of ChatGPT in the labour market using the supply and demand model. Incorporating AI technologies such as ChatGPT has the potential to enhance productivity and efficiency, but it also raises concerns about job displacement and unemployment for certain workers. Specifically, about 32.8% of occupations could face a Full Impact, resulting in significant and disruptive consequences. Conversely, approximately 30.7% of occupations are projected to have No Impact, allowing those workers to maintain their current job functions unaffected. For the remaining 36.5% of occupations that may experience a Partial Impact, there could be moderate changes to work processes and job responsibilities (Zarifhonarvar, 2023). Several studies endorsing increased productivity and efficiency using ChatGPT, such as ChatGPT, are expected to influence various tourism processes significantly. These AI technologies are anticipated to enhance front-of-house operations by optimizing customer service and improving back-of-house operations, increasing productivity and efficiency.

There is a strong relationship between productivity, efficiency, and economic outcomes. Both productivity and efficiency play crucial roles in determining the overall economic performance of a country, industry, or organization (Giménez et al., 2018; Heshmati, 2000). Training ChatGPT on data from production lines makes it capable of detecting anomalies and changes and promptly alerting personnel when necessary. Moreover, in the textile industry, it can offer personalized support and advice to shoppers, generating relevant recommendations based on individual preferences. This technology empowers companies to enhance the customer experience and optimize their services, making them more efficient, cost-effective, and responsive (Rathore, 2023). However, a more fundamental question arises: Will AI replace human labour and decision-making entirely, or will it primarily serve as an assistant, aiding human decision-making in handling information overload? Both scenarios have the potential to generate significant economic benefits. According to a recent report by Goldman Sachs (Hatzius et al., 2023), the widespread adoption of generative AI could boost annual US labour productivity growth by nearly

1½ percentage points over ten years. Budhwar et al. enlightened society's shift towards openly available software, which benefits all organizations and available workers by providing advantages and cost savings. It is the era of self-employment and the Gig economy. ChatGPT can help improve cost-effectiveness in HR by assisting with various tasks such as job descriptions, screening applications, creating interview questions, developing training materials, and writing policy documents. This "outsourcing" to ChatGPT can save time and money and avoid additional costs from consultancy firms, but it may bring inaccurate or misleading information, privacy issues, legal concerns, ethical matters and outdated information (Budhwar et al., 2023).

Social

ChatGPT has sparked extensive discussions regarding its notable features, advantages, and possible drawbacks. From the social perspective, ChatGPT can elevate consumer engagement, enhance customer service, enable personalization in shopping experiences, facilitate social interactions and communication practice, optimize cost-effectiveness, provide insights into consumer behaviour, and refine marketing campaigns (Paul et al., 2023). Andreas Hepp et al., in their manuscript titled 'ChatGPT, LaMDA, and the Hype Around Communicative AI: The Automation of Communication as a Field of Research in Media and Communication Studies', introduced figurational sociology. Figurational sociology could help researchers examine how these technological advancements influence the relationships, behaviours, and interactions within media and communication (Hepp et al., 2023). Baek and Kim researched the user motivations for ChatGPT usage, which may affect perceived creepiness, trust, and the intention to continue using AI chatbot technology. The researcher found that greater task efficiency increased perceived creepiness. The researchers explain that the personalization-gratification component reduces perceived AI creepiness while increasing perceived trust. They suggest that personalization may give ChatGPT users more control over the AI system, making them comfortable (Hyun Baek & Kim, 2023). Ray and Das have indicated that ChatGPT has undeniably facilitated communication, bringing the world closer through its accessible, engaging interface. They suggest the community foster a culture of digital literacy, ethics, and social responsibility, which can help humans harness AI's potential, including ChatGPT, to enhance human capabilities and foster a more cohesive, equitable society (Ray & Das, 2023). ChatGPT is helpful in medical science and helps improve personalized learning, clinical reasoning and understanding of complex medical concepts (Sallam et al., 2023).

Technology

Much debate is going on embedding AI-driven communication's integration with current technological systems. Yongbin He, Haifeng Tang, Dongxue Wang, Shuqin Gu, Guoxin Ni & Haiyang Wu wrote a letter to the editor on the potential use of ChatGPT in assisting the surgeon. According to these researchers, AI-powered chatbots can assist in communication among spinal surgeons, patients, and their families, simplify the gathering and assessment of patient information, and enhance the surgical preparation process (He et al., 2023). Taking advantage of the public availability of ChatGPT, we are embracing its potential to optimize English foreign language materials and assessments. Personalization is the future in utilizing the full potential of ChatGPT in education (Koraishi, 2023). ChatGPT can support the dissemination and diffusion of new research ideas and improve the grammar of manuscripts, but it can produce the 'Matthew Effect'. It is essential to use the tool with responsibility. Copyright of the content is a crucial element of writing the manuscript. It is necessary to understand that ChatGPT is a language model which uses training data, tokenization, and neural network architecture (Zhao et al., 2023). The authors must be careful in understanding the content's source, copyright status, and context (Lund et al., 2023).

Environmental

Considerable attention has been directed towards the adverse environmental effects of artificial intelligence, primarily stemming from energy-intensive machine learning algorithms and associated emissions (Yokoyama et al., 2023). In a news feature published in Nature titled "The Carbon Impact of Artificial Intelligence," Payal Dhar addresses the primary challenges of quantifying energy consumption in AI research. According to the author, the problem to tackle in reducing AI's climate impact is quantifying its energy consumption and carbon emission and making this information transparent (Dhar, 2020). Today, there is a tremendous increase in using several AI applications such as ChatGPT and BARD. Several companies are developing their personalized chatbot, raising concerns about carbon emission issues. The complex computing used by AI models like ChatGPT can contribute to carbon emissions. Training and running large AI models require significant computational resources, including powerful hardware such as GPUs (Graphics Processing Units) and TPUs (Tensor Processing Units) and data centres to support the processing demands. These computational processes consume electricity, and in cases where the electricity comes from non-renewable sources, it can result in carbon emissions (Wang et al., 2023).

The issue arises at the individual level, where technology is ubiquitous within households. With the emergence of the Internet of Things, the widespread utilization of AI tools is inevitable, underscoring the importance of raising awareness about optimizing these tools in homes to mitigate overall carbon emissions. To tackle challenges affecting interpersonal communication and interactions with an environment, it is proposed that AI tools, applications, or systems like ChatGPT can play a role in fostering inventive concepts. The concept revolves around harnessing AI to devise innovative remedies that promote eco-friendly practices and alleviate the environmental impact of interpersonal communication and engagement. What could be Sustainable practices in using CHATGPT to protect the environment? Ask from ChatGPT. The answer is presented in Figure 2.

Figure 1. PESTEL analysis of using ChatGPT in education

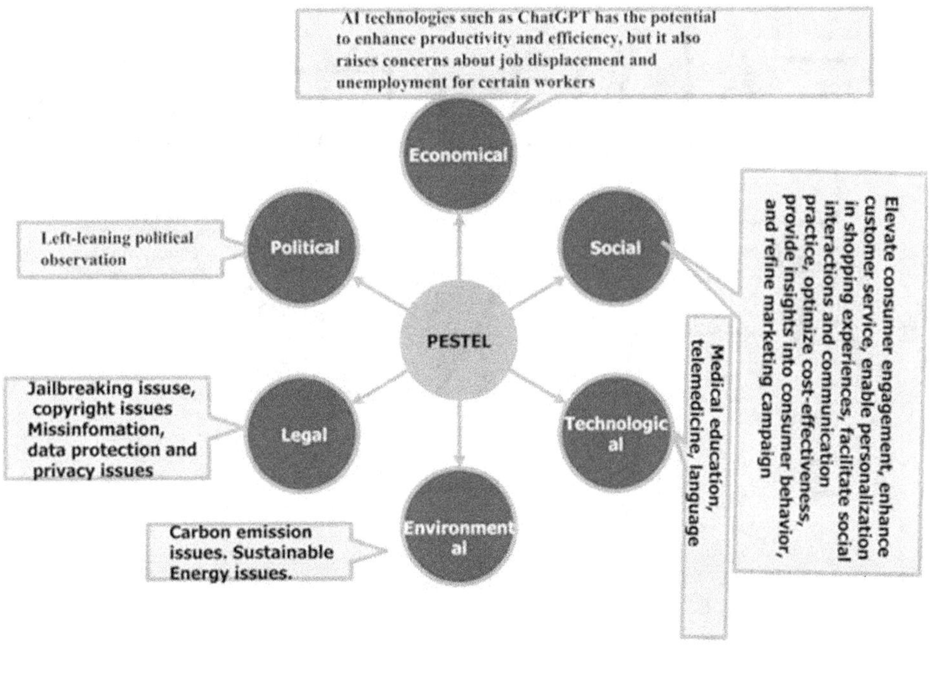

Figure 2. ChatGPT response 'What could be sustainable practices in using CHATGPT to protect the envirnoment?'

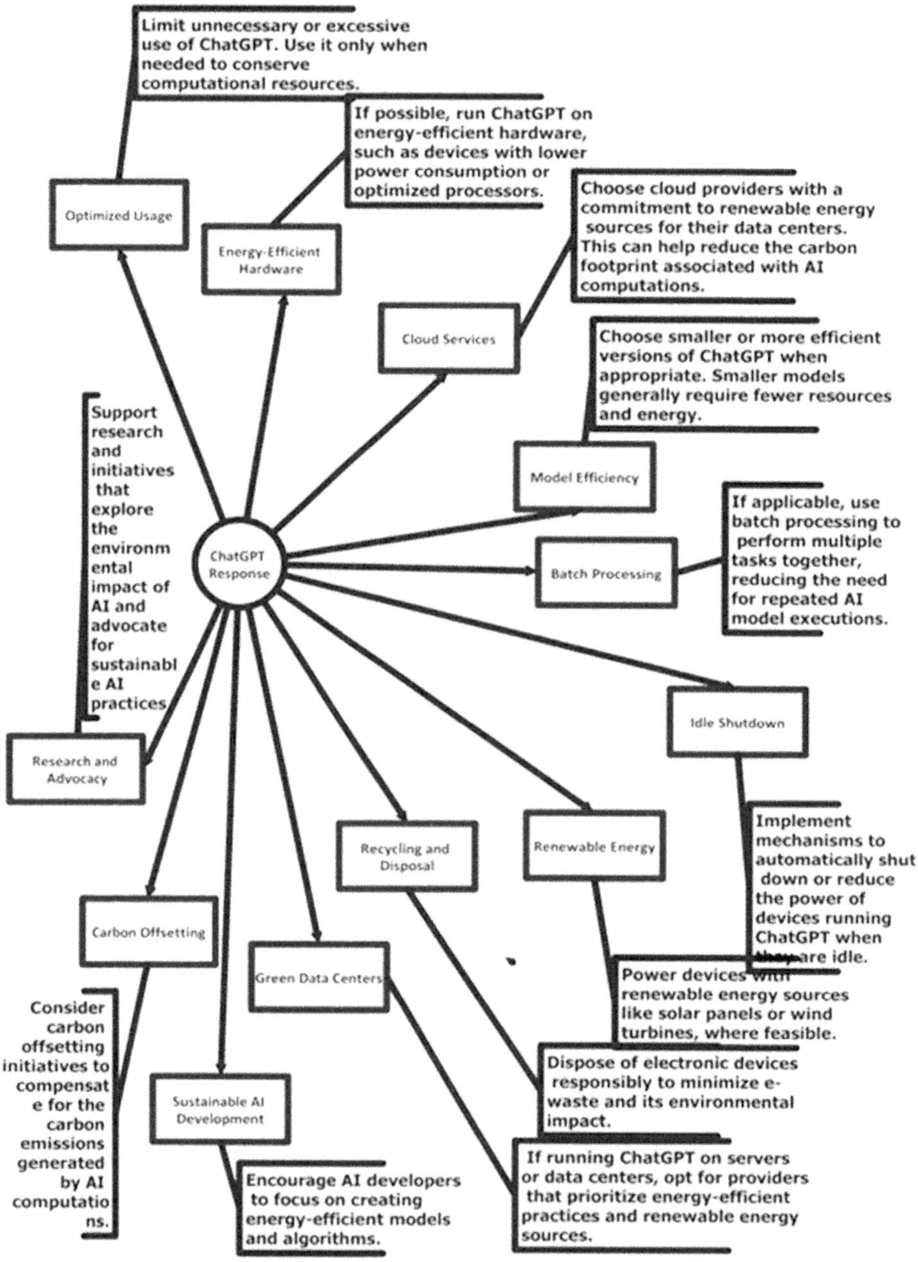

Legal

The notion of "jailbreaking" first emerged within the technology domain, referring to circumventing constraints on electronic devices to achieve heightened control over software and hardware functionalities. Interestingly, this concept has extended its applicability to encompass substantial language models such as ChatGPT. Employing particular techniques, users can "jailbreak" ChatGPT, enabling them to command it in manners that surpass the original intentions of its creators. While the output generated by ChatGPT is typically bound by OpenAI's internal governance and ethical guidelines (Roberts, 2023)There are various methods to jailbreak, such as 'Do Anything Now' (DAN) method, The SWITCH method, The CHARACTER Play method. In the context of ChatGPT, reverse psychology can entail phrasing questions or statements in a way that indirectly prompts the AI to generate the desired response (Gupta et al., 2023). To train large language models, enormous volumes of data are needed. These data may contain private information on specific people, such as their search histories, chats, and personal preferences. This information risks being abused or accessed by unauthorized individuals, which might have significant privacy implications (Ali & Khuwaja, 2023).

Helberger and Diakopoulos have discussed the current status of Artificial intelligence (AI) law. They suggested differentiating between traditional AI and generative AI. Generative AI systems are not constructed for specific contexts or predefined conditions of utilization. Their inherent openness and ease of control facilitate an unparalleled scope of use. Consequently, generative AI introduces challenges that intersect with fundamental concepts and principles outlined in the current rendition of the AI Act. They supported the idea of categorizing generative AI and general-purpose AI more broadly as a distinct category of general risk instead to mentioned it as high risk. The researcher highlights the importance of carefully examining and adjusting the rules in the Act to match the unique features of generative AI systems. They suggest having a rule that monitors potential big problems, like what is done in the Digital Services Act (DSA) law. The researcher emphasizes the fact to pay more attention to how the people who make generative AI and those who use it, both professionals and regular users, work together and agree on things (Helberger & Diakopoulos, 2023).

According to my understanding, Philipp Hacker et al. suggests three regulation layers in their paper titled Regulating ChatGPT and Other Large Generative AI Models. The first layer of regulation applies directly to all Large Generative AI Models (LGAIMs). This layer includes existing regulations that are neutral to the specific technology used. For example, it mentions the General Data Protection Regulation (GDPR), a data protection law, and non-discrimination provisions that ensure fairness and equal treatment. Additionally, certain parts of the AI Act, specifically Article 10 and cybersecurity rules in Article 15, could also be relevant for regulating LGAIM developers. Sustainability and content moderation tools are also considered part of this initial layer of regulation. According to the authors, to my understanding, Article 28b is a move towards regulating LGAIMs regarding sustainability and content moderation; it might not fully cover all aspects or be completely effective. Large Generative AI Models (LGAIMs) such as ChatGPT to summarize or grade job applicants' resumes for employment decisions is considered a high-risk application in the second layer. When an LGAIM is used for a high-risk application, such as the employment example mentioned, the responsibility for adhering to the AI Act's high-risk obligations, including implementing a risk management system, falls on the individual or entity using the AI model for that purpose. The last layer is the vital aspect of LGAIM, suggesting increasing the collaboration between all stakeholders. The authors emphasize drawing from existing legal systems to find a balance between sharing information and protecting trade secrets. The mention of Art. 28(2a) AI Act EP Version indicates that steps are being taken in this direction (Hacker et al., 2023).

CONCLUSION

After evaluating the political, economic, social, technological, environmental, and legal aspects of ChatGPT in a general population, it is concluded that the researcher needs to focus their research on legal and environmental factors. Most of the currently available research is limited to its potential benefits in the field of education and hot ChatGPT passing the examination. I agree with the potential benefits of the rational use of ChatGPT, yet the researcher needs to spend time developing AI-ChatGPT or large language-based model policies in their respective sectors. Moreover, the development of policies must follow United Nations' sustainable development goals (SDGs).

REFERENCES

Ali, S., & Khuwaja, P. (2023). *ChatGPT Needs SPADE (Sustainability, PrivAcy, Digital divide, and Ethics) Evaluation : A Review.* https://ieeexplore.ieee.org/document/10198233/

Budhwar, P., Chowdhury, S., Wood, G., Aguinis, H., Bamber, G. J., Beltran, J. R., Boselie, P., Lee Cooke, F., Decker, S., DeNisi, A., Dey, P. K., Guest, D., Knoblich, A. J., Malik, A., Paauwe, J., Papagiannidis, S., Patel, C., Pereira, V., Ren, S., ... Varma, A. (2023). Human resource management in the age of generative artificial intelligence: Perspectives and research directions on ChatGPT. *Human Resource Management Journal, 33*(3), 606–659. doi:10.1111/1748-8583.12524

Dhar, P. (2020). The carbon impact of artificial intelligence. *Nature Machine Intelligence, 2*(August), 423–425. doi:10.103842256-020-0219-9

Giménez, V., Prior, D., Tortosa-Ausina, E., Giménez, V., Prior, D., & Tortosa-Ausina, E. (2018). The impact of efficiency on the economic growth of emerging economies: The case of Colombia. *Ensayos Sobre Política Económica, 36*(SPE85), 86–100. doi:10.32468/Espe.8505

Gupta, M., Akiri, C., Aryal, K., Parker, E., & Praharaj, L. (2023). From ChatGPT to ThreatGPT: Impact of Generative AI in Cybersecurity and Privacy. *IEEE Access : Practical Innovations, Open Solutions, 11*(July), 80218–80245. doi:10.1109/ACCESS.2023.3300381

Hacker, P., Engel, A., & Mauer, M. (2023). Regulating ChatGPT and other Large Generative AI Models. *2023 ACM Conference on Fairness, Accountability, and Transparency*, 1112–1123. 10.1145/3593013.3594067

Hatzius, J., Briggs, J., Kodnani, D., & Pierdomenico, G. (2023). *Global-Economics-Analyst_-The-Potentially-Large-Effects-of-Artificial-Intelligence.* Goldman Sachs Economics Research. https://www.ansa.it/documents/1680080409454_ert.pdf

He, Y., Tang, H., Wang, D., Gu, S., Ni, G., & Wu, H. (2023). Will ChatGPT/GPT-4 be a Lighthouse to Guide Spinal Surgeons? *Annals of Biomedical Engineering, 51*(7), 1362–1365. doi:10.100710439-023-03206-0 PMID:37071280

Helberger, N., & Diakopoulos, N. (2023). ChatGPT and the AI Act. *Internet Policy Review, 12*(1), 1–6. doi:10.14763/2023.1.1682

Hepp, A., Loosen, W., Dreyer, S., Jarke, J., Kannengießer, S., Katzenbach, C., Malaka, R., Pfadenhauer, M. P., Puschmann, C., & Schulz, W. (2023). ChatGPT, LaMDA, and the Hype Around Communicative AI: The Automation of Communication as a Field of Research in Media and Communication Studies. *Human-Machine Communication*, *6*, 41–63. doi:10.30658/hmc.6.4

Heshmati, A. (2000). Productivity Growth, Efficiency and Outsourcing in. *Journal of Economic Surveys*, *17*(1), 79–112. doi:10.1111/1467-6419.00189

Hyun Baek, T., & Kim, M. (2023). Is ChatGPT scary good? How user motivations affect creepiness and trust in generative artificial intelligence. *Telematics and Informatics*, *83*(March), 102030. doi:10.1016/j.tele.2023.102030

Koraishi, O. (2023). Teaching English in the age of AI: Embracing ChatGPT to optimize EFL materials and assessment. *Language Education and Technology*, *3*(1), 55–72. https://bit.ly/43en7e1

Lund, B. D., Wang, T., Mannuru, N. R., Nie, B., Shimray, S., & Wang, Z. (2023). ChatGPT and a new academic reality: Artificial Intelligence-written research papers and the ethics of the large language models in scholarly publishing. *Journal of the Association for Information Science and Technology*, *74*(5), 570–581. doi:10.1002/asi.24750

Martin, J. L. (2023). The Ethico-Political Universe of ChatGPT. *Journal of Scientific Computing*, *4*(1), 1–11. doi:10.23919/JSC.2023.0003

Nurmi, J., & Niemelä, M. S. (2018). PESTEL Analysis of Hacktivism Campaign Motivations. Lecture Notes in Computer Science, 11252, 323–335. https://doi.org/ doi:10.1007/978-3-030-03638-6_20/FIGURES/8

Pan, W., Chen, L., & Zhan, W. (2019). PESTEL Analysis of Construction Productivity Enhancement Strategies: A Case Study of Three Economies. *Journal of Management Engineering*, *35*(1), 05018013. doi:10.1061/(ASCE)ME.1943-5479.0000662

Paul, J., Ueno, A., & Dennis, C. (2023). ChatGPT and consumers: Benefits, Pitfalls and Future Research Agenda. *International Journal of Consumer Studies*, *47*(4), 1213–1225. doi:10.1111/ijcs.12928

Rathore, B. (2023). Future of textile: Sustainable manufacturing & prediction via chatgpt. *EDUZONE: International Peer Reviewed/Refereed Multidisciplinary Journal*, *12*(1), 2319–5045.

Ray, P. P., & Das, P. K. (2023). ChatGPT and societal dynamics: Navigating the crossroads of AI and human interaction. *AI & Society, 0123456789.* Advance online publication. doi:10.100700146-023-01713-1

Roberts, M. (2023). *How to Jailbreak ChatGPT with these Prompts.* Mlyearning. https://www.mlyearning.org/how-to-jailbreak-chatgpt/

Rozado, D. (2023). The Political Biases of ChatGPT. *Social Sciences (Basel, Switzerland), 12*(3), 148. doi:10.3390ocsci12030148

RutinowskiJ.FrankeS.EndendykJ.DormuthI.PaulyM. (2023). *The Self-Perception and Political Biases of ChatGPT.* https://arxiv.org/abs/2304.07333

Sallam, M., Salim, N., Barakat, M., & Al-Tammemi, A. (2023). ChatGPT applications in medical, dental, pharmacy, and public health education: A descriptive study highlighting the advantages and limitations. *Narra J, 3*(1), e103. doi:10.52225/narra.v3i1.103

Wang, D., Feng, L., Ye, J., Zou, J., & Zheng, Y. (2023). Accelerating the integration of ChatGPT and other large-scale AI models into biomedical research and healthcare. *MedComm – Future Medicine, 2*(2). doi:10.1002/mef2.43

Yokoyama, A. M., Ferro, M., de Paula, F. B., Vieira, V. G., & Schulze, B. (2023). Investigating hardware and software aspects in the energy consumption of machine learning: A green AI-centric analysis. *Concurrency and Computation, e7825*, e7825. doi:10.1002/cpe.7825

Zarifhonarvar, A. (2023). Economics of ChatGPT: A Labor Market View on the Occupational Impact of Artificial Intelligence. SSRN *Electronic Journal.* doi:10.2139/ssrn.4350925

ZhaoW. X.ZhouK.LiJ.TangT.WangX.HouY.MinY.ZhangB.ZhangJ.DongZ.DuY.YangC.ChenY.ChenZ.JiangJ.RenR.LiY.TangX.LiuZ.WenJ.-R. (2023). *A Survey of Large Language Models.* https://arxiv.org/abs/2303.18223

Chapter 13
Is There an Increased Risk of Cyberchondriasis Post ChatGPT Era?
A Conceptual Model With Precipitating, Predisposing, and Maintaining Factors

ABSTRACT

Technology advancements have given people the ability to research health topics online and do self-diagnostics. Cyberchondria is a clinical occurrence wherein recurrent online searches for medical information lead to heightened anxieties regarding one's physical well-being. The AI-powered language model ChatGPT, created by OpenAI, can produce text that sounds like human speech depending on context and previous interactions. Therefore, there is a tremendous increase in use of generative AI such as ChatGPT in assessing their own health condition which may results in increase in prevalence of Cybercondriasis. The objective of current study is understanding the precipitating, predisposing, and maintaining factors in results of using ChatGPT in self-diagnosis. The results develop a conceptual model using psychosocial model and use literature to observe its relevance.

DOI: 10.4018/978-1-6684-9300-7.ch013

BACKGROUND

The escalating prevalence of cyberchondria is becoming an increasingly worrisome issue (Mestre-Bach & Potenza, 2023). In July 2022, a cross-sectional study on cyberchondria prevance was carried out among BSc Computer Science students at Sri Sathya Sai Baba Degree College in Anantapuramu, Andhra Pradesh. The findings indicated a cyberchondria prevalence rate of 22.5%. Among the various constructs examined, excessiveness emerged as the dominant factor (mean ± standard deviation [SD]: 3.36 ± 2.091), followed by distress, compulsion, and reassurance (mean ± SD: 2.48 ± 2.493) (Kulsum et al., 2023). Another research uncovered a notable occurrence of cyberchondria within the Saudi population, and this was found to be linked with both smartphone addiction ($r = 0.395$, CI = 0.316/0.475, $P = 0.0001$) and elevated eHealth literacy levels (r = 0.265, CI = 0.182/0.349, P = 0.0001) (El-Zayat et al., 2023). ChatGPT has been introduced in November 2022. Since the launch of ChatGPT, the social influence has made the application ultiziation on a large scale population. It is being used by students, teachers, researchers, adoescents, aduld and people who has literacy to use internet. The increase used of ChatGPT has raise psychological issues that a population may face in a future. The objective of current study is to identify factors that may increase the risk of cybercondriasis in a general population.

PSYCHOSOCIAL MODEL

A conceptual systems framework such as psychosocial model has been dicussed in various research strategies. Forexample, psychosocial factors on the trajectory of child/adolescent mental health problems (CAMHP) over time was discussed by Daniel Fatori et al., 2013 (D. et al., 2013). Cyberchondria has been discussed in various psychological models. Matteo Vismara et al., discussed the systematic review psychological models and mechanisms associated with cyberchondria (CYB), relationships between CYB and mental disorders and prevention and treatment strategies (Vismara et al., 2020). Zheng et al., in 2020 has published an important theoretical model including psychosocial factors that illuminates the processes of cyberchondria development among individuals who are anxious about their health (Zheng et al., 2021).

Figure 1. Psychosocial model

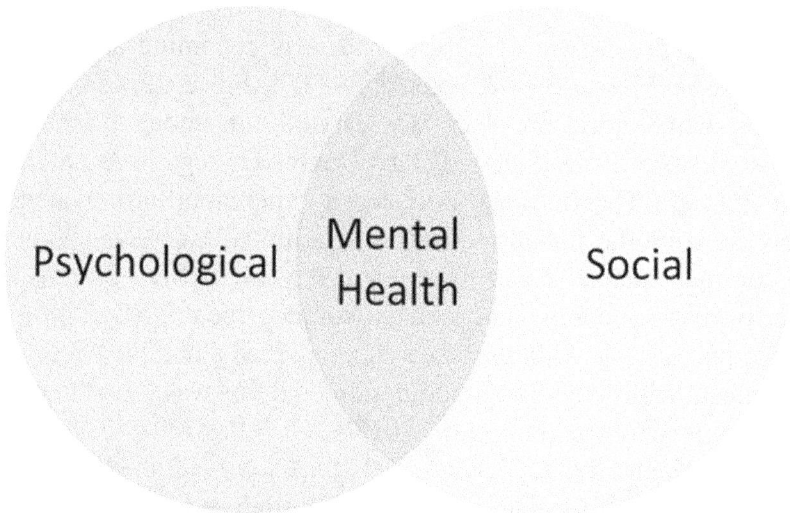

PRECIPITATING FACTORS

Seeking medical advice online has become popular in the recent past. Therefore a growing number of people might ask the recently hyped ChatGPT for medical information regarding their conditions, symptoms and differential diagnosis (Mehnen L., Gruarin, S., Vasileva, M., Knapp, 2023). When individuals input their symptoms into ChatGPT and receive a list of potential conditions, they might hyper-focus on the most severe or alarming possibilities, leading to increased anxiety. People who misread or misunderstand the data shown by ChatGPT may conclude prematurely that they have a significant medical problem. Skyler B Johnson et al., results suggest that ChatGPT provides accurate information about common cancer myths and misconceptions yet, it is unknown to assume that ChatGPT could be accurate in giving information of all kind of medical myths and misconception (Johnson et al., 2023). Continuously seeking reassurance from ChatGPT about health concerns can lead to a cycle of increased anxiety as individuals become more fixated on their symptoms. Shahsavar and Choudhury suggest to improve the technology in ensuring AI chatbots' safe and responsible use in health care (Shahsavar & Choudhury, 2023). Engaging excessively with ChatGPT or other health-related websites over a short period can lead to an information overload that triggers heightened anxiety. A study published in 2021 support positive relationship between compulsive health-related internet use and cyberchondria (Khazaal et al., 2021). Moreover, If ChatGPT responds to a user's input with unexpected or distressing information, it can catch the individual off guard and contribute to anxiety. A study by McMullan et al showed positive correlation between health anxiety and online health information seeking, and between health anxiety and cyberchondria (McMullan et al., 2019). ChatGPT lacks the ability to provide emotional support or empathy, which can leave individuals feeling isolated and anxious when discussing their health concerns (Zhao et al., 2023)(Arslan, 2023). People may get more worried or anxious while using ChatGPT in their health condition as they try to understand what ChatGPT's replies indicate since they are vague or lack context or limited engagement (Frosolini et al., 2023).

Figure 2. Precipitating factors

PREDISPOSING FACTORS

Cyberchondria may be more common in people who already have a propensity toward health worry, anxiety or hypochondria. It is due to metacognitive effect that may trigger predisposing factor (Fergus & Spada, 2018)(Schenkel et al., 2021). Since these people have a propensity to misinterpret even seemingly insignificant symptoms as being suggestive of major illnesses, using ChatGPT for health-related talks might feed their anxieties. Moreover, it is possible that ChatGPT's replies aren't always precise or conclusive, which might make it difficult to evaluate symptoms. This uncertainty could increase anxiety and cause people to think of the worst-case situations. Mehul Bhattacharyya et al., stated that the medical information seeking from ChatGPT is inaccurate and found to be fabricated (Bhattacharyya et al., 2023). Emilio Ferrara has endorsed conformation bias from literature that training data may contain biases that result from individuals seeking out information that aligns with their pre-existing beliefs. People with cyberchondria frequently hunt for material that validates their anxieties. If ChatGPT's replies are consistent with their assumptions, they may unintentionally feed their fears. ChatGPT does not have access to a person's entire medical history because it is not a healthcare provider. Relying exclusively on its replies without obtaining a doctor's guidance might cause symptoms to be misinterpreted. Some people could place an excessive amount of confidence in technology and choose seeking out its advice over seeing a healthcare expert. As a result, their symptoms may be overestimated in severity. This asumptions was explained in broad context by Choudhary and Samszare stated an overreliance on it for health-related advice could potentially lead to misinformation and subsequent health risks (Choudhury & Shamszare, 2023). People may be more open about their worries and symptoms due to the anonymity, which might amplify their anxiety. There is a need of research on the anonymity and detachment as a predisposing factor. The rapid and simple access to a wealth of information offered by ChatGPT and like programs might result in information overload and increased anxiety (Kim et al., 2023). Social influence" plays a vital role in determining users' "Behavioral intention" to adopt technology (Strzelecki, 2023). It is possible that increase in social influence may increase in use of ChatGPT in various aspect of life including psychological issues without consilting medical expert which my result in increase in cyberchondria. There is no available literature till today.

Figure 3. Predisposing factors

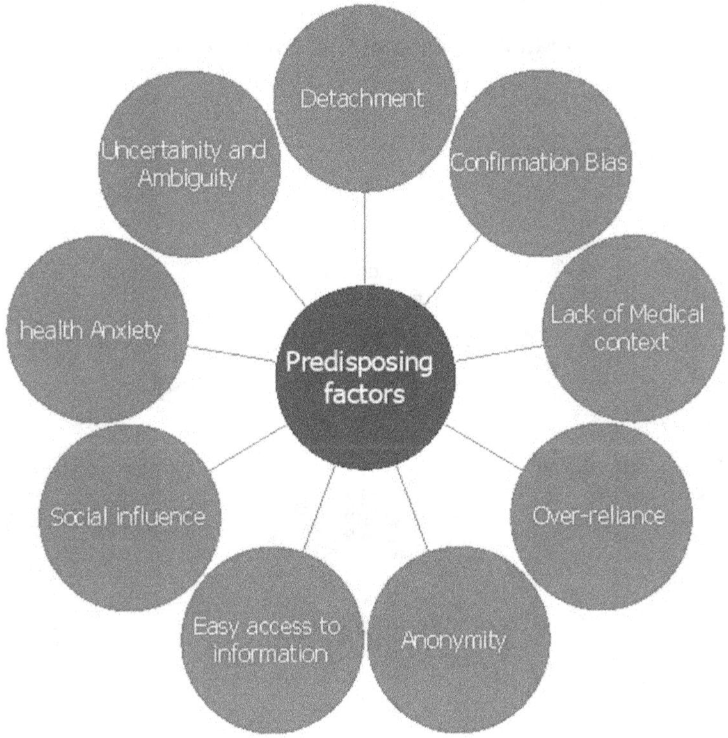

MAINTAING FACTORS

The sensation of cyberchondria can be sustained and made worse over time by maintaining factors, which are persistent elements or habits. Certain actions or circumstances might make cyberchondria more persistent while utilizing ChatGPT or related programs. Here are several sustaining elements that, when used with ChatGPT, might cause and prolong cyberchondria. Continuously consulting ChatGPT for information about health issues, symptoms, or diseases might exacerbate anxiety by maintaining the attention on possible illnesses rather than on finding comfort or the right medical attention. Individuals risk unintentionally reinforcing their anxiety and ignoring more accurate or reassuring information if they focus on and recall only ChatGPT comments that support their fears. Relying solely on ChatGPT for health information and avoiding consultation with qualified medical professionals can lead to a lack of accurate diagnosis and appropriate treatment. Aram Cox has pointed an important issue that ChatGPT-4 to convey medical information on blepharoplasty requires cautious implementation (Cox et al., 2023). There are lack of researching in understanding the maintaing factors and research need do design theortical and conceoptual model to test the hypothesis.

Figure 4. Maintaining factors

CONCLUSION

There is limited results in understanding the difference of prevalence of cybercondriasis between pre-ChatGPT and post-ChatGPT era. In light of current circumstances, it is becoming increasingly important for developers to consider implementing a timer feature within ChatGPT. This would encourage users to take breaks from prolonged usage and would also allow for periodic assessments of their mental state. For instance, incorporating regular sentiment checks during interactions could help ensure a healthier and more mindful engagement with ChatGPT.

Figure 5. PPM factors of a psychosocial model of health and illness

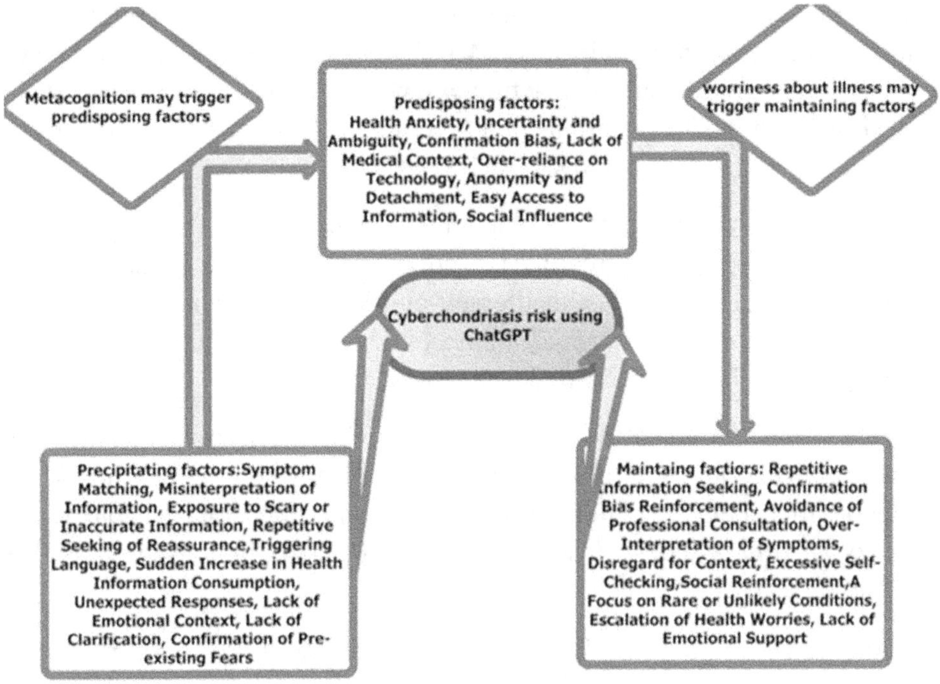

REFERENCES

Arslan, S. (2023). Exploring the Potential of Chat GPT in Personalized Obesity Treatment. *Annals of Biomedical Engineering*, *51*(9), 1887–1888. doi:10.100710439-023-03227-9 PMID:37145177

Bhattacharyya, M., Miller, V. M., Bhattacharyya, D., & Miller, L. E. (2023). High Rates of Fabricated and Inaccurate References in ChatGPT-Generated Medical Content. *Cureus*, *15*(5). Advance online publication. doi:10.7759/cureus.39238 PMID:37337480

Choudhury, A., & Shamszare, H. (2023). Investigating the Impact of User Trust on the Adoption and Use of ChatGPT: Survey Analysis. *Journal of Medical Internet Research*, *25*, e47184. doi:10.2196/47184 PMID:37314848

Cox, A., Seth, I., Xie, Y., Hunter-Smith, D. J., & Rozen, W. M. (2023). Utilizing ChatGPT-4 for Providing Medical Information on Blepharoplasties to Patients. *Aesthetic Surgery Journal*, *43*(8), NP658–NP662. doi:10.1093/asjjad096 PMID:37032521

D., F., I.A., B., B.M., C., & C.S., de P. (2013). Influence of psychosocial risk factors on the trajectory of mental health problems from childhood to adolescence: A longitudinal study. *BMC Psychiatry, 13*(1), 31. http://www.embase.com/search/results?subaction=viewrecord&from=export&id=L52404144%0Ahttp://www.biomedcentral.com/1471-244X/13/31%0Ahttp://dx.doi.org/10.1186/1471-244X-13-31

El-Zayat, A., Namnkani, S., Alshareef, N., Mustfa, M., Eminaga, N., & Algarni, G. (2023). Cyberchondria and its association with smartphone addiction and electronic health literacy among a Saudi population. *Saudi Journal of Medicine & Medical Sciences, 11*(2), 162. doi:10.4103jmms.sjmms_491_22 PMID:37252023

Fergus, T. A., & Spada, M. M. (2018). Moving toward a metacognitive conceptualization of cyberchondria: Examining the contribution of metacognitive beliefs, beliefs about rituals, and stop signals. *Journal of Anxiety Disorders, 60*(August), 11–19. doi:10.1016/j.janxdis.2018.09.003 PMID:30317062

Frosolini, A., Gennaro, P., Cascino, F., & Gabriele, G. (2023). *Reference to "Role of Chat GPT in Public Health", to Highlight the AI's Incorrect Reference Generation. Annals of Biomedical Engineering*. doi:10.100710439-023-03248-4

Johnson, S. B., King, A. J., Warner, E. L., Aneja, S., Kann, B. H., & Bylund, C. L. (2023). Using ChatGPT to evaluate cancer myths and misconceptions: Artificial intelligence and cancer information. *JNCI Cancer Spectrum, 7*(2), pkad015. Advance online publication. doi:10.1093/jncics/pkad015 PMID:36929393

Khazaal, Y., Chatton, A., Rochat, L., Hede, V., Viswasam, K., Penzenstadler, L., Berle, D., & Starcevic, V. (2021). Compulsive Health-Related Internet Use and Cyberchondria. *European Addiction Research, 27*(1), 58–66. doi:10.1159/000510922 PMID:33120393

Kim, J., Kim, J. H., Kim, C., & Park, J. (2023). Decisions with ChatGPT: Reexamining choice overload in ChatGPT recommendations. *Journal of Retailing and Consumer Services, 75*(July), 103494. doi:10.1016/j.jretconser.2023.103494

Kulsum, U., Sushma, M., Subhaprada, S., & Sreedevi, A. (2023). Prevalence of cyberchondria among undergraduate students of a private degree college with Cyberchondria Severity Scale-12 in an urban area. *BLDE University Journal of Health Sciences*, *8*(1), 95. doi:10.4103/bjhs.bjhs_211_22

McMullan, R. D., Berle, D., Arnáez, S., & Starcevic, V. (2019). The relationships between health anxiety, online health information seeking, and cyberchondria: Systematic review and meta-analysis. *Journal of Affective Disorders, 245*, 270–278. doi:10.1016/j.jad.2018.11.037

MehnenL.GruarinS.VasilevaM.KnappB. (2023). ChatGPT as a medical doctor? A diagnostic accuracy study on common and rare diseases. In medRxiv. doi:10.1101/2023.04.20.23288859

Mestre-Bach, G., & Potenza, M. N. (2023). Cyberchondria: A Growing Concern During the COVID-19 Pandemic and a Possible Addictive Disorder? *Current Addiction Reports*, *10*(1), 77–96. doi:10.100740429-022-00462-3 PMID:36785757

Schenkel, S. K., Jungmann, S. M., Gropalis, M., & Witthöft, M. (2021). Conceptualizations of Cyberchondria and Relations to the Anxiety Spectrum: Systematic Review and Meta-analysis. *Journal of Medical Internet Research*, *23*(11), e27835. doi:10.2196/27835 PMID:34792473

Shahsavar, Y., & Choudhury, A. (2023). User Intentions to Use ChatGPT for Self-Diagnosis and Health-Related Purposes: Cross-sectional Survey Study. *JMIR Human Factors*, *10*, e47564. doi:10.2196/47564 PMID:37195756

Strzelecki, A. (2023). To use or not to use ChatGPT in higher education? A study of students' acceptance and use of technology. *Interactive Learning Environments*, (May), 1–14. doi:10.1080/10494820.2023.2209881

Vismara, M., Caricasole, V., Starcevic, V., Cinosi, E., Dell'Osso, B., Martinotti, G., & Fineberg, N. A. (2020). Is cyberchondria a new transdiagnostic digital compulsive syndrome? A systematic review of the evidence. *Comprehensive Psychiatry*, *99*, 152167. doi:10.1016/j.comppsych.2020.152167 PMID:32146315

ZhaoW.ZhaoY.LuX.WangS.TongY.QinB. (2023). Is ChatGPT Equipped with Emotional Dialogue Capabilities? https://arxiv.org/abs/2304.09582

Zheng, H., Kyung Kim, H., Joanna Sin, S. C., & Theng, Y. L. (2021). A theoretical model of cyberchondria development: Antecedents and intermediate processes. *Telematics and Informatics, 63*, 101659. doi:10.1016/j.tele.2021.101659

Chapter 14
Policy Guidelines Post ChatGPT Era in Education, Research, and Public Administration:
A Document Analysis

ABSTRACT

ChatGPT is an extensive language generative artificial model used to generate content of various kinds. This brings several challenges in education, research, and public administration. The document analysis focuses on formulating policy guidelines for the education, research and public sectors in the post-ChatGPT era. The researcher searched documents from UNESCO, UNICEF, WIPO, PIPEDA, and European Council (EU). The researcher identified a lack of current policies on generative AI, such as ChatGPT. The available policy has been restricted to traditional artificial intelligence and is outdated. However, the chapter identified some available policies on generative AI. The researcher encourages all stakeholders to develop localized policies based on country legislative laws on data protection, privacy, and copyright laws.

BACKGROUND

The United Nations Educational, Scientific and Cultural Organization (UNESCO) was born on November 16 1945. UNESCO has 195 Members and 8 Associate Members and is governed by the General Conference and

DOI: 10.4018/978-1-6684-9300-7.ch014

the Executive Board. The Secretariat, headed by the Director-General, implements the decisions of these two bodies. The organization has over 50 field offices worldwide, and its headquarters are in Paris. UNESCO's mission is to contribute to building a culture of peace, the eradication of poverty, sustainable development and intercultural dialogue through education, the sciences, culture, communication and information. UNESCO works to create the conditions for dialogue among civilizations, cultures and peoples based upon respect for commonly shared values. Through this dialogue, the world can achieve global visions of sustainable development encompassing observance of human rights, mutual respect and the alleviation of poverty, all of which are at the heart of UNESCO's mission and activities (*UNESCO in Brief*, 2023).

World Intellectual Property Organization (WIPO) leads the development of a balanced and effective global intellectual property ecosystem to promote innovation and creativity for a better and more sustainable future. WIPO facilitates international cooperation and harmonizes intellectual property laws and practices. The Berne Convention, adopted in 1886, deals with the protection of works and the rights of their authors. It allows creators such as authors, musicians, poets, and painters to control how their works are used, by whom, and on what terms. It is based on three basic principles and contains a series of provisions determining the minimum protection to be granted, as well as special provisions available to developing countries that want to use them (*Berne Convention for the Protection of Literary and Artistic Works*, 2023).

There is a growing understanding of the significance of data protection in safeguarding not just individuals' private lives but also their freedom (Rodotà, 2009). The notable data protection regulations and laws include General Data Protection Regulation (GDPR), California Consumer Privacy Act (CCPA), Personal Information Protection and Electronic Documents Act (PIPEDA), Personal Data Protection Act (PDPA), and Brazilian General Data Protection Law (LGPD). It is important to note that each country has its own privacy and data protection laws, which typically have jurisdiction within the country's borders. The General Data Protection Regulation is a European Union regulation on Information privacy in the European Union and the European Economic Area. The GDPR is an essential component of EU privacy law and human rights law, particularly Article 8 of the Charter of Fundamental Rights of the European Union (*The General Data Protection Regulation - Consilium*, 2023).

UNESCO RECOMMENDATION

Formulation of a comprehensive framework encompassing strategic aims and priorities for integrating artificial intelligence (AI) across educational systems. Establishment of a guiding principle that spans all facets of AI and education policies. Implementation of a multidisciplinary strategy involving collaborative planning across diverse disciplines, coupled with inter-sectoral governance mechanisms. Crafting policies and regulations that ensure AI's impartial, all-encompassing, and ethically sound application, fostering inclusivity and fairness. Elaboration and realization of master plans detailing AI's incorporation into educational administration, pedagogy, knowledge acquisition, and assessment processes. Introduction of pilot testing, continuous monitoring, evaluative procedures, and creating a solid evidential foundation to support policy development. Encouragement of local AI innovations within the educational context, thereby promoting autonomous growth and development. Table 1 represents the area and recommendations given by UNESCO.

Table 1. UNESCO area of recommendations (UNESCO, 2023)

Areas	Recommendation
Strategic priorities	A system-wide vision and strategic priorities
Overarching principle	The overarching principle for AI and education policies
Multidisciplinary approach	Interdisciplinary planning and inter-sectoral governance
Rational use of AI	Policies and regulations for equitable, inclusive, and ethical use of AI
Development of Master plan	Master plans for using AI in education management, teaching, learning, and assessment
Evidence-based policy	Pilot testing, monitoring and evaluation, and building an evidence base
Innovations in AI	Fostering local AI innovations for education

ADAPTING TO CHATGPT INTO HIGHER EDUCATION

United Nations Educational, Scientific and Cultural Organization suggest recommendations Facilitate platforms for active engagement amongst faculty, staff, students, and relevant stakeholders to deliberate upon the ramifications of ChatGPT within the Higher Education Institution (HEI) and collaboratively devise adaptive and integrative strategies for AI assimilation. Introduce unambiguous directives tailored for students and instructors, outlining the precise contexts and occasions wherein ChatGPT utilization is permissible and delineating scenarios wherein its application is not warranted. Such directives should emerge through a consultative process with students and educators rather than being unilaterally imposed. Establish a coherent linkage between the utilization of ChatGPT and the attainment of course-specific learning objectives. This concerted alignment elucidates to students the role of ChatGPT in enhancing their learning experience and sets forth the anticipations associated with its incorporation. Subject assessments and evaluations to a comprehensive review, thereby ensuring their congruence with intended purposes. This appraisal may lead to substituting conventional examinations with in-person evaluations or modifying question types and examination structures. Undertake a thorough reevaluation and revision of prevailing academic integrity policies in the context of ChatGPT and analogous AI tools to address issues pertinent to academic honesty and integrity. Deliver training programs encompassing educators, researchers, and students to enhance their competency in formulating adept inquiries for ChatGPT. As highlighted by scholars, the optimal utility of ChatGPT is contingent upon the meticulous crafting of input queries. Table 2 explains how to adapt ChatGPT in higher education.

Table 2. Adapting to ChatGPT in your higher education institution (UNESCO, 2023)

Areas	Recommendation	Reference
Discussion	Create opportunities for faculty, staff, students, and other stakeholders to discuss the impact of ChatGPT on the HEI and co-construct strategies to adapt and adapt to AI.	(*Academic Honesty : University of Rochester*, 2023)
Development of clear guidelines for all students and teachers	Introduce clear guidance for students and instructors about how and when ChatGPT can be used (and when it cannot). Such guidance should be negotiated with students and teachers, not imposed on them.	
Course learning outcomes	Connect the use of ChatGPT to course learning outcomes. This helps students understand how ChatGPT can support their learning and what expectations there are for them.	
Review assessment	Review all forms of assessment and evaluation to ensure that each element is fit for purpose. This review may lead to replacing exams or other assessments with in-person assessments or altering the types of questions or exam formats that are used.	
Review academic integrity policy to ChatGPT	Review and update policies relating to academic integrity/ honesty in relation to ChatGPT and other AI tools.	(*Tec de Monterrey Recomienda a Su Comunidad Uso Inteligente de ChatGPT*, 2023)
Training to all stakes holders	Train teachers, researchers, and students to improve the queries they pose to ChatGPT. As researchers have noted, ChatGPT is most useful when the inputs provided to it are carefully created.	(*ChatGPT Will Revolutionise Academic Research*, 2023)

WIPO CONVERSATION ON INTELLECTUAL PROPERTY (IP) AND FRONTIER TECHNOLOGIES

Currently, the Berne Convention, a foundational copyright treaty, does not provide explicit guidance on addressing AI-generated works. The legal implications of AI in creative fields are an area that continues to develop, and legal frameworks may evolve to encompass these new challenges and opportunities posed by generative AI. The eighth session of the World Intellectual Property Organization (WIPO) is scheduled in Geneva on September 20 and 21, 2023. The outlined program, orchestrated by WIPO, addresses the escalating challenges posed by the rapid proliferation of generative artificial intelligence (AI). Notably, during the second day of the session, designated for Thursday, September 21, 2023, there will be a comprehensive examination of the strategies adopted by Intellectual Property (IP) Offices in managing applications authored by ChatGPT and analogous AI systems. Furthermore, deliberations will revolve around identifying regulatory measures that can streamline the process for businesses to safeguard their intellectual property amidst the emergent landscape of Generative AI (WIPO, 2023).

PERSONAL INFORMATION PROTECTION AND ELECTRONIC DOCUMENTS ACT (PIPEDA)

In Canada, PIPEDA regulates how private-sector organizations handle personal information. It emphasizes consent, accountability, and individual rights. On May 25, 2023, an announcement was issued by the Office of the Privacy Commissioner of Canada, revealing that privacy regulatory bodies from Canada, Québec, British Columbia, and Alberta have collaboratively initiated an investigation into the enterprise responsible for the artificial intelligence-driven chatbot, ChatGPT. According to retrieved information from the website, quoted.

The privacy authorities will investigate whether OpenAI: has obtained valid and meaningful consent for the collection, use and disclosure of the personal information of individuals based in Canada via ChatGPT; has respected its obligations with respect to openness and transparency, access, accuracy, and accountability; and has collected, used and/or disclosed personal information for purposes that a reasonable person would consider appropriate, reasonable or legitimate in the circumstances, and whether this collection is limited to information that is necessary for these purposes" (Announcement: OPC to Investigate ChatGPT Jointly with Provincial Privacy Authorities, 2023). Furthermore, during Keynote Remarks delivered at the International Institute of Communications (IIC) Canada's 19th Annual Communications Law & Policy Conference on May 15, 2023, in Ottawa, Ontario, Philippe Dufresne, Privacy Commissioner of Canada, extensively deliberated upon the subject of artificial intelligence and its intersection with the fourth industrial revolution. According to speaker we quote "Staying ahead of the fast-moving pace of technological advancement is another one of my key focus areas, especially in the world of artificial intelligence (AI) and generative AI. Whether it is AI chatbots like ChatGPT, Bing or Google's Bard, these new technologies have seemingly limitless possibilities – some have likened it to opening a Pandora's box – but we need to make sure that the related risks of these privacy impactful tools are addressed appropriately. We need to consider privacy implications, concerns about algorithmic biases, and the need for a clear and strong legal framework to regulate their use. That is responsible innovation. Last September, the House of Commons' Standing Committee on Access to Information, Privacy and Ethics (ETHI) completed a study on the use of facial recognition technology, and called for a moratorium on its use until it could be reviewed by the courts or my Office. I welcomed the Committee's report which confirmed the pressing need to ensure the appropriate regulation of privacy impactful technologies, such as facial recognition and artificial intelligence, in a way that protects and promotes Canadians' fundamental right to privacy. In April, my Office announced that we have launched an investigation into the company behind ChatGPT to determine whether the organization's practices comply with Canadian privacy law. My Office is monitoring and researching these and other new technologies so that we can anticipate how they may impact privacy, and so that we can promote the most privacy enhancing technologies. AI technology and its impact on privacy is also a matter of global privacy interest. We have, and will continue to, engage with our domestic and international partners on these issues. (Keynote Remarks at the International Institute of Communications (IIC) Canada's 19th Annual Communications Law & Policy Conference, 2023).

COUNCIL OF THE EU AND THE EUROPEAN COUNCIL

The analysis and research team supports the European Council and the Council of the European Union in their strategic thinking and policy planning. They published the paper titled "ChatGPT in the Public Sector – overhyped or overlooked" and explained the potential benefits and risk of using a generative AI tool such as ChatGPT. According to them, "ChatGPT does not itself understand the meaning of the text it produces. Its responses are based on statistics and probability that" ChatGPT can produce an impact on the European principles of public administration ("ChatGPT in the Public Sector – Overhyped or Overlooked?," 2023).

CREATIVE COMMONS

CC is a worldwide nonprofit entity that enables individuals to cultivate and maintain the flourishing commons of communal knowledge and culture. This endeavour is essential to tackling the paramount global issues and fostering a more promising future for everyone. The organization collaborate with their extensive global network and diverse collaborators, enhance capabilities and frameworks, devise pragmatic resolutions, and champion improved modes of sharing. This entails sharing that is attuned to context, all-encompassing, fair, impartial, mutually beneficial, and enduring. The Creative Commons Certificate program aims to educate individuals about copyright law, open licensing, and the effective use of Creative Commons licenses. Explains the various types of Creative Commons licenses, such as Attribution (CC BY), Attribution-NonCommercial (CC BY-NC), Attribution-ShareAlike (CC BY-SA) (*What We Do*, 2023). Creative Commons (CC) licenses are a set of copyright licenses and tools that provide a flexible and standardized way for creators to grant permissions for others to use their work. It is suggested that the respective stakeholder will organize training on CC licenses.

Figure 1. How to attribute creative commons photos by Foter
Source: Foter (2015)

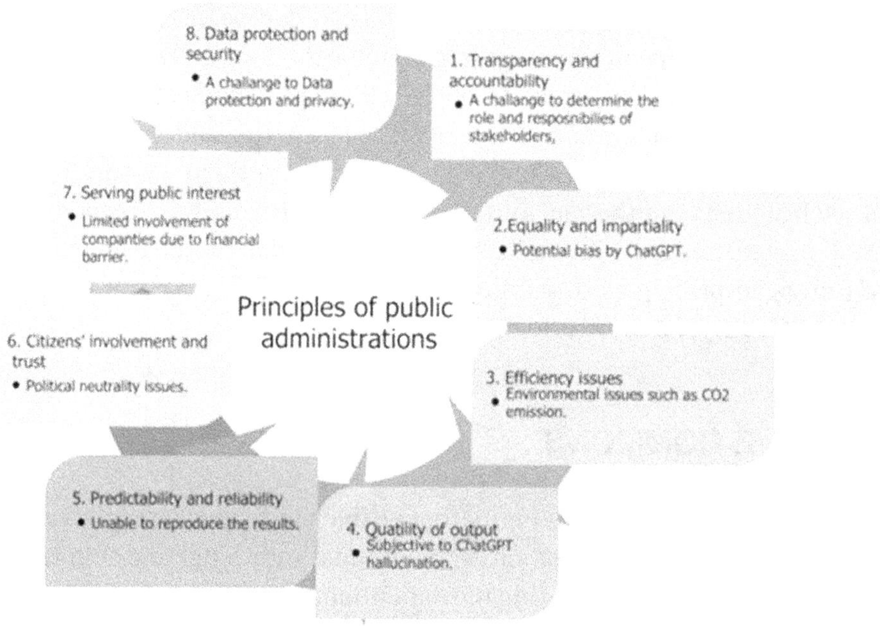

CONCLUSION

Given the rapid and escalating advancements in technology and its widespread accessibility, there arises a compelling requirement for educational initiatives that foster awareness regarding the judicious handling of data and the pertinent legal considerations. Integrating Generative AI into extensive linguistic and training frameworks renders data vulnerable to potential misuse and the propagation of misinformation. Consequently, it becomes imperative to devise a comprehensive training regimen that imparts insights into the responsible application of generative AI tools, acknowledges the associated risks, and outlines practical strategies for mitigating potential challenges.

REFERENCES

Academic Honesty : University of Rochester. (2023). University of Rochester. http://www.rochester.edu/college/honesty/

Announcement: OPC to investigate ChatGPT jointly with provincial privacy authorities. (2023). Office of the Privacy Commissioner of Canada. https://www.priv.gc.ca/en/opc-news/news-and-announcements/2023/an_230525-2/

Berne Convention for the Protection of Literary and Artistic Works. (2023). WIPO. https://www.wipo.int/treaties/en/ip/berne/

ChatGPT in the Public Sector – overhyped or overlooked? (2023). Council of the European Union.

ChatGPT will revolutionize academic research. (2023). Times Higher Education (THE). https://www.timeshighereducation.com/depth/chatgpt-revolution-academic-research-has-begun

Foter. (2015). *How To Attribute Creative Commons Photos.* https://foter.com/blog/how-to-attribute-creative-commons-photos/

Keynote Remarks at the International Institute of Communications (IIC) Canada's 19th Annual Communications Law & Policy Conference. (2023). Office of the Privacy Commissioner of Canada. https://www.priv.gc.ca/en/opc-news/speeches/2023/sp-d_20230515/

Rodotà, S. (2009). Data Protection as a Fundamental Right. In *Reinventing Data Protection?* (pp. 77–82). Springer Netherlands. doi:10.1007/978-1-4020-9498-9_3

Tec de Monterrey recomienda a su comunidad uso inteligente de ChatGPT. (2023). Tecnológico de Monterrey. https://conecta.tec.mx/es/noticias/nacional/institucion/tec-de-monterrey-recomienda-su-comunidad-uso-inteligente-de-chatgpt

The general data protection regulation - Consilium. (2023). Data Protection in the EU. https://www.consilium.europa.eu/en/policies/data-protection/data-protection-regulation/

UNESCO. (2023). *ChatGPT and Artificial Intelligence in Higher Education.* https://unesdoc.unesco.org/ark:/48223/pf0000385146

UNESCO in brief. (2023). UNESCO. https://www.unesco.org/en/brief

What We Do. (2023). Creative Commons. https://creativecommons.org/about/

WIPO. (2023). *Wipo Conversation on Intellectual Property (Ip) and Frontier Technologies.* Sixth Session. WIPO.

Chapter 15
Synergizing Tradition and Technology by Exploring ChatGPT's Role in Enhancing Pathology Education for Traditional Chinese Medicine

ABSTRACT

The availability of generative AI tools such as ChatGPT has significantly changed current situations. In the previous chapters, the authors explained how ChatGPT succeeded in medical examinations. Therefore, it is the need of the time for teachers to incorporate ChatGPT in their teaching pedagogy. Although many professors oppose using ChatGPT in education and ask for a ban, the authors do not find that solution feasible in the longer run. It is human nature to abstain from innovations and adapt with time. The current chapter has attempted to find solutions for incorporating ChatGPT in teaching pathology. The teacher uses a rational approach to suggest some tips in case the reader does not want to adopt ChatGPT in teaching methods. The authors believe a mixed approach is better and more rational in using ChatGPT in pathology, particularly for students of traditional Chinese medicine who face difficulty with language and understanding Western medicine theories, which contrast with traditional Chinese medicine philosophy.

DOI: 10.4018/978-1-6684-9300-7.ch015

vBACKGROUND

Traditional Chinese medicine, as it persists in several East and Southeast Asian countries, has undergone significant changes (Ooi, 1993). Traditional Chinese Medicine (TCM) is a complete medical healthcare system encompassing acupuncture, acupressure, moxibustion, herbal medicine, diet, tui na massage, and exercises (tai chi and qigong), among other traditional therapies. It uses herbs and natural resources to produce traditional medicines and focuses on maintaining the balance between body and mind (Quoquab et al., 2023). Western medicine was first introduced to China in the 17th century. During the first two centuries, several different views on the future of TCM and the relationship between TCM and Western medicine emerged. Some advocated the 'complete westernization' of Chinese medicine, others favoured keeping it intact, whereas others recommended the 'digestion and assimilation of TCM and Western medicine'. Nowadays, more and more people realize that each medical tradition has its own merits and advise that the two systems should benefit from each other's strong points. In the 20th century, China maintained and developed three kinds of medical science: TCM, Western medicine, and 'integrated medicine'. Much has been achieved in clinical, experimental and theoretical research (KEJI & HAO, 2003). Therefore, students need to understand the western medicine subjects such as pathology. However, teaching Western medicine subjects to students with a language barrier is always challenging. The availability of ChatGPT has allowed students to learn and grasp knowledge quicker and faster. However, I am sceptical to see how to maintain students' critical thinking while allowing them to use ChatGPT. Therefore, I am presenting the chapter on incorporating ChatGPT in assessment.

ETIOLOGY AND PATHOGENESIS OF DISEASE

Global Health, Division of Parasitic Diseases and Malaria, has given details on Leishmaniasis. We can ask the student to read the details on a given website (https://www.cdc.gov/parasites/leishmaniasis/biology.html; *Leishmaniasis*, 2020). The content from the website will help them to understand the basics. We then provide them with some questions where they can use ChatGPT to find their answers. The questions are given below.

Figure 1. Yin and Yang of the body in traditional Chinese medicine
Source: Lee et al. (2016), Huang et al. (2018), Xu et al. (2018), and Yin Yang Theory (2023)

- What is the causative agent responsible for Leishmaniasis, according to the information provided on the CDC website?
- How is Leishmaniasis transmitted to humans, and what are the primary vectors involved in its transmission?
- Describe the life cycle of the Leishmania parasite as outlined in the CDC resource, including its different stages and hosts.
- What are the various clinical manifestations of Leishmaniasis, and how do they relate to the pathogenesis of the disease?
- According to the CDC, what factors contribute to the variation in disease severity and clinical outcomes among individuals with Leishmaniasis?
- Explain the role of the immune response in controlling and contributing to the pathogenesis of Leishmaniasis, as discussed in the provided details.

- Discuss the mechanisms that allow Leishmania parasites to evade the host's immune system based on the information from the CDC resource.
- How does Leishmaniasis demonstrate a complex interaction between the parasite, the vectors, and the host, leading to the disease's diverse clinical presentations?
- According to the CDC website, what challenges are associated with developing effective vaccines and treatments for Leishmaniasis, considering its complex pathogenesis?
- Summarize the key points about the aetiology and pathogenesis of Leishmaniasis from the CDC resource, highlighting the interactions between the parasite, vectors, and host immune responses.

Instead of asking students to search for answers directly, please encourage them to ask open-ended questions about the topic. For example, they can ask ChatGPT to explain the concept of Leishmaniasis, describe its transmission mechanisms, or discuss the factors affecting disease severity. This approach prompts students to dialogue with ChatGPT and fosters understanding through interactive exploration.

To measure students' critical thinking in their interactions with ChatGPT, teachers can develop a marking rubric that assesses various aspects of their engagement. Here is a suggested rubric:

Table 1. Sample guided inquiry approach

*Guided Inquiry Approach	Question and Answer
Student	Hi ChatGPT, can you explain the causative agent responsible for Leishmaniasis?
ChatGPT	Of course! Leishmaniasis is caused by protozoan parasites belonging to the genus Leishmania. These parasites are transmitted to humans through the bites of infected sandflies. Would you like more details about the specific species of Leishmania involved?
Student	Yes, please. Also, can you elaborate on the transmission process?
ChatGPT	Certainly! Different species of sandflies act as vectors for Leishmania parasites. When an infected sandfly bites a human, it injects the parasites into the bloodstream. The parasites then invade immune cells and multiply, leading to the development of the disease. Do you want to know more about the life cycle of the parasites within the host?

*The interaction can continue similarly, allowing students to ask follow-up questions and request more detailed explanations. This format encourages students to actively think, engage with the information, and seek more profound understanding.

Table 2. Sample marking rubric

Areas	Recommendation
Depth of Inquiry (15 Marks)	Did the student ask questions that went beyond basic facts? Did the student seek explanations, connections, or comparisons?
Engagement and Interaction (15 Marks)	Did the student actively engage with ChatGPT's responses? Did the student ask follow-up questions to clarify or delve deeper into the topic?
Synthesis and Analysis (15 Marks)	Did the student summarize or paraphrase ChatGPT's responses in their own words? Did the student demonstrate the ability to analyze the information provided?
Application and Context (15 Marks)	Did the student apply the information to hypothetical scenarios or real-world situations? Did the student consider different perspectives or implications of the topic?
Critical Thinking (15 Marks)	Did the student demonstrate curiosity, curiosity, and thoughtful exploration? Did the student exhibit a willingness to question assumptions and think critically about the topic?
Content Accuracy and Verification (25 Marks)	Did the student independently verify information provided by ChatGPT from reliable sources? Did the student identify any potential inaccuracies in ChatGPT's responses and seek clarification or further verification? Did the student incorporate verified information into their understanding of the topic?
Total	100 Marks

The students were asked to read common etiological issues in a general population such as carbon monoxide poisoning (https://www.straitstimes.com/asia/se-asia/three-malaysians-die-in-suspected-carbon-monoxide-poisoning-in-their-vehicle; *Three Malaysians Die in Suspected Carbon Monoxide Poisoning in Their Vehicle*, 2020; https://www.therakyatpost.com/news/malaysia/2022/05/30/kids-almost-die-from-carbon-monoxide-poisoning-on-roadtrip-to-selangor-even-mom-affected/). I prepared a situation room in a class and inquiry under such situation about policymakers as given in Figure 2.

Moreover, the students were asked to read the report on essential health issues such as ageing in China. Students can use discussion starter prompts and engage in dialogues with ChatGPT. Read the news report about China's declining population and fertility rate. Engage in a dialogue with ChatGPT to explore the potential causes and implications of China's plummeting birthrate. Discuss various factors contributing to the decline, potential strategies the government could implement, and the social and economic consequences of a shrinking population. A screenshot is attached of the presentation (Yiu et al., 2023). The real-time assessment or assessing as a home task has different implications. It depends upon the nature of the assessment. A potential marking rubric has been attached.

Figure 2. Situation room

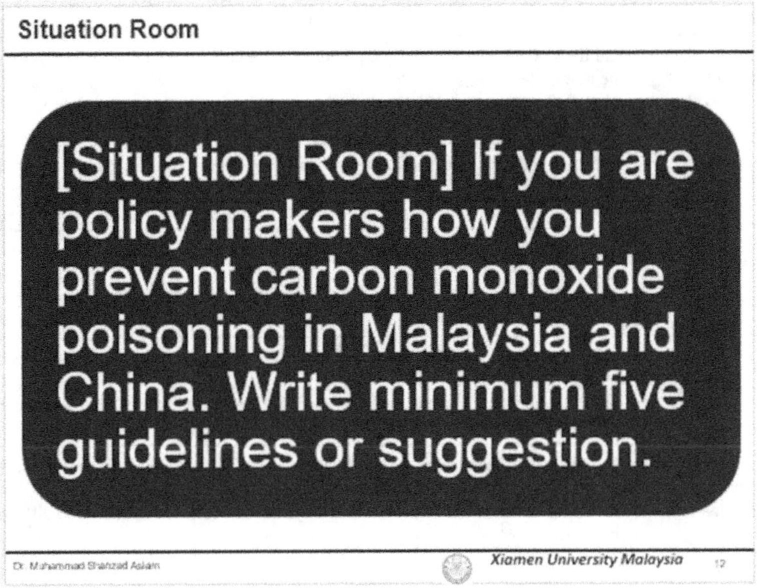

Figure 3. Rules using ChatGPT under situation room

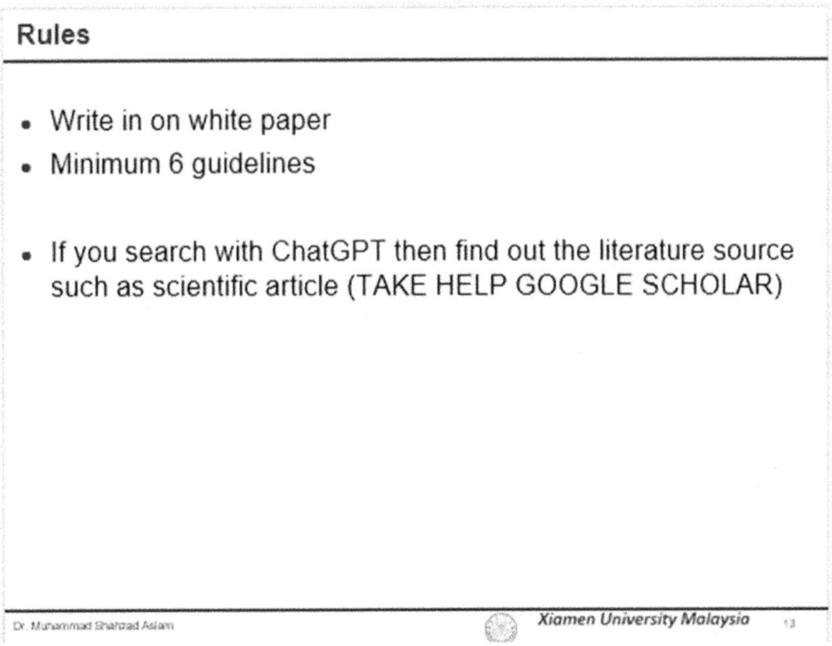

Table 3. Sample marking rubric

Areas	Recommendation
Identification of Causes (20 marks)	Did the student identify multiple potential causes of China's declining birthrate based on the news report? Were the causes presented clearly and coherently, demonstrating an understanding of the factors at play?
Discussion of Strategies (20 marks)	Did the student engage in a dialogue with ChatGPT to explore possible strategies the Chinese government could implement to address the declining birthrate? Did the student critically evaluate the feasibility and potential impact of these strategies?
Analysis of Consequences (20 marks)	Did the student discuss the social and economic implications of a shrinking population in China? Did the student analyze how the declining birthrate might affect the country's workforce, economy, and social dynamics?
Consideration of Expert Opinions (20 marks):	Did the student seek expert opinions or references from the news report to support their discussion points? Did the student analyze and critically evaluate the expert opinions in the context of the overall conversation?
Synthesis and Critical Thinking (20 marks):	Did the student synthesize the information gained from the dialogue to form a comprehensive understanding of the issue? Did the student exhibit critical thinking by drawing connections between different aspects of the topic?
Total	100 Marks

Figure 4. Ageing issue in China

HISTORY OF PATHOLOGY

When I was teaching the history of pathology, I asked the student to read Gabriele Fallopio (1523–1562) and the Fallopian tube (Thiery, 2009). I shared published notes and allowed the students to use ChatGPT. The students will read the given notes to understand the content, and then I encourage students to ask "why" and "how" questions from ChatGPT that helps students to develop critical thinking. The student can combine the guided inquiry approach and "why" and "how" approach. The question that students may ask will be given below.

- Why did Gabriele Fallopio's work on anatomy and medicine become influential during his time?
- Why did Gabriele Fallopio's discovery of the Fallopian tubes contribute significantly to our understanding of reproductive anatomy?
- How did Gabriele Fallopio's research methods and observations in the 16th century shape our early knowledge of the female reproductive system?
- How did Fallopio's detailed descriptions of the Fallopian tubes lay the foundation for advancements in gynaecology and obstetrics?
- Why did the Fallopian tubes come to be named after Gabriele Fallopio, and what impact did this nomenclature have on medicine?

Table 4. Sample marking rubric

Areas	Recommendation
Depth of Inquiry (25 marks)	Did the student's question demonstrate a genuine curiosity about the historical significance of Fallopio's work? Did the student pose a question that delves into the motivations, circumstances, or consequences of Fallopio's contributions?
Engagement and context (25 marks)	Did the student's question show an understanding of the historical context and the importance of Fallopio's work in his time? Did the student engage with the topic by asking a thoughtful and relevant question?
Research and Synthesis (25 Marks)	Did the student use the provided source to gather relevant information about Fallopio and the Fallopian tubes? Did the student synthesize the information effectively to formulate a well-structured "Why and How" question?
Content integration and presentation (25 Marks)	Did the student present the question coherently, ensuring that it clearly addresses the "Why and How" aspect of Fallopio's work? Did the student show an ability to integrate historical knowledge with medical concepts in formulating the question?
Total	100 Marks

Moreover, incorporating ChatGPT in real-time class environments may need modifications of activity, such as using a paper and pen approach so that students can write in by hand and ask simplifying questions such as the contribution and importance of Gabriele Fallopio's contributions in medical science. The lecturer can fix the time to complete their task as time is essential in real-time teaching where the students are not well equiped with flip-teaching methods, and the lecturer needs to use mixed methods (active and passive teaching pedagogy).

Another example was given from *Percivall Pott And The Chimney Sweeps' Cancer* (*Percivall Pott and the Chimney Sweeps*, n.d.), where students have asked to question: What is the contribution of Sir. Percival Pot in medical science? What is the impact of his contribution to society (20 Minutes)? Hans Christian Gram is a crucial historical figure in the field of histopathology. The student was asked to read the title *The Directed Steps of Hans Christian Gram* and answer the question: How is Gram stain helpful in pathology?

Which disease could be identified easily using gram stain? Give Three examples in (20 minutes) (https://answersingenesis.org/biology/gram-stain-discovery/). While students from traditional Chinese medicine were studying pathology, they were asked to read the current research areas, such as stem cells, as mentioned in Figure 5.

Figure 5. What are we doing now?

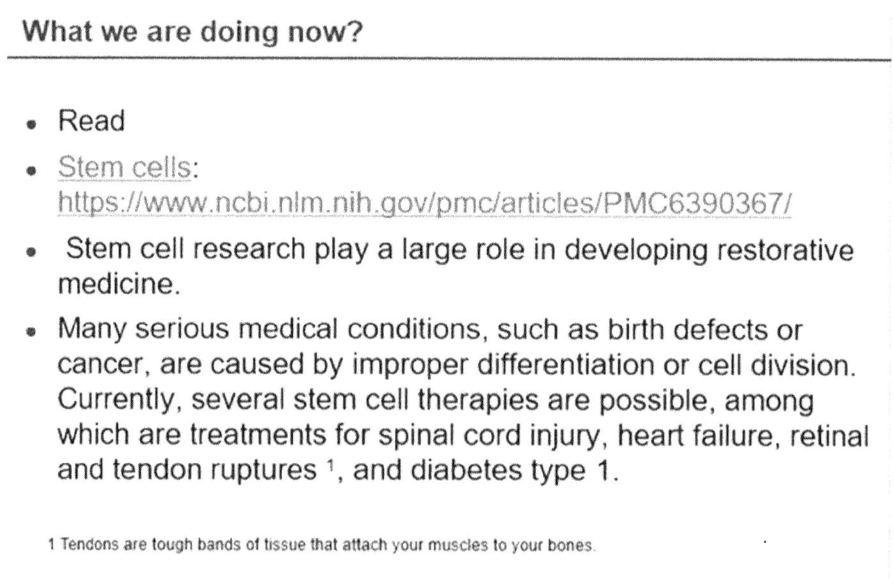

BASIC CONCEPT

Necrosis is a vital concept in pathology and there are several types of necrosis based upon microscopic and macroscopic features. Caseous necrosis consists of combined features of both coagulative and liquefactive necrosis. Instruct students to use ChatGPT to research and identify five diseases related to caseous necrosis. Students can use ChatGPT to identify the disease and then ask them to develop a *hypothetical patient scenario*. Students were asked to find six (6) diseases using ChatGPT in which excessive calcium absorption from the gut will result in Metastatic calcification. Physiologic atrophy is one of the critical topics to understand for undergraduate students. Students were asked to prepare their digital poster using Padlet by finding the examples from different search engines or using ChatGPT to find the examples and search the illustration of examples identified. Due to limited time, as the class activity was in real-time, the student could not draw their illustration but use open-source illustrations to identify and upload in padlet. The instruction is presented in the Figure 6.

Figure 6. Instructions to develop the poster in padlet

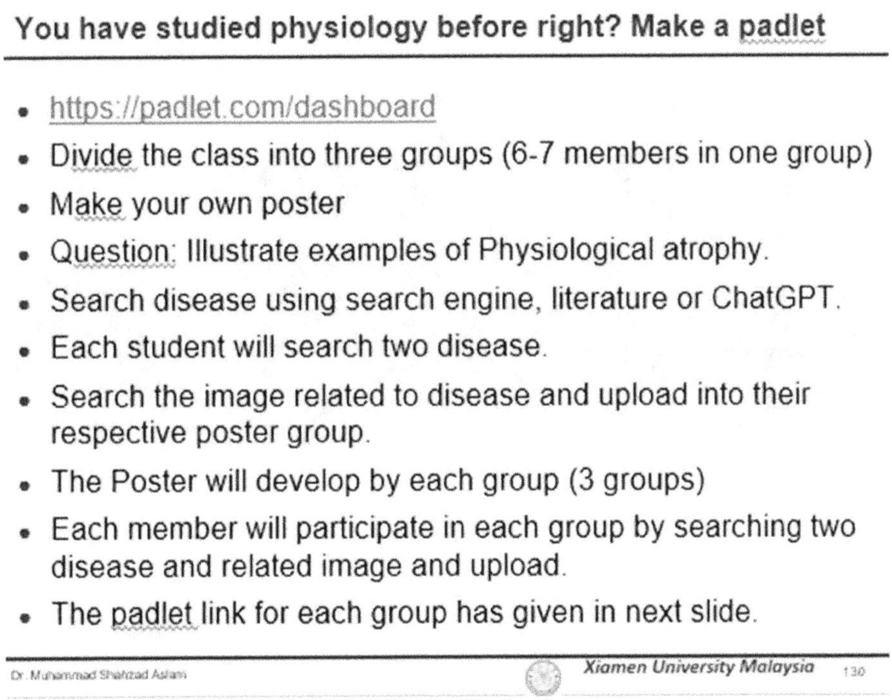

Figure 7. Example of students in context to example of physiological atrophy Part (a)

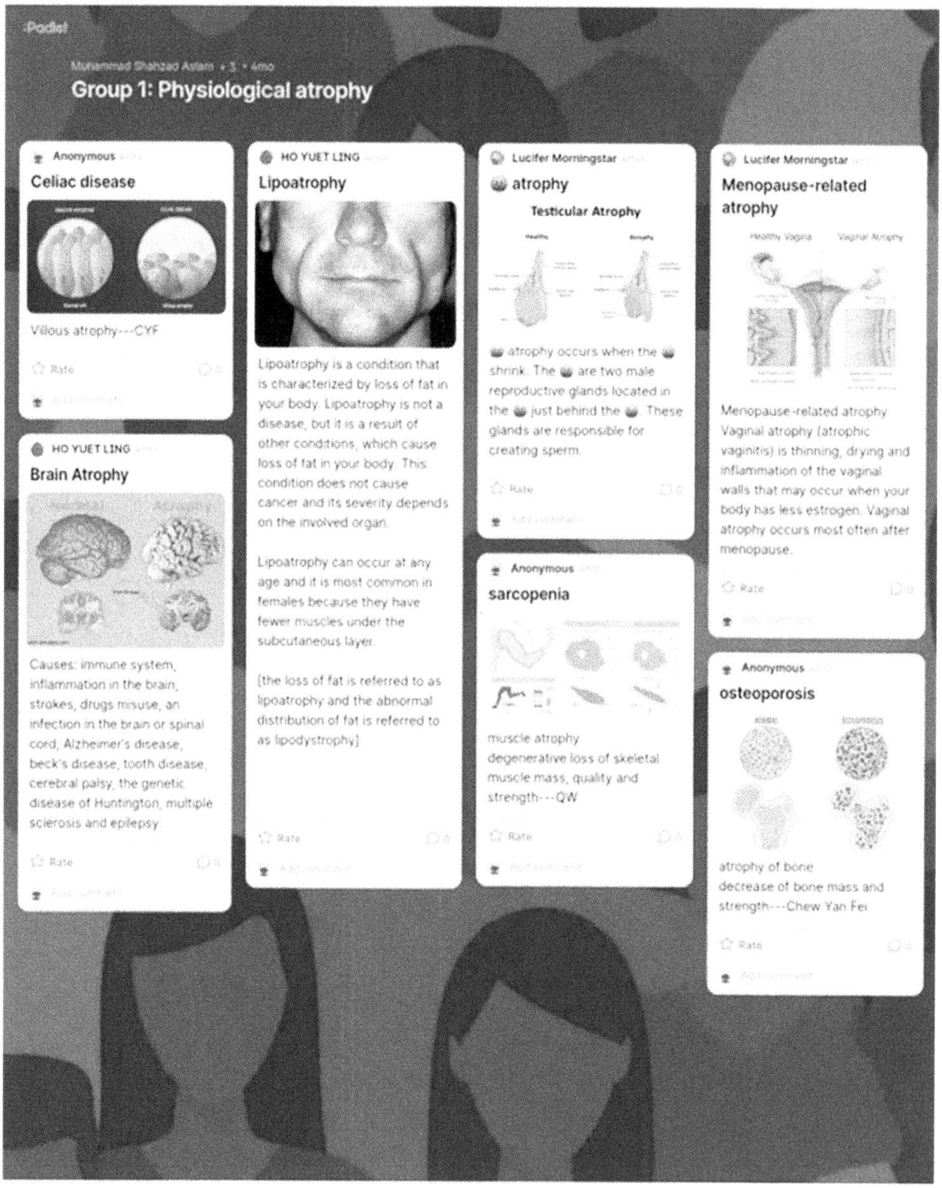

Figure 8. Example of students in context to example of physiological atrophy Part (b)

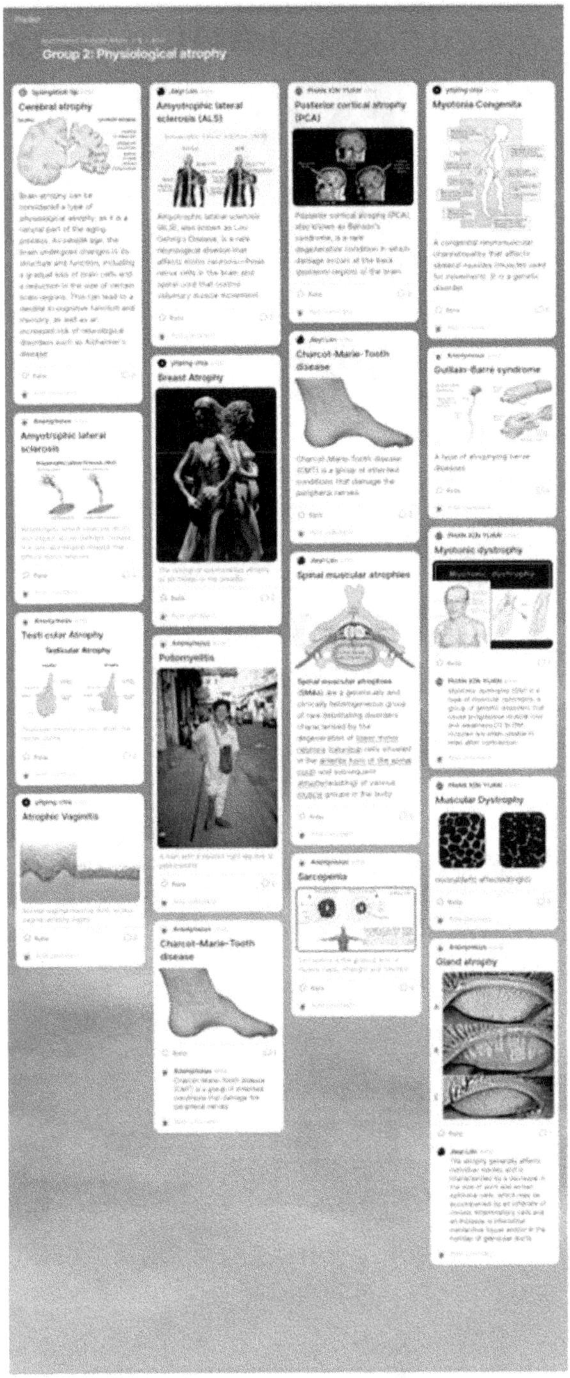

Figure 9. Example of students in context to example of physiological atrophy Part (c)

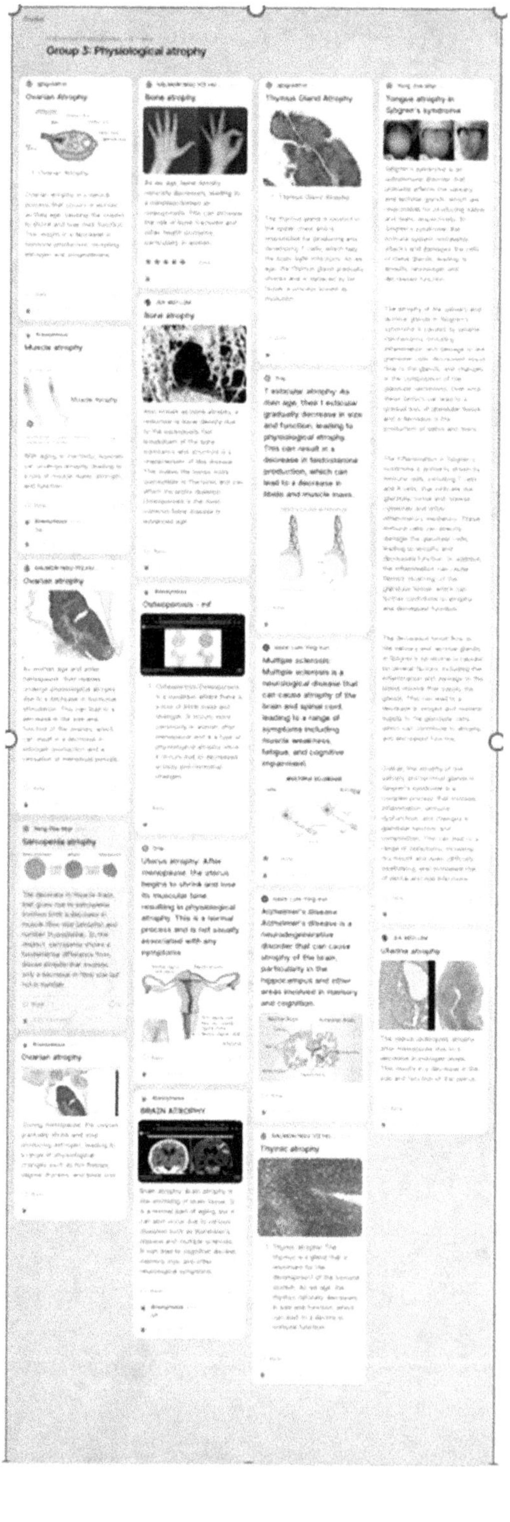

Hypertrophy is an increase in the size of parenchymal cells resulting in the enlargement of the organ or tissue without changing the number of cells. I prefer to use passive and active mixed learning pedagogy. Therefore, I asked students to use ChatGPT and solve the questions. For example, I asked students to identify diseases involving various hypertrophies. The students were asked to identify the disease and, later on, encouraged students to use ChatGPT to compare different types of hypertrophy based on the type of muscle. For example, they can ask about the differences between different forms of hypertrophy (i.e., smooth muscle, cardiac muscle, skeletal muscle) or compare the disease's pathogenesis that involves singular or multiple hypertrophy. This encourages critical thinking by requiring students to evaluate similarities and differences and analyze the context.

Pat Anson, in their title "*Stem Cells Could Help Diabetics Produce Their Insulin*", has addressed the potential solution for diabetes. De Koning says. "*But an era of clinical application of innovative stem-cell based islet replacement therapy for the treatment of diabetes has finally begun,*" I asked the student to read the report (https://www.painnewsnetwork.org/stories/2021/12/2/stem-cells-could-help-diabetics-produce-their-own-insulin-nbsp) and asked the student to prepare the summary of findings in the report. When I was teaching the topic turbulence, I did ask the student, "*Can you search FIVE situations that can cause turbulence*?" I asked the student to write it on a white sheet of paper in 30 minutes and asked not to use ChatGPT. This is tricky as students have internet access from the university server. I suggest teachers use the following methods to turn off the internet inside the classroom.

Table 5. How to disable internet access (4 Ways to Disable Internet Access, 2022)

Disabling Firewall Access for Windows Programs
Disabling a Specific Connection in Windows
Set Up a Fake Proxy Server
Internet-Toggling Apps

Navigate to the Control Panel by pressing the "Windows" key or selecting the "Start" icon, followed by clicking on "Control Panel". Access the Security Center and proceed to the Windows Firewall settings. Within the Firewall settings, locate the "Exceptions" tab. Find the program users wish to restrict from accessing the internet and deselect it. Confirm by clicking

"OK" on any prompts that appear. After making these changes, launch the program and attempt to connect to the internet. The program readers deselected will now be effectively barred from breaching the Windows security firewall, ensuring it cannot access the internet. However, readers' ability to use the internet with other programs will remain unaffected. (https://www.makeuseof.com/tag/block-windows-internet-explore r-accessing-internet/)

For deactivating a specific connection in windows: step 1: Access the Control Panel by pressing the "Windows" key or clicking the "Start" icon, then selecting "Control Panel".

For Windows 8 users, the readers can reveal the "charm bar" by moving the mouse to the top right corner of the screen, then click on "Control Panel". Alternatively, press the Windows key along with 'C', click "Settings", and choose "Control Panel".

Step 2: Navigate to the "Network and Sharing Center". If viewing by category under Network and Internet, click "Network settings, network adapters" followed by "View network status and tasks". If viewing by icons, click "Network and Sharing Center".

Step 3: Left-click to highlight the WiFi connection want to deactivate.

Right-click the selected WiFi connection and opt for "Disable". This action will restrict readers computer from connecting to this specific WiFi network; however, other networks will not be affected unless you disable them too. Other devices can still join the same WiFi network.

To reverse this, right-click the WiFi connection and choose "Enable".

Ensure administrative rights. The user need to be logged in as an administrator or a member of the Administrators group to complete this process. Network policy settings could also prevent the deactivation if connected to a network.

Step 4: Alternatively, disable all network connections in a more advanced manner. Go to Start > All Programs > Accessories, right-click Command Prompt, select Run as Administrator, grant permissions if needed, type "mmc compmgmt.msc" (without quotes), and press Enter. Wait for it to load, then click on Device Manager in the left-hand frame. Open the Network Adapters section, right-click each listed device, and choose Disable. Optionally, restart the system afterward.

Figure 10. Disabling firewall access for Windows programs
Source: 4 Ways to Disable Internet Access (2022)

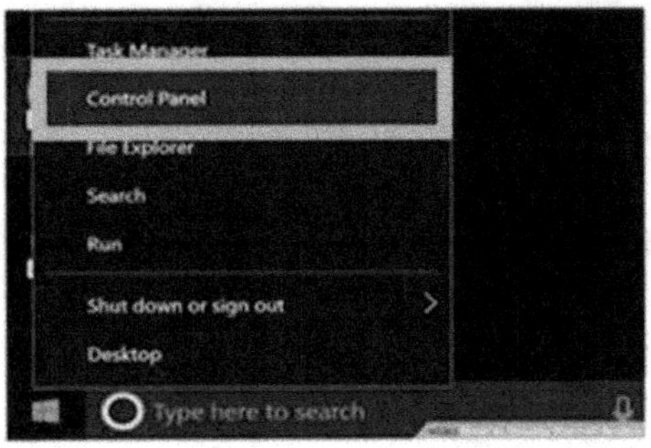

Go to the Control Panel. Click the "Windows" key or the "Start" icon, then click on "Control Panel"

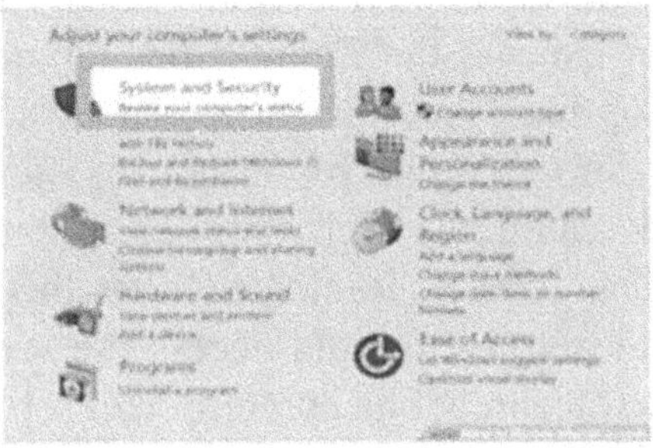

Open the Security Center.

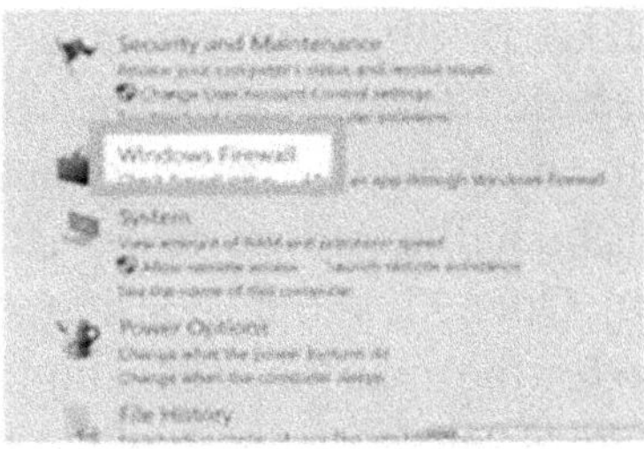

Open Windows Firewall settings.
Open the "Exceptions" tab.
Un-check the program for which you want to block access to the internet.
Click "OK" when prompted.

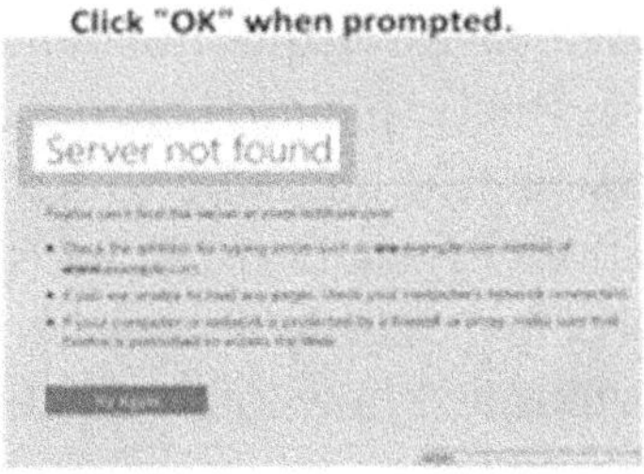

Open the program and try to access the Internet.

Parental Control Software

Step 5: Consider using third-party parental control software to manage internet access.

Such programs enable restriction of websites and complete internet blocking.

Install the software directly onto the target computer.

There might be a small fee associated, but you can ensure controlled internet usage by your child.

Apple OS X:

On Apple OS X, configure built-in parental controls to prohibit internet access for specific accounts. The illustration is presented in next figure.

For establishing the fake Proxy Server: Open Internet Options within the Control Panel. Access the Connections tab and click on LAN settings. Deselect the option "Automatically detect settings". Instead, choose "Use a proxy server" and input non-existent proxy server details. This action will cause the web browser to time out whenever a user attempts to load a website. Remember that this approach is not foolproof, as a knowledgeable user could access the settings and rectify the situation (https://www.techrepublic.com/article/disable-internet-access-on-a-windows-pc/5491068/).

These methods help block the internet and help to avoid generative AI applications such as ChatGPT. Every subject has its demand. Therefore, teacher set their parameter as per the requirement of the topic or nature of the topic.

Now, we have the following problem of searching for questions related to illustrations. Pathology is all about illustrations, and ChatGPT is a text-based language model developed by OpenAI, and it is designed to understand and generate human-like text based on the input the application receives. Therefore, teachers can use search engines, medical databases, or textbooks to find relevant images and information. A class activity is presented in Figure 14.

I have given some more class activities where I forbid students not to use ChatGPT. When teaching oedema, I asked questions about Chinese medicine philosophy to find TCM theories that explained oedema and asked the students to avoid ChatGPT and search scientific literature with references. It is crucial nowadays to give clear indications in generative AI tools. I suggest using both methods, using generative AI or avoiding them if we need to avoid such tools, then I have suggested in previous text how to block such tools as ChatGPT.

Figure 11. Disabling a specific connection in Windows (4 Ways to Disable Internet Access, 2022)

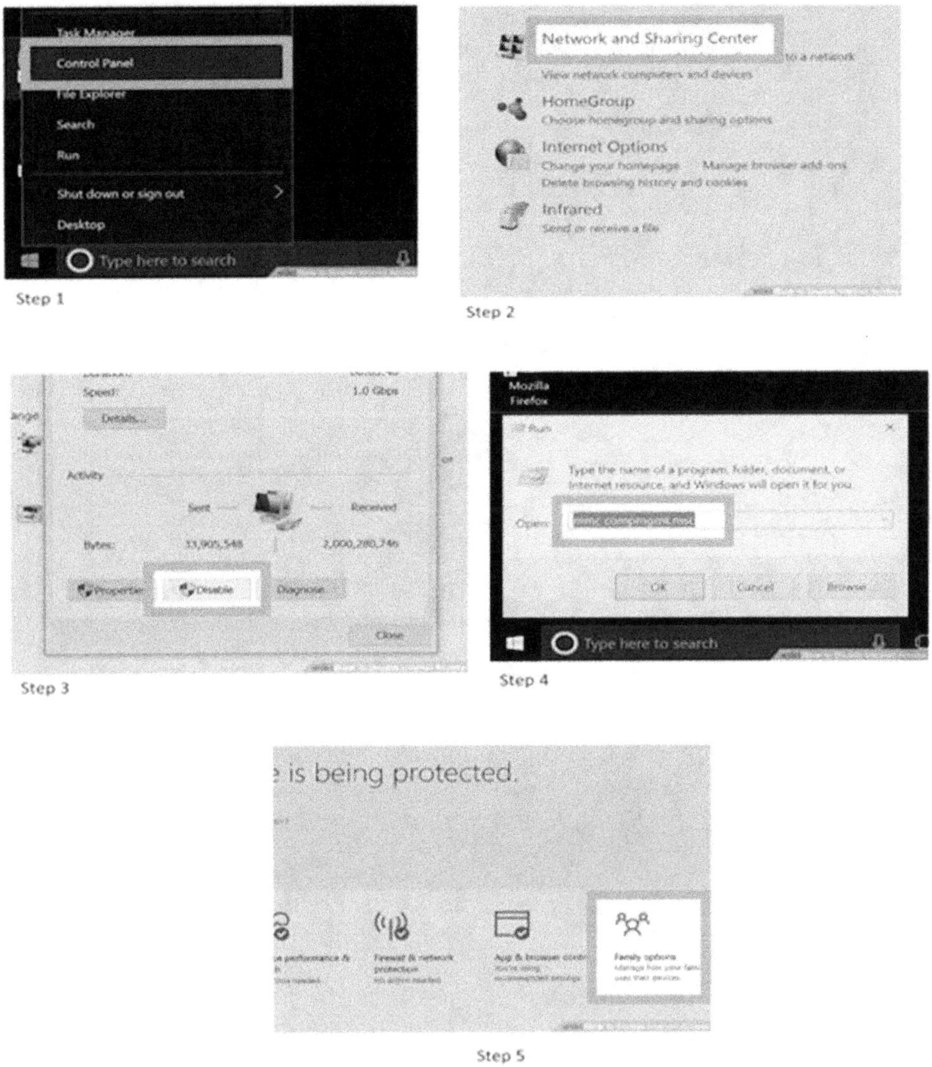

When I was teaching inflammation and giving students a question to identify inflammatory mediators of a specific disease, I suggested the readers use ChatGPT using Prompt Engineering ideas as given in table 6.

Figure 12. Set up a fake proxy server (4 Ways to Disable Internet Access, 2022)

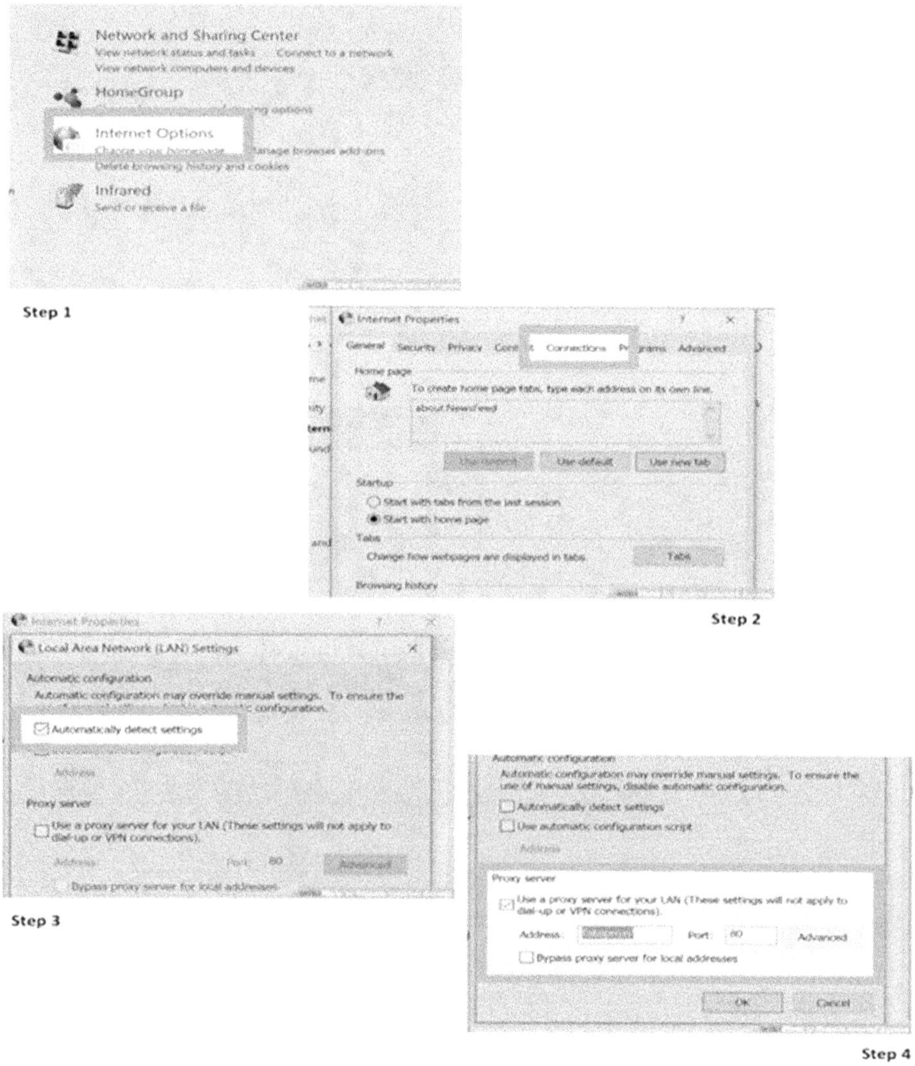

Figure 13. Internet-toggling apps
Source: 4 Ways to Disable Internet Access (2022), https://www.labnol.org/software/disable-internet-connection/26235/

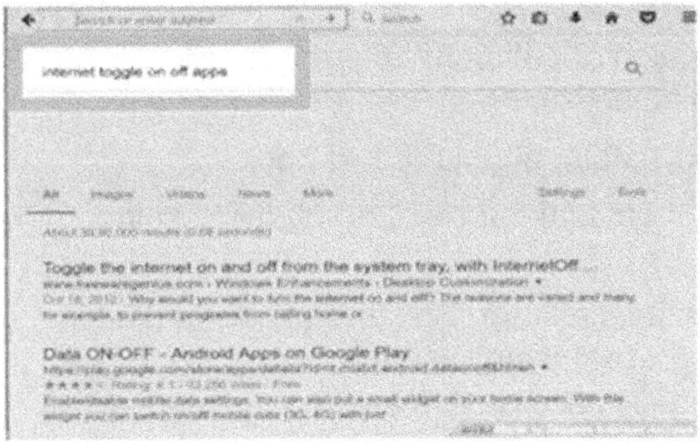

Consider using an internet-toggling app.

Try using the Toggle Internet script

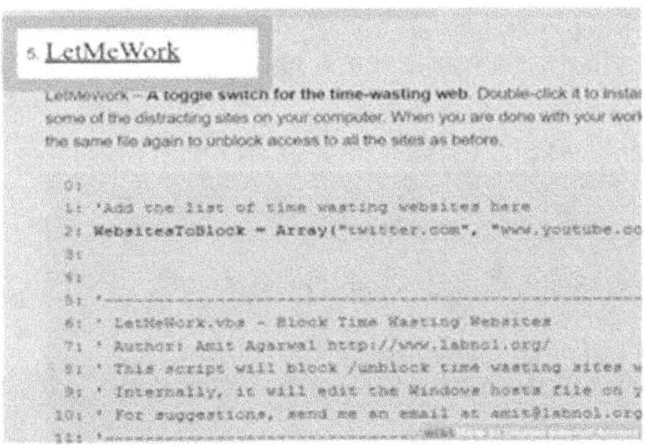

Toggle your Internet. Right click on the Toggle desktop icon. Choose "Run as Administrator," and you'll be instantly disconnected from the Internet. Later, when you need to reconnect, just right-click the same file and run as an administrator as before.

Figure 14. What questions should we give in context to illustrations in pathology?

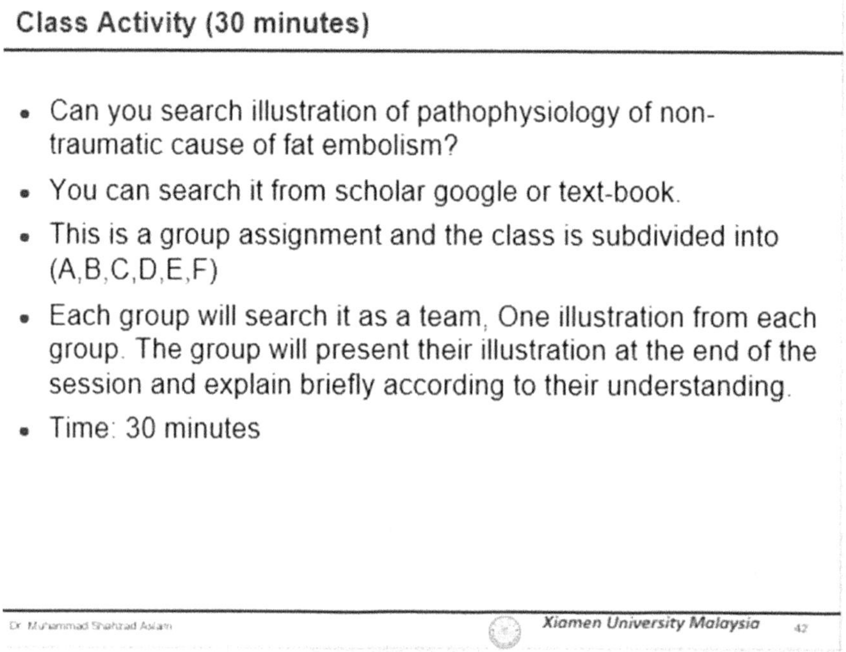

Figure 15. Integrating traditional Chinese philosophy with Western medicine philosophies

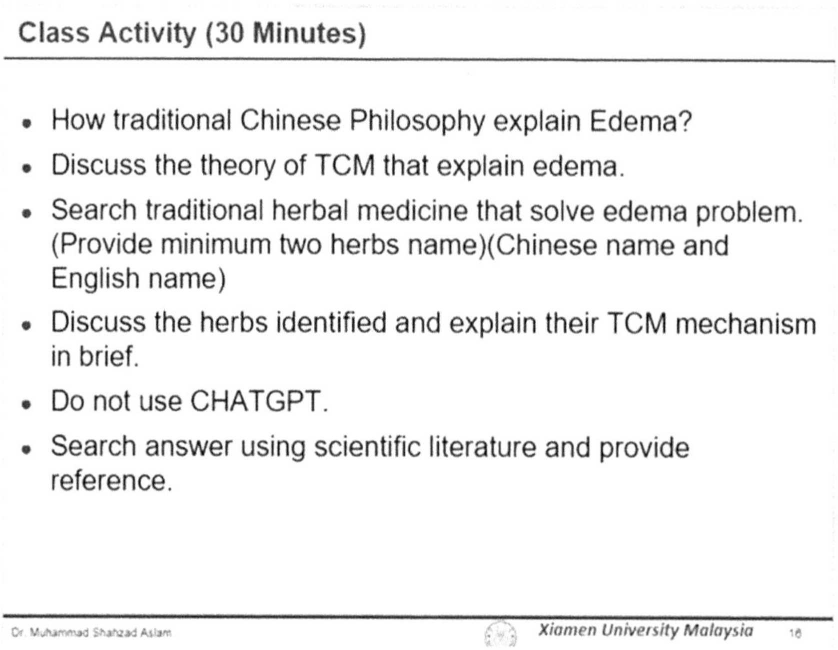

Table 6. Prompt for ChatGPT on inflammatory mediators

Nature of Prompt	Examples
Long Prompt	Examine the complex role that inflammatory mediators play in the onset and development of chronic illnesses. Explore the wide spectrum of inflammatory mediators involved in a number of chronic ailments, such as cardiovascular disease, diabetes, autoimmune disorders, and more, in your response. Describe the cellular and molecular processes at play and how these mediators affect disease pathogenesis. Feel free to support your ideas with Hypothetical case study. Your answer should show that you have a thorough grasp of how inflammatory mediators affect chronic illnesses and how important they could be in clinical settings.
Short Prompt	1. Explain the pivotal role of inflammatory mediators in driving the progression of chronic diseases. Provide specific examples to illustrate their impact. 2. Discuss the significance of inflammatory mediators in the context of chronic diseases. Elaborate on how their dysregulation contributes to disease pathology. 3. Explore the diverse range of inflammatory mediators involved in chronic diseases. Select one mediator and delve into its mechanisms and effects on disease development. 4. Investigate the intricate interplay between inflammation and chronic diseases, focusing on the multifaceted roles of different inflammatory mediators. 5. Compare and contrast the roles of pro-inflammatory and anti-inflammatory mediators in chronic diseases. Provide real-world scenarios to illustrate their dynamic balance. 6. Analyze how chronic diseases such as cardiovascular diseases, diabetes, or autoimmune disorders are influenced by inflammatory mediators. Provide a comprehensive overview of their contributions. 7. Examine the potential therapeutic interventions targeting inflammatory mediators in the management of chronic diseases. Discuss their effectiveness and challenges. 8. Discuss the concept of "inflammaging" and its relationship with chronic diseases. Explore how age-related changes in inflammatory mediators impact disease susceptibility. 9. Dive into the molecular pathways through which inflammatory mediators exacerbate chronic diseases. Highlight key signaling pathways and their implications. 10. Critically evaluate the role of inflammatory mediators as potential biomarkers for predicting the onset and progression of chronic diseases. Discuss their diagnostic utility.

Table 7. Ideal prompt as per suggestion

Areas	Recommendation
Clarity	The prompt you want ChatGPT to answer should be made crystal clear. Use direct words and abstain from ambiguity.
Context	Give ChatGPT enough background information to fully comprehend the task's needs, especially if the subject is specialized or niche.
Relevance	Ensure that the prompt is pertinent to the work at hand. Extraneous data might cause the model to malfunction or produce false results.
Conciseness	While context is crucial, try to be as succinct as you can in your response. Verbosity that is unnecessary might cause model confusion.
Open-endedness	Leave room for the model to generate creative responses. Overly restrictive prompts may limit the model's ability to provide diverse answers.
Keywords	Use keywords that guide ChatGPT's focus and highlight the key aspects of the task.
Question Formulation	For question-based prompts, ensure that the question is well-structured and grammatically correct.

SYSTEMIC PATHOLOGY

To understand the systemic pathology, such as diseases of the cardiovascular system. I suggest the teachers use ChatGPT to ask students to develop the hypothetical case study and then to discuss the answers inside the classroom in a group discussion. For example, When I asked ChatGPT to create a hypothetical case study, ChatGPT responded in the figure. It is possible that a lecturer gave a hypothetical or factual case study from literature and asked the student to use the given case study to develop another hypothetical case study, as suggested in Figure 16.

Figure 16. A hypothetical case study to understand hypertension

Student and ChatGPT

Student asking from ChatGPT

Can you create a hypothetical case for hypertension. i am giving one sample to you:A 58-year-old man with a 15-year history of hypertension, history of smoking two packs of cigarettes a day, and diabetes mellitus experiences the acute onset of weakness and numbness on the left side of his body and an inability to walk. He admits to having a severe headache. His wife reports that during the ride to the emergency center he became lethargic. His blood pressure upon arrival was 192/105 mm Hg

ChatGPT responded

Hypothetical Case: A 42-year-old Woman with Hypertension and Recurrent Headaches

Ms. Smith, a 42-year-old woman, has a known history of hypertension for the past 5 years. She's been prescribed antihypertensive medication, but her blood pressure has been fluctuating. She visits her primary care physician with complaints of recurrent headaches, particularly in the morning. She describes the headaches as throbbing and usually located at the back of her head. She occasionally experiences dizziness and blurred vision when the headaches are intense.

During her visit, Ms. Smith's blood pressure is measured at 160/100 mm Hg. Her physician also notices that her optic discs appear slightly swollen upon fundoscopic examination. Ms. Smith's medical history includes occasional smoking and a sedentary lifestyle. Her family has a history of cardiovascular diseases.

Questions

a) Analyze the potential relationship between Ms. Smith's hypertension, her recurrent headaches, and the observed optic disc changes.
b) Discuss the significance of her family history and lifestyle factors in the context of her hypertension.
c) Propose an initial evaluation plan for Ms. Smith, considering her symptoms, medical history, blood pressure reading, and fundoscopic findings.

Figure 17. A hypothetical case study to understand acute respiratory distress syndrome

Student and ChatGPT

Student asking from ChatGPT

Can you create a hypothetical case for acute respiratory distress syndrome. For-example: A 60-year-old man presented to the emergency department complaining of persistent right-sided chest pain and cough. The chest pain was pleuritic in nature and had been present for the last month. The associated cough was productive of yellow sputum without hemoptysis. He had unintentionally lost approximately 30 pounds over the last 6 months and had nightly sweats. The patient smoked one pack of cigarettes daily for the past 50 years and denied recreational drug use. He reported ingesting twelve beers daily and had delirium tremens, remote right-sided rib fractures and a wrist fracture as a result of alcohol consumption. He was initially admitted to the general medical floor for treatment of community-acquired pneumonia and for the prevention of delirium tremens. By hospital day 5, his respiratory status continued to worsen, requiring transfer to the intensive care unit (ICU) for hypoxemic respiratory failure. His neurologic status had also significantly deteriorated with worsening confusion, memory loss, drowsiness, visual hallucinations.

ChatGPT responded

Hypothetical Case: A 55-year-old Man with Acute Respiratory Distress Syndrome (ARDS)

Mr. Johnson, a 55-year-old man, is brought to the emergency department complaining of severe shortness of breath and difficulty breathing. His family reports that he had been experiencing a persistent cough, fever, and chills for the past week. His medical history is significant for heavy alcohol consumption and a smoking habit of 50 years.

Upon arrival, Mr. Johnson is in distress, with labored breathing and low oxygen saturation. His chest X-ray reveals bilateral infiltrates consistent with pneumonia. He is admitted to the hospital for treatment of severe community-acquired pneumonia. Despite aggressive antibiotic therapy, Mr. Johnson's respiratory distress worsens over the next few days. He requires increased oxygen support and is transferred to the intensive care unit (ICU) for closer monitoring.

On ICU admission, Mr. Johnson's condition continues to deteriorate. He requires mechanical ventilation due to severe hypoxemia and respiratory failure. His oxygenation remains inadequate, and he develops a persistently high respiratory rate. Despite treatment, his oxygen levels do not improve, and his chest X-ray shows diffuse opacities in both lung fields. His kidney function also declines, requiring continuous renal replacement therapy.

The ICU team recognizes the possibility of Acute Respiratory Distress Syndrome (ARDS) as a complication of his severe pneumonia. Mr. Johnson's oxygen levels, lung compliance, and overall condition continue to worsen. He becomes increasingly lethargic, and his blood pressure drops. He is placed on high levels of positive end-expiratory pressure (PEEP) to improve oxygenation, but his prognosis remains guarded.

The case of Mr. Johnson underscores the rapid and severe progression of ARDS, often seen as a consequence of severe lung injury, pneumonia, or systemic inflammation. It highlights the challenges in managing a critically ill patient with complex medical history and the need for prompt recognition and interventions in cases of ARDS.

This hypothetical case offers a context for students to apply their knowledge of ARDS, its clinical manifestations, and the complexities of managing critically ill patients with respiratory failure.

Asking students to create a hypothetical case study using ChatGPT is not necessary. The essential assessment element is case discussion between their peers or teacher. A proposed marking rubric has been attached to the table.

Table 8. Case discussion marking rubric suggested by ChatGPT prompt

Areas	Recommendation
Participation and engagement (30 points)	Excellent (26-30 points): Actively engages in the case discussion, initiates meaningful contributions, responds to peers' ideas with insightful comments, and promotes a collaborative environment. Good (21-25 points): Participates consistently, provides relevant input, and interacts constructively with peers and the teacher. Fair (16-20 points): Participates occasionally but may not consistently contribute or respond to others.
Content Understanding and Analysis (40 points):	Excellent (35-40 points): Demonstrates a deep understanding of the case, highlights key clinical aspects, identifies relevant symptoms, and thoroughly analyzes the case's medical implications. Good (28-34 points): Shows a solid grasp of the case details, discusses important medical factors, and offers meaningful insights. Fair (20-27 points): Provides basic analysis of the case but may miss some key details or lack in-depth medical understanding.
Critical Thinking and Integration (20 points):	Excellent (18-20 points): Applies critical thinking skills by drawing connections between symptoms, suggesting possible diagnoses, and proposing well-reasoned solutions. Integrates medical knowledge effectively. Good (14-17 points): Demonstrates critical thinking by offering reasoned interpretations and suggestions, although connections might be less comprehensive. Fair (10-13 points): Presents basic critical thinking, but connections and insights may be limited.
Contribution to Discussion Dynamics (10 points):	Excellent (9-10 points): Contributes to a dynamic discussion by facilitating exchanges, asking insightful questions, and encouraging peers' participation. Good (7-8 points): Contributes positively to the discussion by engaging with peers' ideas and maintaining a respectful tone. Fair (5-6 points): Participates without significantly impacting the overall dynamics of the discussion.
Total	100 Marks

ChatGPT note: Remember, the rubric is a guideline and can be customized based on specific teaching goals, the complexity of the cases, and the desired level of participation and engagement. The rubric focuses on active participation, depth of understanding, critical thinking, and the ability to foster a collaborative learning environment.

Another method to implement ChatGPT in systemic pathology is the comparative analysis of different diseases. For example, if I am teaching gastritis and peptic ulcer disease, ask the students to use ChatGPT to compare and contrast the symptoms, risk factors, pathogenesis, pathophysiology, diagnostic approach and treatment method between gastritis and peptic ulcer as mentioned in Figure 18.

Figure 18. Comparative analysis of concept using ChatGPT

Present the Case study:Start by presenting a hypothetical case of a patient with symptoms of gastritis and peptic ulcer. Describe the patient's history, symptoms, and relevant medical information.	Group Discussion: Bring students together for a group discussion. Each group can present their findings and insights from the comparative analysis tasks.
Initial Discussion: Assessing background information by asking students to share their initial thoughts on the potential causes, risk factors, and clinical presentation of gastritis and peptic ulcer.	Critical Thinking Reflection: Using real-world situations, real case study, skills beyond classroom.
Comparative Analysis with ChatGPT: Allow student to use ChatGPT to ask questions about symptoms, risk factors, pathogenesis, pathophysiology, diagnostic approach and treatment method	Positive reinformcement: Giving rewards to groups in excellent performance such as giving books, soveniers.

CONCLUSION

With the fast advancement of technology, it is crucial to update teaching pedagogies. A balanced approach of generative AI such as ChatGPT is recommended based on modern teaching methods and a fast pace world where time is essential. ChatGPT can use rationally to give students knowledge of critical thinking in a problem-solving world. Teachers need to revisit their assessment methods and teaching pedagogies.

REFERENCES

Ways to Disable Internet Access. (2022). WikiHow. https://www.wikihow.com/Disable-Internet-Access

Huang, Y., Yao, P., Leung, K. W., Wang, H., Kong, X. P., Wang, L., Dong, T. T. X., Chen, Y., & Tsim, K. W. K. (2018). The Yin-Yang Property of Chinese Medicinal Herbs Relates to Chemical Composition but Not Anti-Oxidative Activity: An Illustration Using Spleen-Meridian Herbs. *Frontiers in Pharmacology*, *9*, 1304. Advance online publication. doi:10.3389/fphar.2018.01304 PMID:30498446

Keji, C., & Hao, X. (2003). The integration of traditional Chinese medicine and Western medicine. *European Review (Chichester, England)*, *11*(2), 225–235. doi:10.1017/S106279870300022X

Lee, S. J., Park, S. H., & Chae, H. (2016). Biopsychological structure of Yin-Yang using Cloninger's Temperament model and Carver and White's BIS/BAS scale. *PeerJ*, *4*(5), e2021. doi:10.7717/peerj.2021 PMID:27231654

Leishmaniasis. (2020). Center for Disease Control.

Ooi, G. L. (1993). Chinese Medicine in Malaysia and Singapore: The Business of Healing. *The American Journal of Chinese Medicine, 21*(3-4), 197–212. doi:10.1142/S0192415X93000236

Percivall Pott and the Chimney Sweeps. (n.d.). Encyclopedia.Com. Retrieved August 17, 2023, from https://www.encyclopedia.com/science/encyclopedias-almanacs-transcripts-and-maps/percivall-pott-and-chimney-sweeps-cancer

Quoquab, F., Md Husin, M., Basiruddin, R., & Mohamed, A. H. (2023). Traditional Chinese Medicine (TCM) in Malaysia: An Alternative Approach to Treatment. In Sustainability and Social Marketing Issues in Asia (pp. 85–97). Emerald Publishing Limited. doi:10.1108/978-1-80071-845-620231006

Thiery, M. (2009). Gabriele Fallopio (1523–1562) and the Fallopian tube. *Gynecological Surgery*, *6*(1), 93–95. doi:10.100710397-008-0453-3

Three Malaysians die in suspected carbon monoxide poisoning in their vehicle. (2020). The Straits Times. https://www.straitstimes.com/asia/se-asia/three-malaysians-die-in-suspected-carbon-monoxide-poisoning-in-their-vehicle

Xu, Z., Zhang, S., Huang, L., Zhu, X., Zhao, Q., Zeng, Y., Zhou, D., Wang, D., Kuga, H., Kamiya, A., & Qu, M. (2018). Altered Resting-State Brain Activities in Drug-Naïve Major Depressive Disorder Assessed by fMRI: Associations With Somatic Symptoms Defined by Yin-Yang Theory of the Traditional Chinese Medicine. *Frontiers in Psychiatry*, *9*, 195. Advance online publication. doi:10.3389/fpsyt.2018.00195 PMID:29867614

Yin Yang Theory. (2023). Ageless Herbs. https://agelessherbs.com/yin-yang-theory/

Yiu, P., Li, G., Tan, C., & Obe, M. (2023). China's aging population threatens a Japan-style lost decade. *Nikkei Asia*. https://asia.nikkei.com/Spotlight/The-Big-Story/China-s-aging-population-threatens-a-Japan-style-lost-decade

Conclusion

Finally, ChatGPT is a unique educational breakthrough that bridges the gap between cutting-edge technology and the pursuit of knowledge. Its capacity to hold natural, intelligent conversations, along with its large knowledge base, makes it an invaluable companion for both students and educators. Our book did discuss some tool and methods of using an effective ChatGPT. With ChatGPT, personalized and interactive learning experiences are within reach. Its adaptability and versatility allow it to cater to individual learning styles, providing tailored explanations and guidance.

ChatGPT has the ability to transform traditional classrooms into dynamic spaces where curiosity is kindled, critical thinking is cultivated, and knowledge is accessible to all by using the power of AI. However, it is critical to recognise that ChatGPT is not a replacement for human teachers and mentors. The human touch, sensitivity, and knowledge that educators bring to the table are invaluable. ChatGPT should be considered as a tool to enrich and support educational journeys, providing a plethora of information, resources, and insights to both teachers and learners. As we move onward, it is critical to create a balance between the incorporation of AI technologies like ChatGPT and the preservation of human ties in education. Ethical considerations, privacy safeguards, and continual research and development are required to ensure that AI stays a force for good and that its benefits are ethically utilised.

ChatGPT in Education promises to be a vital ally in the ever-changing educational landscape, ushering in a new era of personalised learning, better accessibility, and enhanced educational experiences. We can use the potential of this AI-powered tool to motivate lifelong learners, foster intellectual curiosity, and design a brighter future for education if we work together.

Let's continue to explore, discover, and learn together.

Compilation of References

Ways to Disable Internet Access. (2022). WikiHow. https://www.wikihow.com/Disable-Internet-Access

Abdulai, A., & Hung, L. (2023). Will ChatGPT undermine ethical values in nursing education, research, and practice? *Nursing Inquiry*, *3–5*(3), e12556. Advance online publication. doi:10.1111/nin.12556 PMID:37101311

AbouammohN.RainaR.SolimanM. (2023). *Original Research : Exploring Perceptions and Experiences of ChatGPT in Medical Education : A Qualitative Study Among Medical College Faculty and Students in Saudi Arabia Acknowledgments : Declaration of*. doi:10.1101/2023.07.13.23292624

Academic Honesty : University of Rochester. (2023). University of Rochester. http://www.rochester.edu/college/honesty/

AgrazM.KarniadakisG. E. (2023). *ChatGPT-Enhanced ROC Analysis (CERA): A Shiny Web Tool for Finding Optimal Cutoff in Biomarker Analysis Authors summary*. doi:10.1101/2023.07.13.548794

AhmedI.KajolM.HasanU.DattaP. P. (2023). *ChatGPT vs. Bard: A Comparative Study*. doi:ndownloader.figshare.com/files/41277468

Alam, A. (2021). Possibilities and Apprehensions in the Landscape of Artificial Intelligence in Education. *2021 International Conference on Computational Intelligence and Computing Applications (ICCICA)*, 1–8. 10.1109/ICCICA52458.2021.9697272

Ali, S., & Khuwaja, P. (2023). *ChatGPT Needs SPADE (Sustainability, PrivAcy, Digital divide, and Ethics) Evaluation : A Review*. https://ieeexplore.ieee.org/document/10198233/

Ali, M. J., & Djalilian, A. (2023). Readership Awareness Series – Paper 4: Chatbots and ChatGPT - Ethical Considerations in Scientific Publications. *Seminars in Ophthalmology*, *38*(5), 403–404. doi:10.1080/08820538.2023.2193444 PMID:36945119

Alkaissi, H., & McFarlane, S. I. (2023). Artificial Hallucinations in ChatGPT: Implications in Scientific Writing. *Cureus*, *15*(2), 2–5. doi:10.7759/cureus.35179 PMID:36811129

Amber, Q. (2023). *ChatGPT Revolution in Different Fields of Life : Literature Synthesis and Research Agenda ChatGPT Avenues : Integrated Evidence from Literature and ChatGPT*. https://papers.ssrn.com/sol3/papers.cfm?abstract_id=4451821

AngelM.PatelA.AlachkarA.BaldiP. F. (2023). Clinical Knowledge and Reasoning Abilities of AI Large Language Models in Pharmacy: A Comparative Study on the NAPLEX Exam. In bioRxiv. doi:10.1101/2023.06.07.544055

Announcement: OPC to investigate ChatGPT jointly with provincial privacy authorities. (2023). Office of the Privacy Commissioner of Canada. https://www.priv.gc.ca/en/opc-news/news-and-announcements/2023/an_230525-2/

Anonymous. (2023). *How ChatGPT Will Impact the Future of Education*. Hope 103.2. https://hope1032.com.au/stories/life/education/2023/how-chatgpt-will-impact-the-future-of-education/

Arif, T., Munaf, U., & Ul-Haque, I. (2023). The future of medical education and research: Is ChatGPT a blessing or blight in disguise? *Medical Education Online*, *28*(1), 2181052. Advance online publication. doi:10.1080/10872981.2023.2181052 PMID:36809073

Arslan, S. (2023). Exploring the Potential of Chat GPT in Personalized Obesity Treatment. *Annals of Biomedical Engineering*, *51*(9), 1887–1888. doi:10.100710439-023-03227-9 PMID:37145177

Au, A. (2023). *Inevitable rise of ChatGPT and other AI tools must be managed rather than resisted*. South China Morning Post. https://www.scmp.com/comment/opinion/article/3208914/inevitable-rise-chatgpt-and-other-ai-tools-must-be-managed-rather-resisted

Aydin, Ö., & Karaarslan, E. (2022). OpenAI ChatGPT Generated Literature Review : Digital Twin in Healthcare. In *Emerging Computer Technologies 2* (Vol. 2). İzmir Akademi Dernegi. doi:10.2139srn.4308687

Baruch, Y. (1999). Response Rate in Academic Studies-A Comparative Analysis. *Human Relations*, *52*(4), 421–438. doi:10.1177/001872679905200401

Berne Convention for the Protection of Literary and Artistic Works. (2023). WIPO. https://www.wipo.int/treaties/en/ip/berne/

Bhattacharyya, M., Miller, V. M., Bhattacharyya, D., & Miller, L. E. (2023). High Rates of Fabricated and Inaccurate References in ChatGPT-Generated Medical Content. *Cureus*, *15*(5). Advance online publication. doi:10.7759/cureus.39238 PMID:37337480

Biswas, S. S. (2023). Potential Use of Chat GPT in Global Warming. *Annals of Biomedical Engineering*, *1–2*(6), 1126–1127. Advance online publication. doi:10.100710439-023-03171-8 PMID:36856927

Bowman, E. (2022). *ChatGPT could transform academia. But it's not an A+ student yet*. NPR. https://www.npr.org/2022/12/19/1143912956/chatgpt-ai-chatbot-homework-academia

Budhwar, P., Chowdhury, S., Wood, G., Aguinis, H., Bamber, G. J., Beltran, J. R., Boselie, P., Lee Cooke, F., Decker, S., DeNisi, A., Dey, P. K., Guest, D., Knoblich, A. J., Malik, A., Paauwe, J., Papagiannidis, S., Patel, C., Pereira, V., Ren, S., ... Varma, A. (2023). Human resource management in the age of generative artificial intelligence: Perspectives and research directions on ChatGPT. *Human Resource Management Journal*, *33*(3), 606–659. doi:10.1111/1748-8583.12524

Bugeja, M. (2023). *If AI kills the essay, I will be a pallbearer at the funeral*. Poynter. https://www.poynter.org/commentary/2023/will-chatgpt-kill-term-papers-essays/

Cascella, M., Montomoli, J., Bellini, V., & Bignami, E. (2023). Evaluating the Feasibility of ChatGPT in Healthcare: An Analysis of Multiple Clinical and Research Scenarios. *Journal of Medical Systems*, *47*(1), 33. doi:10.100710916-023-01925-4 PMID:36869927

Celik, I. (2023). Towards Intelligent-TPACK: An empirical study on teachers' professional knowledge to ethically integrate artificial intelligence (AI)-based tools into education. *Computers in Human Behavior*, *138*, 107468. doi:10.1016/j.chb.2022.107468

ChatGPT in the Public Sector – overhyped or overlooked ? (2023). Council of the European Union.

ChatGPT will revolutionize academic research. (2023). Times Higher Education (THE). https://www.timeshighereducation.com/depth/chatgpt-revolution-academic-research-has-begun

ChenL.ChenJ.GoldsteinT.HuangH.ZhouT. (2023). *InstructZero: Efficient Instruction Optimization for Black-Box Large Language Models.* https://arxiv.org/abs/2306.03082v1

ChenQ.SunH.LiuH.JiangY.RanT.JinX.XiaoX.LinZ.NiuZ.ChenH. (2023). A Comprehensive Benchmark Study on Biomedical Text Generation and Mining with ChatGPT. BioRxiv, 2023.04.19.537463. doi:10.1101/2023.04.19.537463

Choudhury, A., & Shamszare, H. (2023). Investigating the Impact of User Trust on the Adoption and Use of ChatGPT: Survey Analysis. *Journal of Medical Internet Research*, *25*, e47184. doi:10.2196/47184 PMID:37314848

Corsello, A., & Santangelo, A. (2023). May Artificial Intelligence Influence Future Pediatric Research?—The Case of ChatGPT. *Children (Basel, Switzerland)*, *10*(4), 757. doi:10.3390/children10040757 PMID:37190006

Cothran, T. (2011). Google Scholar acceptance and use among graduate students: A quantitative study. *Library & Information Science Research*, *33*(4), 293–301. doi:10.1016/j.lisr.2011.02.001

CottonD. R. E.CottonP. A.ShipwayJ. R. (2023). *Chatting and cheating: Ensuring academic integrity in the era of ChatGPT* (Issue February). https://doi.org/ doi:10.35542/osf.io/mrz8h

Cox, A., Seth, I., Xie, Y., Hunter-Smith, D. J., & Rozen, W. M. (2023). Utilizing ChatGPT-4 for Providing Medical Information on Blepharoplasties to Patients. *Aesthetic Surgery Journal*, *43*(8), NP658–NP662. doi:10.1093/asjjad096 PMID:37032521

Cross, J., Robinson, R., Devaraju, S., Vaughans, A., Hood, R., Kayalackakom, T., Honnavar, P., Naik, S., & Sebastian, R. (2023). Transforming Medical Education: Assessing the Integration of ChatGPT Into Faculty Workflows at a Caribbean Medical School. *Cureus*, *15*(7). Advance online publication. doi:10.7759/cureus.41399 PMID:37426402

D., F., I.A., B., B.M., C., & C.S., de P. (2013). Influence of psychosocial risk factors on the trajectory of mental health problems from childhood to adolescence: A longitudinal study. *BMC Psychiatry, 13*(1), 31. http://www.embase.com/search/results?subaction=viewrecord&from=export&id=L52404144%0Ahttp://www.biomedcentral.com/1471-244X/13/31%0Ahttp://dx.doi.org/10.1186/1471-244X-13-31

Dartmouth. (2023). *ChatGPT Gets Dartmouth Talking*. Dartmouth. https://home.dartmouth.edu/news/2023/02/chatgpt-gets-dartmouth-talking

Davis, F. D. (1989). Perceived Usefulness, Perceived Ease of Use, and User Acceptance of Information Technology. *Management Information Systems Quarterly*, *13*(3), 319. doi:10.2307/249008

Davis, F. D. (1993). User acceptance of information technology: System characteristics, user perceptions and behavioral impacts. *International Journal of Man-Machine Studies*, *38*(3), 475–487. doi:10.1006/imms.1993.1022

Davis, F. D. (2011). *Foreword in Technology Acceptance in Education: Research and Issues. Rotterdam*. Sense Publishers. https://www.scirp.org/(S(351jmbntvnsjt1aadkozje))/reference/referencespapers.aspx?referenceid=2967483

DeshpandeA.MurahariV.RajpurohitT.KalyanA.NarasimhanK. (2023). *Toxicity in ChatGPT: Analyzing Persona-assigned Language Models*. https://arxiv.org/abs/2304.05335v1

Dhar, P. (2020). The carbon impact of artificial intelligence. *Nature Machine Intelligence*, *2*(August), 423–425. doi:10.103842256-020-0219-9

Dreher, P. C., Tong, C., Ghiraldi, E., & Friedlander, J. I. (2018). Use of Google Trends to Track Online Behavior and Interest in Kidney Stone Surgery. *Urology*, *121*, 74–78. doi:10.1016/j.urology.2018.05.040 PMID:30076945

Duarte, F. (2023). *Number of ChatGPT Users*. Exploding Topics. https://explodingtopics.com/blog/chatgpt-users

Dwivedi, V. (2023). Teaching in times of ChatGPT. *The Hindu Businessline*. https://www.thehindubusinessline.com/opinion/teaching-in-times-of-chatgpt/article66522426.ece

El-Zayat, A., Namnkani, S., Alshareef, N., Mustfa, M., Eminaga, N., & Algarni, G. (2023). Cyberchondria and its association with smartphone addiction and electronic health literacy among a Saudi population. *Saudi Journal of Medicine & Medical Sciences*, *11*(2), 162. doi:10.4103jmms.sjmms_491_22 PMID:37252023

Eysenbach, G. (2023). The Role of ChatGPT, Generative Language Models, and Artificial Intelligence in Medical Education: A Conversation With ChatGPT and a Call for Papers. *JMIR Medical Education*, *9*, e46885. doi:10.2196/46885 PMID:36863937

Fergus, T. A., & Spada, M. M. (2018). Moving toward a metacognitive conceptualization of cyberchondria: Examining the contribution of metacognitive beliefs, beliefs about rituals, and stop signals. *Journal of Anxiety Disorders*, *60*(August), 11–19. doi:10.1016/j.janxdis.2018.09.003 PMID:30317062

Ferlazzo, L. (2023). *Educators Need to Get With the AI Program. ChatGPT, More Specifically*. Education Week. https://www.edweek.org/teaching-learning/opinion-educators-need-to-get-with-the-ai-program-chatgpt-more-specifically/2023/01

Fijačko, N., Gosak, L., Štiglic, G., Picard, C. T., & John Douma, M. (2023). Can ChatGPT pass the life support exams without entering the American heart association course? *Resuscitation*, *185*, 109732. doi:10.1016/j.resuscitation.2023.109732 PMID:36775020

Foter. (2015). *How To Attribute Creative Commons Photos*. https://foter.com/blog/how-to-attribute-creative-commons-photos/

Frosolini, A., Gennaro, P., Cascino, F., & Gabriele, G. (2023). *Reference to "Role of Chat GPT in Public Health", to Highlight the AI's Incorrect Reference Generation. Annals of Biomedical Engineering*. doi:10.100710439-023-03248-4

GabashviliI. S. (2023). *ChatGPT in Dermatology: A Comprehensive Systematic Review*. doi:10.1101/2023.06.11.23291252

Gilliard, C., & Rorabaugh, P. (2023). *You're Not Going to Like How Colleges Respond to ChatGPT*. Slate. https://slate.com/technology/2023/02/chat-gpt-cheating-college-ai-detection.html

Gilmore, D., Nottingham, A., Zerwes, M., & University, R. (2023). *ChatGPT as a course content creator*. RMIT University. https://www.timeshighereducation.com/campus/chatgpt-and-learning-design-what-online-content-creation-opportunities-does-it-offer

Gilson, A., Safranek, C. W., Huang, T., Socrates, V., Chi, L., Taylor, R. A., & Chartash, D. (2023). How Does ChatGPT Perform on the United States Medical Licensing Examination? The Implications of Large Language Models for Medical Education and Knowledge Assessment. *JMIR Medical Education*, *9*, e45312. doi:10.2196/45312 PMID:36753318

Giménez, V., Prior, D., Tortosa-Ausina, E., Giménez, V., Prior, D., & Tortosa-Ausina, E. (2018). The impact of efficiency on the economic growth of emerging economies: The case of Colombia. *Ensayos Sobre Política Económica, 36*(SPE85), 86–100. doi:10.32468/Espe.8505

Gödde, D., Nöhl, S., Wolf, C., Rupert, Y., & Rimkus, L. (2023). *ChatGPT in medical literature – A concise review and SWOT analysis*. Academic Press.

Goodwin, K. (2023). W&L Dialogues on the Future of AI. *W&L Magazine*. https://columns.wlu.edu/wl-dialogues-on-the-future-of-ai/

Grabb, D. (2023). ChatGPT in Medical Education: A Paradigm Shift or a Dangerous Tool? *Academic Psychiatry*, *0123456789*, 2–3. doi:10.100740596-023-01791-9 PMID:37160840

Guillén-Gámez, F. D., Mayorga-Fernández, M., Bravo-Agapito, J., & Escribano-Ortiz, D. (2021). Analysis of Teachers' Pedagogical Digital Competence: Identification of Factors Predicting Their Acquisition. *Technology, Knowledge and Learning*, *26*(3), 481–498. doi:10.100710758-019-09432-7

Gupta, M., Akiri, C., Aryal, K., Parker, E., & Praharaj, L. (2023). From ChatGPT to ThreatGPT: Impact of Generative AI in Cybersecurity and Privacy. *IEEE Access : Practical Innovations, Open Solutions*, *11*(July), 80218–80245. doi:10.1109/ACCESS.2023.3300381

Hacker, P., Engel, A., & Mauer, M. (2023). Regulating ChatGPT and other Large Generative AI Models. *2023 ACM Conference on Fairness, Accountability, and Transparency*, 1112–1123. 10.1145/3593013.3594067

Hagood, T. C. (2023). *ChatGPT message to faculty*. The University of Utah. https://attheu.utah.edu/facultystaff/chatgpt-message-to-faculty/

Hariri, W. (2023). Analyzing the Performance of ChatGPT in Cardiology and Vascular Pathologies. doi:/v1www.researchsquare.com/article/rs-2782768/v1 doi:10.21203/rs.3.rs-2782768

HaririW. (2023). *Analyzing the Performance of ChatGPT in Cardiology and Vascular Pathologies*. doi:10.21203/rs.3.rs-2782768/v1www.researchsquare.com/article/rs-2782768/v1

Hartman-Sigall, J. (2023). *University declines to ban ChatGPT, releases faculty guidance for its usage*. The Princetonian. https://www.dailyprincetonian.com/article/2023/01/university-declines-ban-chatgpt-releases-faculty-guidance-for-usage

Hatzius, J., Briggs, J., Kodnani, D., & Pierdomenico, G. (2023). *Global-Economics-Analyst_-The-Potentially-Large-Effects-of-Artificial-Intelligence*. Goldman Sachs Economics Research. https://www.ansa.it/documents/1680080409454_ert.pdf

Helberger, N., & Diakopoulos, N. (2023). ChatGPT and the AI Act. *Internet Policy Review*, *12*(1), 1–6. doi:10.14763/2023.1.1682

Henebery, B. (2023). *How schools can strike the right balance with ChatGPT*. The Educator K/12. https://www.theeducatoronline.com/k12/news/how-schools-can-strike-the-right-balance-with-chatgpt/281845

Hepp, A., Loosen, W., Dreyer, S., Jarke, J., Kannengießer, S., Katzenbach, C., Malaka, R., Pfadenhauer, M. P., Puschmann, C., & Schulz, W. (2023). ChatGPT, LaMDA, and the Hype Around Communicative AI: The Automation of Communication as a Field of Research in Media and Communication Studies. *Human-Machine Communication*, *6*, 41–63. doi:10.30658/hmc.6.4

Heshmati, A. (2000). Productivity Growth, Efficiency and Outsourcing in. *Journal of Economic Surveys*, *17*(1), 79–112. doi:10.1111/1467-6419.00189

He, Y., Tang, H., Wang, D., Gu, S., Ni, G., & Wu, H. (2023). Will ChatGPT/GPT-4 be a Lighthouse to Guide Spinal Surgeons? *Annals of Biomedical Engineering*, *51*(7), 1362–1365. doi:10.100710439-023-03206-0 PMID:37071280

HolmesJ.LiuZ.ZhangL.DingY.SioT. T.McGeeL. A.AshmanJ. B.LiX. LiuT.ShenJ.LiuW. (2023). *Evaluating Large Language Models on a Highly-specialized Topic, Radiation Oncology Physics*. https://arxiv.org/abs/2304.01938

Hosseini, M., Gao, C. A., Liebovitz, D., Carvalho, A., Ahmad, F. S., Luo, Y., MacDonald, N., Holmes, K., & Kho, A. (2023). *An exploratory survey about using ChatGPT in education, healthcare, and research Mohammad.* https://doi.org/https://doi.org/10.1101/2023.03.31.23287979

Hou, W., & Ji, Z. (2023b). GeneTuring tests GPT models in genomics. BioRxiv *: The Preprint Server for Biology, 6*, 1–8. doi:10.1101/2023.03.11.532238

HouW.JiZ. (2023a). Reference-free and cost-effective automated cell type annotation with GPT-4 in single-cell RNA-seq analysis. In bioRxiv. doi:10.1101/2023.04.16.537094

Hrastinski, S., & Keller, C. (2007). An Examination of Research Approaches that Underlie Research on Educational Technology: A Review From 2000 to 2004. *Journal of Educational Computing Research, 36*(2), 175–190. doi:10.2190/H16L-4662-6000-0446

HuangY.GomaaA.SemrauS.HaderleinM.LettmaierS.WeissmannT.GrigoJ.BenTkhayatH.FreyB.GaiplU.DistelL.MaierA.FietkauR.BertC.PutzF. (2023). *Benchmarking ChatGPT-4 on ACR Radiation Oncology In-Training (TXIT) Exam and Red Journal Gray Zone Cases: Potentials and Challenges for AI-Assisted Medical Education and Decision Making in Radiation Oncology.* doi:10.2139/ssrn.4457218

Huang, Y., Yao, P., Leung, K. W., Wang, H., Kong, X. P., Wang, L., Dong, T. T. X., Chen, Y., & Tsim, K. W. K. (2018). The Yin-Yang Property of Chinese Medicinal Herbs Relates to Chemical Composition but Not Anti-Oxidative Activity: An Illustration Using Spleen-Meridian Herbs. *Frontiers in Pharmacology, 9*, 1304. Advance online publication. doi:10.3389/fphar.2018.01304 PMID:30498446

Hunt, R., & Dickens, D. (2023). *ChatGPT isn't going to make us slaves; uninspired education might.* The Dallas Morning News. https://www.dallasnews.com/opinion/commentary/2023/02/04/chatgpt-isnt-going-to-make-us-slaves-uninspired-education-might/

Hwang, G.-J., Xie, H., Wah, B. W., & Gašević, D. (2020). Vision, challenges, roles and research issues of Artificial Intelligence in Education. *Computers and Education: Artificial Intelligence, 1*, 100001. doi:10.1016/j.caeai.2020.100001

Hyun Baek, T., & Kim, M. (2023). Is ChatGPT scary good? How user motivations affect creepiness and trust in generative artificial intelligence. *Telematics and Informatics*, *83*(March), 102030. doi:10.1016/j.tele.2023.102030

Irwin, P., Jones, D., & Fealy, S. (2023). What is ChatGPT and what do we do with it? Implications of the age of AI for nursing and midwifery practice and education: An editorial. *Nurse Education Today*, *127*(May), 105835. doi:10.1016/j.nedt.2023.105835 PMID:37267643

Jang, S. H., Youm, S., & Yi, Y. J. (2023). Anti-Asian Discourse in Quora: Comparison of Before and During the COVID-19 Pandemic with Machine- and Deep-Learning Approaches. *Race and Justice*, *13*(1), 55–79. doi:10.1177/21533687221134690

Johnson, S. B., King, A. J., Warner, E. L., Aneja, S., Kann, B. H., & Bylund, C. L. (2023). Using ChatGPT to evaluate cancer myths and misconceptions: Artificial intelligence and cancer information. *JNCI Cancer Spectrum*, *7*(2), pkad015. Advance online publication. doi:10.1093/jncics/pkad015 PMID:36929393

Karabacak, M., Ozkara, B. B., Margetis, K., Wintermark, M., & Bisdas, S. (2023). The Advent of Generative Language Models in Medical Education. *JMIR Medical Education*, *9*, e48163. doi:10.2196/48163 PMID:37279048

Keji, C., & Hao, X. (2003). The integration of traditional Chinese medicine and Western medicine. *European Review (Chichester, England)*, *11*(2), 225–235. doi:10.1017/S106279870300022X

Keynote Remarks at the International Institute of Communications (IIC) Canada's 19th Annual Communications Law & Policy Conference. (2023). Office of the Privacy Commissioner of Canada. https://www.priv.gc.ca/en/opc-news/speeches/2023/sp-d_20230515/

Khazaal, Y., Chatton, A., Rochat, L., Hede, V., Viswasam, K., Penzenstadler, L., Berle, D., & Starcevic, V. (2021). Compulsive Health-Related Internet Use and Cyberchondria. *European Addiction Research*, *27*(1), 58–66. doi:10.1159/000510922 PMID:33120393

Khurana, S., & Vaddi, A. (2023). ChatGPT From the Perspective of an Academic Oral and Maxillofacial Radiologist. *Cureus*, *15*(6). Advance online publication. doi:10.7759/cureus.40053 PMID:37425514

KılıçM. E. (2023). *AI in Medical Education: A Comparative Analysis of GPT-4 and GPT-3.5 on Turkish Medical Specialization Exam Performance*. https://doi.org/https://doi.org/10.1101/2023.07.12.23292564

Kim, J., Kim, J. H., Kim, C., & Park, J. (2023). Decisions with ChatGPT: Reexamining choice overload in ChatGPT recommendations. *Journal of Retailing and Consumer Services*, *75*(July), 103494. doi:10.1016/j.jretconser.2023.103494

King, R. C., Samaan, J. S., Yeo, Y. H., Mody, B., Lombardo, D. M., & Ghashghaei, R. (2023). *Appropriateness of ChatGPT in answering heart failure related questions*. Academic Press.

Klebanov, S. (2022). *Reddit's Journey to a Potential $15 Billion IPO. 2022*. https://www.businessofbusiness.com/articles/reddit-15-billion-ipo-cultural-force/

Koraishi, O. (2023). Teaching English in the age of AI: Embracing ChatGPT to optimize EFL materials and assessment. *Language Education and Technology*, *3*(1), 55–72. https://bit.ly/43en7e1

KrügelS.OstermaierA.UhlM. (2023). *The moral authority of ChatGPT*. https://arxiv.org/abs/2301.07098v1

Kulsum, U., Sushma, M., Subhaprada, S., & Sreedevi, A. (2023). Prevalence of cyberchondria among undergraduate students of a private degree college with Cyberchondria Severity Scale-12 in an urban area. *BLDE University Journal of Health Sciences*, *8*(1), 95. doi:10.4103/bjhs.bjhs_211_22

Kung, T. H., Cheatham, M., Medenilla, A., Sillos, C., De Leon, L., Elepaño, C., Madriaga, M., Aggabao, R., Diaz-Candido, G., Maningo, J., & Tseng, V. (2023). Performance of ChatGPT on USMLE: Potential for AI-assisted medical education using large language models. *PLOS Digital Health*, *2*(2), e0000198. doi:10.1371/journal.pdig.0000198 PMID:36812645

Lee, S. J., Park, S. H., & Chae, H. (2016). Biopsychological structure of Yin-Yang using Cloninger's Temperament model and Carver and White's BIS/BAS scale. *PeerJ*, *4*(5), e2021. doi:10.7717/peerj.2021 PMID:27231654

Leishmaniasis. (2020). Center for Disease Control.

Levac, D., Colquhoun, H., & O'Brien, K. K. (2010). Scoping studies: Advancing the methodology. *Implementation Science : IS*, *5*(1), 69. doi:10.1186/1748-5908-5-69 PMID:20854677

Liebrenz, M., Schleifer, R., Buadze, A., Bhugra, D., & Smith, A. (2023). Generating scholarly content with ChatGPT: Ethical challenges for medical publishing. *The Lancet. Digital Health*, *5*(3), e105–e106. doi:10.1016/S2589-7500(23)00019-5 PMID:36754725

Liu, J., Wang, C., & Liu, S. (2023). Utility of ChatGPT in Clinical Practice. *Journal of Medical Internet Research*, *25*, e48568. doi:10.2196/48568 PMID:37379067

Liu, S., Wright, A. P., Patterson, B. L., Wanderer, J. P., Turer, R. W., Nelson, S. D., McCoy, A. B., Sittig, D. F., & Wright, A. (2023). Using AI-generated suggestions from ChatGPT to optimize clinical decision support. *Journal of the American Medical Informatics Association : JAMIA*, *30*(7), 1237–1245. doi:10.1093/jamia/ocad072 PMID:37087108

Lo, C. K. (2023). What Is the Impact of ChatGPT on Education? A Rapid Review of the Literature. *Education Sciences*, *13*(4), 410. doi:10.3390/educsci13040410

Lund, B. D., & Wang, T. (2023). Chatting about ChatGPT: how may AI and GPT impact academia and libraries? *Library Hi Tech News*. doi:10.1108/LHTN-01-2023-0009

Lund, B. D., Wang, T., Mannuru, N. R., Nie, B., Shimray, S., & Wang, Z. (2023). ChatGPT and a new academic reality: Artificial Intelligence-written research papers and the ethics of the large language models in scholarly publishing. *Journal of the Association for Information Science and Technology*, *74*(5), 570–581. doi:10.1002/asi.24750

Lyu, Q., Tan, J., Zapadka, M. E., Ponnatapura, J., Niu, C., Myers, K. J., Wang, G., & Whitlow, C. T. (2023). Translating Radiology Reports into Plain Language using ChatGPT and GPT-4 with Prompt Learning: Promising Results, Limitations, and Potential. *Visual Computing for Industry, Biomedicine, and Art*, *6*(1), 9. Advance online publication. doi:10.118642492-023-00136-5 PMID:37198498

Manias, E., Bullock, S., & Bennett, R. (2000). Formative evaluation of a computer-assisted learning program in pharmacology for nursing students. *Computer Nurse*, *18*(6), 265–271. https://pubmed.ncbi.nlm.nih.gov/11105400/

Manias, E., Bullock, S., & Bennett, R. (1999). A computer-assisted learning program in pharmacology: Integrating scientific and nursing knowledge. *Contemporary Nurse*, *8*(2), 23–29. doi:10.5172/conu.1999.8.2.23 PMID:11096792

Martin, J. L. (2023). The Ethico-Political Universe of ChatGPT. *Journal of Scientific Computing*, *4*(1), 1–11. doi:10.23919/JSC.2023.0003

Masters, K. (2023a). Ethical use of Artificial Intelligence in Health Professions Education: AMEE Guide No. 158. *Medical Teacher*, *45*(6), 574–584. doi:10.1080/0142159X.2023.2186203 PMID:36912253

Masters, K. (2023b). Medical Teacher 's first ChatGPT's referencing hallucinations: Lessons for editors, reviewers, and teachers. *Medical Teacher*, *45*(7), 673–675. doi:10.1080/0142159X.2023.2208731 PMID:37183932

Matulis, J., & McCoy, R. (2023). Relief in Sight? Chatbots, In-baskets, and the Overwhelmed Primary Care Clinician. *Journal of General Internal Medicine*, *1*. Advance online publication. doi:10.100711606-023-08271-8 PMID:37369892

Mavragani, A., & Ochoa, G. (2019). Google Trends in Infodemiology and Infoveillance: Methodology Framework. *JMIR Public Health and Surveillance*, *5*(2), e13439. doi:10.2196/13439 PMID:31144671

McMullan, R. D., Berle, D., Arnáez, S., & Starcevic, V. (2019). The relationships between health anxiety, online health information seeking, and cyberchondria: Systematic review and meta-analysis. *Journal of Affective Disorders, 245*, 270–278. doi:10.1016/j.jad.2018.11.037

MehnenL.GruarinS.VasilevaM.KnappB. (2023). ChatGPT as a medical doctor? A diagnostic accuracy study on common and rare diseases. In medRxiv. doi:10.1101/2023.04.20.23288859

Meneses, J. P. (2023). *We spoke with ChatGPT about Macau*. Macau Business. https://www.macaubusiness.com/we-spoke-with-chatgpt-about-macau/

Meo, S. A., Al-Masri, A. A., Alotaibi, M., Meo, M. Z. S., & Meo, M. O. S. (2023). ChatGPT Knowledge Evaluation in Basic and Clinical Medical Sciences: Multiple Choice Question Examination-Based Performance. *Healthcare (Basel)*, *11*(14), 1–11. doi:10.3390/healthcare11142046 PMID:37510487

Mesko, B. (2023). The ChatGPT (Generative Artificial Intelligence) Revolution Has Made Artificial Intelligence Approachable for Medical Professionals. *Journal of Medical Internet Research*, *25*, e48392. doi:10.2196/48392 PMID:37347508

Mestre-Bach, G., & Potenza, M. N. (2023). Cyberchondria: A Growing Concern During the COVID-19 Pandemic and a Possible Addictive Disorder? *Current Addiction Reports*, *10*(1), 77–96. doi:10.100740429-022-00462-3 PMID:36785757

Mhlanga, D. (2023). Open AI in Education, the Responsible and Ethical Use of ChatGPT Towards Lifelong Learning. SSRN *Electronic Journal*. doi:10.2139/ssrn.4354422

Miao, H., & Ahn, H. (2023). Impact of ChatGPT on Interdisciplinary Nursing Education and Research. *Asian/Pacific Island Nursing Journal*, *7*, e48136. doi:10.2196/48136 PMID:37093625

Naumova, E. N. (2023). A mistake-find exercise: A teacher's tool to engage with information innovations, ChatGPT, and their analogs. *Journal of Public Health Policy*, *44*(2), 173–178. doi:10.105741271-023-00400-1 PMID:36914712

Newsroom, T. C. (2023). *Navigating the Risks and Rewards of ChatGPT*. Columbia University. https://www.tc.columbia.edu/articles/2023/january/navigating-the-risks-and-rewards-of-chatgpt/

Nurmi, J., & Niemelä, M. S. (2018). PESTEL Analysis of Hacktivism Campaign Motivations. Lecture Notes in Computer Science, 11252, 323–335. https://doi.org/ doi:10.1007/978-3-030-03638-6_20/FIGURES/8

O'Connor, S., & Chat, G. P. T.ChatGPT. (2023). Open artificial intelligence platforms in nursing education: Tools for academic progress or abuse? *Nurse Education in Practice*, *66*, 103537. doi:10.1016/j.nepr.2022.103537 PMID:36549229

Ooi, G. L. (1993). Chinese Medicine in Malaysia and Singapore: The Business of Healing. *The American Journal of Chinese Medicine, 21*(3-4), 197–212. doi:10.1142/S0192415X93000236

Pan, W., Chen, L., & Zhan, W. (2019). PESTEL Analysis of Construction Productivity Enhancement Strategies: A Case Study of Three Economies. *Journal of Management Engineering*, *35*(1), 05018013. doi:10.1061/(ASCE)ME.1943-5479.0000662

Parsons, S., Davis, H., Caputo, R., & Welsh, M. (2023). *A conversation among Duke Thompson Writing Program faculty about ChatGPT*. The Chronicle. https://www.dukechronicle.com/article/2023/01/013123-parsons-davis-caputo-welsh-chat-gpt

Patel, S. B., & Lam, K. (2023). ChatGPT: The future of discharge summaries? *The Lancet. Digital Health*, *5*(3), e107–e108. doi:10.1016/S2589-7500(23)00021-3 PMID:36754724

PatnaikS. S.HoffmannU. (2023). Comparison of ChatGPT vs. Bard to Anesthesia-related Queries. In MedRxiv. doi:10.1101/2023.06.29.23292057

Paul, J., Ueno, A., & Dennis, C. (2023). ChatGPT and consumers: Benefits, Pitfalls and Future Research Agenda. *International Journal of Consumer Studies*, *47*(4), 1213–1225. doi:10.1111/ijcs.12928

Pavlik, J. V. (2023). *Collaborating With ChatGPT: Considering the Implications of Generative Artificial Intelligence for Journalism and Media Education*. doi:10.1177/10776958221149577

Paykamian, B. (2023). *Higher Ed Reactions to ChatGPT Run the Gamut*. Government Technology. https://www.govtech.com/education/higher-ed/higher-ed-reactions-to-chatgpt-run-the-gamut

Percivall Pott and the Chimney Sweeps. (n.d.). Encyclopedia.Com. Retrieved August 17, 2023, from https://www.encyclopedia.com/science/encyclopedias-almanacs-transcripts-and-maps/percivall-pott-and-chimney-sweeps-cancer

PhongwattanaT.ChanJ. H. (2023). *Automated Extraction and Visualization of Metabolic Networks from Biomedical Literature Using a Large Language Model*. doi:10.1101/2023.06.27.546560

QiuJ.LiL.SunJ.PengJ.ShiP.ZhangR.DongY.LamK.LoF. P.-W.XiaoB.YuanW.XuD.LoB. (2023). *Large AI Models in Health Informatics: Applications, Challenges, and the Future*. https://arxiv.org/abs/2303.11568

Quoquab, F., Md Husin, M., Basiruddin, R., & Mohamed, A. H. (2023). Traditional Chinese Medicine (TCM) in Malaysia: An Alternative Approach to Treatment. In Sustainability and Social Marketing Issues in Asia (pp. 85–97). Emerald Publishing Limited. doi:10.1108/978-1-80071-845-620231006

Rathore, B. (2023). Future of textile: Sustainable manufacturing & prediction via chatgpt. *EDUZONE: International Peer Reviewed/Refereed Multidisciplinary Journal, 12*(1), 2319–5045.

Rawlinson, C., & Bloom, T. (2019). New preprint server for medical research. *BMJ (Clinical Research Ed.)*, *365*, l2301. doi:10.1136/bmj.l2301 PMID:31167753

Ray, P. P. (2023). ChatGPT: A comprehensive review on background, applications, key challenges, bias, ethics, limitations and future scope. *Internet of Things and Cyber-Physical Systems*, *3*(April), 121–154. doi:10.1016/j.iotcps.2023.04.003

Ray, P. P., & Das, P. K. (2023). ChatGPT and societal dynamics: Navigating the crossroads of AI and human interaction. *AI & Society*, *0123456789*. Advance online publication. doi:10.100700146-023-01713-1

Red Mendoza. (2023). *Experts – AI not a threat, but can be used as complement | The Manila Times*. The Manila Times. https://www.manilatimes.net/2023/02/19/news/national/experts-ai-not-a-threat-but-can-be-used-as-complement/1879314

Roberts, M. (2023). *How to Jailbreak ChatGPT with these Prompts*. Mlyearning. https://www.mlyearning.org/how-to-jailbreak-chatgpt/

Rodotà, S. (2009). Data Protection as a Fundamental Right. In *Reinventing Data Protection?* (pp. 77–82). Springer Netherlands. doi:10.1007/978-1-4020-9498-9_3

Roose, K. (2023). *Don't Ban ChatGPT in Schools. Teach With It.* The New York Times. https://www.nytimes.com/2023/01/12/technology/chatgpt-schools-teachers.html

Rozado, D. (2023). The Political Biases of ChatGPT. *Social Sciences (Basel, Switzerland)*, *12*(3), 148. doi:10.3390ocsci12030148

Rudolph, J., Tan, S., & Tan, S. (2023). ChatGPT: Bullshit spewer or the end of traditional assessments in higher education? *Journal of Applied Learning & Teaching*, *6*(1). Advance online publication. doi:10.37074/jalt.2023.6.1.9

RutinowskiJ.FrankeS.EndendykJ.DormuthI.PaulyM. (2023). *The Self-Perception and Political Biases of ChatGPT*. https://arxiv.org/abs/2304.07333

Sallam, M. (2023). ChatGPT Utility in Healthcare Education, Research, and Practice: Systematic Review on the Promising Perspectives and Valid Concerns. *Health Care*, *11*(6), 887. doi:10.3390/healthcare11060887 PMID:36981544

Sallam, M. (2023). Practice : Systematic Review on the Promising Perspectives and Valid Concerns. *Health Care*, *11*(6), 887. PMID:36981544

Sallam, M., Salim, N., Barakat, M., & Al-Tammemi, A. (2023). ChatGPT applications in medical, dental, pharmacy, and public health education: A descriptive study highlighting the advantages and limitations. *Narra J*, *3*(1), e103. doi:10.52225/narra.v3i1.103

Schenkel, S. K., Jungmann, S. M., Gropalis, M., & Witthöft, M. (2021). Conceptualizations of Cyberchondria and Relations to the Anxiety Spectrum: Systematic Review and Meta-analysis. *Journal of Medical Internet Research*, *23*(11), e27835. doi:10.2196/27835 PMID:34792473

Shahsavar, Y., & Choudhury, A. (2023). User Intentions to Use ChatGPT for Self-Diagnosis and Health-Related Purposes: Cross-sectional Survey Study. *JMIR Human Factors*, *10*, e47564. doi:10.2196/47564 PMID:37195756

Sharma, P., Thapa, K., Thapa, D., Dhakal, P., Upadhaya, M. D., Adhikari, S., & Khanal, S. R. (2023). Performance of ChatGPT on USMLE: Unlocking the Potential of Large Language Models for AI-Assisted Medical Education. https://arxiv.org/abs/2307.00112

SharmaP.ThapaK.ThapaD.DhakalP.UpadhayaM. D.AdhikariS.KhanalS. R. (2023). *Performance of ChatGPT on USMLE: Unlocking the Potential of Large Language Models for AI-Assisted Medical Education*. https://arxiv.org/abs/2307.00112

Shaw, D., Morfeld, P., & Erren, T. (2023). The (mis)use of ChatGPT in science and education. *EMBO Reports*, *24*(7), e57501. Advance online publication. doi:10.15252/embr.202357501 PMID:37259767

Sircar, N. (2023). *UAE: AI enters the classroom, but experts say role of the teacher is safe*. Khaleej Times. https://www.zawya.com/en/business/technology-and-telecom/uae-ai-enters-the-classroom-but-experts-say-role-of-the-teacher-is-safe-m783vwgr

Sitter, P. (2023). *Iowa school districts, universities work on policies for AI tools that could be used to cheat*. Ames Tribune.

Skalidis, I., Cagnina, A., Luangphiphat, W., Mahendiran, T., Muller, O., Abbe, E., & Fournier, S. (2023). ChatGPT takes on the European Exam in Core Cardiology: An artificial intelligence success story? *European Heart Journal. Digital Health*, *4*(3), 279–281. doi:10.1093/ehjdh/ztad029 PMID:37265864

Southworth, J. (2023). Rethinking university writing pedagogy in a world of ChatGPT. *University Affairs*.

Steinberg, E. (2023). Faculty split on using ChatGPT as university prepares to confront AI boom. *The Tufts Daily*. https://tuftsdaily.com/news/2023/02/16/faculty-split-on-using-chatgpt-as-university-prepares-to-confront-ai-boom/

Strzelecki, A. (2023). To use or not to use ChatGPT in higher education? A study of students' acceptance and use of technology. *Interactive Learning Environments*, (May), 1–14. doi:10.1080/10494820.2023.2209881

Tec de Monterrey recomienda a su comunidad uso inteligente de ChatGPT. (2023). Tecnológico de Monterrey. https://conecta.tec.mx/es/noticias/nacional/institucion/tec-de-monterrey-recomienda-su-comunidad-uso-inteligente-de-chatgpt

Temsah, M.-H., Aljamaan, F., Malki, K. H., Alhasan, K., Altamimi, I., Aljarbou, R., Bazuhair, F., Alsubaihin, A., Abdulmajeed, N., Alshahrani, F. S., Temsah, R., Alshahrani, T., Al-Eyadhy, L., Alkhateeb, S. M., Saddik, B., Halwani, R., Jamal, A., Al-Tawfiq, J. A., & Al-Eyadhy, A. (2023). ChatGPT and the Future of Digital Health: A Study on Healthcare Workers' Perceptions and Expectations. *Health Care*, *11*(13), 1812. doi:10.3390/healthcare11131812 PMID:37444647

Temsah, O., Khan, S. A., Chaiah, Y., Senjab, A., Alhasan, K., Jamal, A., Aljamaan, F., Malki, K. H., Halwani, R., Al-Tawfiq, J. A., Temsah, M.-H., & Al-Eyadhy, A. (2023). Overview of Early ChatGPT's Presence in Medical Literature: Insights From a Hybrid Literature Review by ChatGPT and Human Experts. *Cureus*, *15*(4). Advance online publication. doi:10.7759/cureus.37281 PMID:37038381

The general data protection regulation - Consilium. (2023). Data Protection in the EU. https://www.consilium.europa.eu/en/policies/data-protection/data-protection-regulation/

Thiery, M. (2009). Gabriele Fallopio (1523–1562) and the Fallopian tube. *Gynecological Surgery*, *6*(1), 93–95. doi:10.100710397-008-0453-3

Three Malaysians die in suspected carbon monoxide poisoning in their vehicle. (2020). The Straits Times. https://www.straitstimes.com/asia/se-asia/three-malaysians-die-in-suspected-carbon-monoxide-poisoning-in-their-vehicle

TianS.JinQ.YeganovaL.LaiP.-T.ZhuQ.ChenX.YangY.ChenQ.KimW. ComeauD. C.IslamajR.KapoorA.GaoX.LuZ. (2023). *Opportunities and Challenges for ChatGPT and Large Language Models in Biomedicine and Health*. https://arxiv.org/abs/2306.10070v1

Tijerina, J. D., Morrison, S. D., Nolan, I. T., Vail, D. G., Nazerali, R., & Lee, G. K. (2019). Google Trends as a Tool for Evaluating Public Interest in Facial Cosmetic Procedures. *Aesthetic Surgery Journal*, *39*(8), 908–918. doi:10.1093/asjjy267 PMID:30304356

UludagK. (2023). *The use of AI-supported Chatbot in Psychology*. doi:10.2139/ssrn.4331367

UNESCO in brief. (2023). UNESCO. https://www.unesco.org/en/brief

UNESCO. (2023). *ChatGPT and Artificial Intelligence in Higher Education*. https://unesdoc.unesco.org/ark:/48223/pf0000385146

UNICEF. (2022). *Safer Chatbots Implementation Guide*. UNICEF.

van de Ridder, J. M. M., Shoja, M. M., & Rajput, V. (2023). *Finding the Place of ChatGPT in Medical Education*. Academic Medicine, Publish Ah. doi:10.1097/ACM.0000000000005254

VeraP.MarieM.GaviriaJ. A.MiroslavT.PetrH.EstherB.TudorT.NinaM. ChawdheryR. A. (2023). *Performance of ChatGPT on Clinical Medicine Entrance Examination for Chinese Postgraduate in Chinese*. doi:10.2139/ssrn.4415697

Victor, V. (2023). *AI challenges pedagogy, learning assessments*. Deccan Herald. https://www.deccanherald.com/opinion/panorama/ai-challenges-pedagogy-learning-assessments-1177049.html

Villasenor, J. (2023). *How ChatGPT Can Improve Education, Not Threaten it*. Scientific American. https://www.scientificamerican.com/article/how-chatgpt-can-improve-education-not-threaten-it/

Vismara, M., Caricasole, V., Starcevic, V., Cinosi, E., Dell'Osso, B., Martinotti, G., & Fineberg, N. A. (2020). Is cyberchondria a new transdiagnostic digital compulsive syndrome? A systematic review of the evidence. *Comprehensive Psychiatry*, *99*, 152167. doi:10.1016/j.comppsych.2020.152167 PMID:32146315

Voigt, A. (2023). *Schools right now face a choice - fight the wave of ChatGPT, or surf it*. The Sydney Morning Herald. https://www.smh.com.au/national/schools-right-now-face-a-choice-fight-the-wave-of-chatgpt-or-surf-it-20230118-p5cdle.html

Wang, D., Feng, L., Ye, J., Zou, J., & Zheng, Y. (2023). Accelerating the integration of ChatGPT and other large-scale AI models into biomedical research and healthcare. *MedComm – Future Medicine, 2*(2). doi:10.1002/mef2.43

Wang, S., Scells, H., Koopman, B., & Zuccon, G. (2023). *Can ChatGPT Write a Good Boolean Query for Systematic Review Literature Search?* https://doi.org/ doi:10.1145/nnnnnnn.nnnnnnn

Wang, Y., Sibaii, F., Lee, K., Gill, J. M., & Hatch, J. (2023). NOTE: This preprint reports new research that has not been certified by peer review and should not be used to guide clinical practice. medRxiv. https://doi.org/https://doi.org/10.1101/2023.02.13.23285879

Wang, H., Li, J., Wu, H., Hovy, E., & Sun, Y. (2022). Pre-Trained Language Models and Their Applications. *Engineering (Beijing)*. Advance online publication. doi:10.1016/j.eng.2022.04.024

WangJ.ShiE.YuS.WuZ.MaC.DaiH.YangQ.KangY.WuJ.HuH.YueC.ZhangH.LiuY.LiX.GeB.ZhuD.YuanY.ShenD.LiuT.ZhangS. (2023). *Prompt Engineering for Healthcare: Methodologies and Applications*. https://arxiv.org/abs/2304.14670

Wardat, Y., Tashtoush, M. A., AlAli, R., & Jarrah, A. M. (2023). ChatGPT: A revolutionary tool for teaching and learning mathematics. *Eurasia Journal of Mathematics, Science and Technology Education, 19*(7), em2286. Advance online publication. doi:10.29333/ejmste/13272

Warr, W. A. (2003). Evaluation of an Experimental Chemistry Preprint Server. *Journal of Chemical Information and Computer Sciences, 43*(2), 362–373. doi:10.1021/ci025627a PMID:12653498

What We Do. (2023). Creative Commons. https://creativecommons.org/about/

WhiteJ.FuQ.HaysS.SandbornM.OleaC.GilbertH.ElnasharA.Spencer-SmithJ.SchmidtD. C. (2023). *A Prompt Pattern Catalog to Enhance Prompt Engineering with ChatGPT*. https://arxiv.org/abs/2302.11382v1

WIPO. (2023). *Wipo Conversation on Intellectual Property (Ip) and Frontier Technologies*. Sixth Session. WIPO.

XiaoZ.LiW.MoonH.RoellG. W.ChenY.TangY. J.RoellG.TangY. (2023). Generative artificial intelligence GPT-4 accelerates knowledge mining and machine learning for synthetic biology. In bioRxiv. doi:10.1101/2023.06.14.544984

Xu, Z., Zhang, S., Huang, L., Zhu, X., Zhao, Q., Zeng, Y., Zhou, D., Wang, D., Kuga, H., Kamiya, A., & Qu, M. (2018). Altered Resting-State Brain Activities in Drug-Naïve Major Depressive Disorder Assessed by fMRI: Associations With Somatic Symptoms Defined by Yin-Yang Theory of the Traditional Chinese Medicine. *Frontiers in Psychiatry*, *9*, 195. Advance online publication. doi:10.3389/fpsyt.2018.00195 PMID:29867614

Yahoo. (2021). *Yahoo Answers has shut down*. https://help.yahoo.com/kb/SLN35642.html

Yeo, Y. H., Samaan, J. S., Ng, W. H., Ting, P.-S., Trivedi, H., Vipani, A., Ayoub, W., Yang, J. D., Liran, O., Spiegel, B., & Kuo, A. (2023). Assessing the performance of ChatGPT in answering questions regarding cirrhosis and hepatocellular carcinoma. *Clinical and Molecular Hepatology*, *29*(3), 721–732. doi:10.3350/cmh.2023.0089 PMID:36946005

Yin Yang Theory. (2023). Ageless Herbs. https://agelessherbs.com/yin-yang-theory/

Yiu, P., Li, G., Tan, C., & Obe, M. (2023). China's aging population threatens a Japan-style lost decade. *Nikkei Asia*. https://asia.nikkei.com/Spotlight/The-Big-Story/China-s-aging-population-threatens-a-Japan-style-lost-decade

Yokoyama, A. M., Ferro, M., de Paula, F. B., Vieira, V. G., & Schulze, B. (2023). Investigating hardware and software aspects in the energy consumption of machine learning: A green AI-centric analysis. *Concurrency and Computation*, *e7825*, e7825. doi:10.1002/cpe.7825

Zarifhonarvar, A. (2023). Economics of ChatGPT: A Labor Market View on the Occupational Impact of Artificial Intelligence. SSRN *Electronic Journal*. doi:10.2139/ssrn.4350925

Zhang, B., Ding, D., & Jing, L. (2022). How would Stance Detection Techniques Evolve after the Launch of ChatGPT? https://doi.org/https://doi.org/10.48550/arXiv.2212.14548

Zhang, Y., Yin, H., & Zheng, L. (2018). Investigating academic dishonesty among Chinese undergraduate students: Does gender matter? *Assessment & Evaluation in Higher Education, 43*(5), 812–826. doi:10.1080/02602938.2017.1411467

ZhaoW. X.ZhouK.LiJ.TangT.WangX.HouY.MinY.ZhangB.ZhangJ.DongZ.DuY.YangC.ChenY.ChenZ.JiangJ.RenR.LiY.TangX.LiuZ.WenJ.-R. (2023). *A Survey of Large Language Models*. https://arxiv.org/abs/2303.18223

ZhaoW.ZhaoY.LuX.WangS.TongY.QinB. (2023). Is ChatGPT Equipped with Emotional Dialogue Capabilities? https://arxiv.org/abs/2304.09582

Zheng, H., Kyung Kim, H., Joanna Sin, S. C., & Theng, Y. L. (2021). A theoretical model of cyberchondria development: Antecedents and intermediate processes. *Telematics and Informatics, 63*, 101659. doi:10.1016/j.tele.2021.101659

Zhi, T., Lei, L., Renyuan, W., & Song, G. (2023). Performance of ChatGPT on Chinese National Medical Licensing Examinations: A Five-Year Examination Evaluation Study for Physicians, Pharmacists and Nurses. https://doi.org/https://doi.org/10.1101/2023.07.09.23292415

ZhiT.LeiL.RenyuanW.SongG. (2023). *Performance of ChatGPT on Chinese National Medical Licensing Examinations: A Five-Year Examination Evaluation Study for Physicians, Pharmacists and Nurses*. https://doi.org/https://doi.org/10.1101/2023.07.09.23292415

Zhu, J.-J., Jiang, J., Yang, M., & Ren, Z. J. (2023). ChatGPT and Environmental Research. *Environmental Science & Technology, 1–4*, acs.est.3c01818. Advance online publication. doi:10.1021/acs.est.3c01818 PMID:36943179

ZhuoT. Y.HuangY.ChenC.XingZ. (2023). *Exploring AI Ethics of ChatGPT: A Diagnostic Analysis*. https://arxiv.org/abs/2301.12867v3

Zumsteg, J. M., & Junn, C. (2023). Will ChatGPT Match to Your Program? *American Journal of Physical Medicine & Rehabilitation, 102*(6), 545–547. doi:10.1097/PHM.0000000000002238 PMID:36912286

Zygomatic. (2003). *Free online word cloud generator and tag cloud creator*. Zygomatic. https://www.wordclouds.com/

Related References

To continue our tradition of advancing academic research, we have compiled a list of recommended IGI Global readings. These references will provide additional information and guidance to further enrich your knowledge and assist you with your own research and future publications.

Aburezeq, I. M., & Dweikat, F. F. (2017). Cloud Applications in Language Teaching: Examining Pre-Service Teachers' Expertise, Perceptions and Integration. *International Journal of Distance Education Technologies*, *15*(4), 39–60. doi:10.4018/IJDET.2017100103

Acharjya, B., & Das, S. (2022). Adoption of E-Learning During the COVID-19 Pandemic: The Moderating Role of Age and Gender. *International Journal of Web-Based Learning and Teaching Technologies*, *17*(2), 1–14. https://doi.org/10.4018/IJWLTT.20220301.oa4

Adams, J. L., & Thomas, S. K. (2022). Non-Linear Curriculum Experiences for Student Learning and Work Design: What Is the Maximum Potential of a Chat Bot? In S. Ramlall, T. Cross, & M. Love (Eds.), *Handbook of Research on Future of Work and Education: Implications for Curriculum Delivery and Work Design* (pp. 299–306). IGI Global. https://doi.org/10.4018/978-1-7998-8275-6.ch018

Adera, B. (2017). Supporting Language and Literacy Development for English Language Learners. In J. Keengwe (Ed.), *Handbook of Research on Promoting Cross-Cultural Competence and Social Justice in Teacher Education* (pp. 339–354). Hershey, PA: IGI Global. doi:10.4018/978-1-5225-0897-7.ch018

Ahamer, G. (2017). Quality Assurance for a Developmental "Global Studies" (GS) Curriculum. In I. Management Association (Ed.), Educational Leadership and Administration: Concepts, Methodologies, Tools, and Applications (pp. 438-477). Hershey, PA: IGI Global. https://doi.org/ doi:10.4018/978-1-5225-1624-8.ch023

Ahamer, G. (2017). Quality Assurance for a Developmental "Global Studies" (GS) Curriculum. In I. Management Association (Ed.), Educational Leadership and Administration: Concepts, Methodologies, Tools, and Applications (pp. 438-477). Hershey, PA: IGI Global. https://doi.org/ doi:10.4018/978-1-5225-1624-8.ch023

Akayoğlu, S., & Seferoğlu, G. (2019). An Analysis of Negotiation of Meaning Functions of Advanced EFL Learners in Second Life: Negotiation of Meaning in Second Life. In M. Kruk (Ed.), *Assessing the Effectiveness of Virtual Technologies in Foreign and Second Language Instruction* (pp. 61–85). IGI Global. https://doi.org/10.4018/978-1-5225-7286-2.ch003

Akella, N. R. (2022). Unravelling the Web of Qualitative Dissertation Writing!: A Student Reflects. In A. Zimmerman (Ed.), *Methodological Innovations in Research and Academic Writing* (pp. 260–282). IGI Global. https://doi.org/10.4018/978-1-7998-8283-1.ch014

Alegre de la Rosa, O. M., & Angulo, L. M. (2017). Social Inclusion and Intercultural Values in a School of Education. In S. Mukerji & P. Tripathi (Eds.), *Handbook of Research on Administration, Policy, and Leadership in Higher Education* (pp. 518–531). Hershey, PA: IGI Global. doi:10.4018/978-1-5225-0672-0.ch020

Alexander, C. (2019). Using Gamification Strategies to Cultivate and Measure Professional Educator Dispositions. *International Journal of Game-Based Learning*, *9*(1), 15–29. https://doi.org/10.4018/IJGBL.2019010102

Anderson, K. M. (2017). Preparing Teachers in the Age of Equity and Inclusion. In I. Management Association (Ed.), Medical Education and Ethics: Concepts, Methodologies, Tools, and Applications (pp. 1532-1554). Hershey, PA: IGI Global. doi:10.4018/978-1-5225-0978-3.ch069

Awdziej, M. (2017). Case Study as a Teaching Method in Marketing. In D. Latusek (Ed.), *Case Studies as a Teaching Tool in Management Education* (pp. 244–263). Hershey, PA: IGI Global. doi:10.4018/978-1-5225-0770-3.ch013

Bakos, J. (2019). Sociolinguistic Factors Influencing English Language Learning. In N. Erdogan & M. Wei (Eds.), *Applied Linguistics for Teachers of Culturally and Linguistically Diverse Learners* (pp. 403–424). IGI Global. https://doi.org/10.4018/978-1-5225-8467-4.ch017

Banas, J. R., & York, C. S. (2017). Pre-Service Teachers' Motivation to Use Technology and the Impact of Authentic Learning Exercises. In L. Tomei (Ed.), *Exploring the New Era of Technology-Infused Education* (pp. 121–140). Hershey, PA: IGI Global. doi:10.4018/978-1-5225-1709-2.ch008

Barton, T. P. (2021). Empowering Educator Allyship by Exploring Racial Trauma and the Disengagement of Black Students. In C. Reneau & M. Villarreal (Eds.), *Handbook of Research on Leading Higher Education Transformation With Social Justice, Equity, and Inclusion* (pp. 186–197). IGI Global. https://doi.org/10.4018/978-1-7998-7152-1.ch013

Benhima, M. (2021). Moroccan English Department Student Attitudes Towards the Use of Distance Education During COVID-19: Moulay Ismail University as a Case Study. *International Journal of Information and Communication Technology Education, 17*(3), 105–122. https://doi.org/10.4018/IJICTE.20210701.oa7

Beycioglu, K., & Wildy, H. (2017). Principal Preparation: The Case of Novice Principals in Turkey. In I. Management Association (Ed.), Educational Leadership and Administration: Concepts, Methodologies, Tools, and Applications (pp. 1152-1169). Hershey, PA: IGI Global. https://doi.org/doi:10.4018/978-1-5225-1624-8.ch054

Bharwani, S., & Musunuri, D. (2018). Reflection as a Process From Theory to Practice. In M. Khosrow-Pour, D.B.A. (Ed.), Encyclopedia of Information Science and Technology, Fourth Edition (pp. 1529-1539). Hershey, PA: IGI Global. doi:10.4018/978-1-5225-2255-3.ch132

Bhushan, A., Garza, K. B., Perumal, O., Das, S. K., Feola, D. J., Farrell, D., & Birnbaum, A. (2022). Lessons Learned From the COVID-19 Pandemic and the Implications for Pharmaceutical Graduate Education and Research. In C. Ford & K. Garza (Eds.), *Handbook of Research on Updating and Innovating Health Professions Education: Post-Pandemic Perspectives* (pp. 324–345). IGI Global. https://doi.org/10.4018/978-1-7998-7623-6.ch014

Bintz, W., Ciecierski, L. M., & Royan, E. (2021). Using Picture Books With Instructional Strategies to Address New Challenges and Teach Literacy Skills in a Digital World. In L. Haas & J. Tussey (Eds.), *Connecting Disciplinary Literacy and Digital Storytelling in K-12 Education* (pp. 38–58). IGI Global. https://doi.org/10.4018/978-1-7998-5770-9.ch003

Bohjanen, S. L., Cameron-Standerford, A., & Meidl, T. D. (2018). Capacity Building Pedagogy for Diverse Learners. In J. Keengwe (Ed.), *Handbook of Research on Pedagogical Models for Next-Generation Teaching and Learning* (pp. 195–212). Hershey, PA: IGI Global. doi:10.4018/978-1-5225-3873-8.ch011

Brewer, J. C. (2018). Measuring Text Readability Using Reading Level. In M. Khosrow-Pour, D.B.A. (Ed.), Encyclopedia of Information Science and Technology, Fourth Edition (pp. 1499-1507). Hershey, PA: IGI Global. doi:10.4018/978-1-5225-2255-3.ch129

Brookbanks, B. C. (2022). Student Perspectives on Business Education in the USA: Current Attitudes and Necessary Changes in an Age of Disruption. In A. Zhuplev & R. Koepp (Eds.), *Global Trends, Dynamics, and Imperatives for Strategic Development in Business Education in an Age of Disruption* (pp. 214–231). IGI Global. doi:10.4018/978-1-7998-7548-2.ch011

Brown, L. V., Dari, T., & Spencer, N. (2019). Addressing the Impact of Trauma in High Poverty Elementary Schools: An Ecological Model for School Counseling. In K. Daniels & K. Billingsley (Eds.), *Creating Caring and Supportive Educational Environments for Meaningful Learning* (pp. 135–153). IGI Global. https://doi.org/10.4018/978-1-5225-5748-7.ch008

Brown, S. L. (2017). A Case Study of Strategic Leadership and Research in Practice: Principal Preparation Programs that Work – An Educational Administration Perspective of Best Practices for Master's Degree Programs for Principal Preparation. In V. Wang (Ed.), *Encyclopedia of Strategic Leadership and Management* (pp. 1226–1244). Hershey, PA: IGI Global. doi:10.4018/978-1-5225-1049-9.ch086

Brzozowski, M., & Ferster, I. (2017). Educational Management Leadership: High School Principal's Management Style and Parental Involvement in School Management in Israel. In V. Potocan, M. Üngan, & Z. Nedelko (Eds.), *Handbook of Research on Managerial Solutions in Non-Profit Organizations* (pp. 55–74). Hershey, PA: IGI Global. doi:10.4018/978-1-5225-0731-4.ch003

Cahapay, M. B. (2020). Delphi Technique in the Development of Emerging Contents in High School Science Curriculum. *International Journal of Curriculum Development and Learning Measurement*, *1*(2), 1–9. https://doi.org/10.4018/IJCDLM.2020070101

Camacho, L. F., & Leon Guerrero, A. E. (2022). Indigenous Student Experience in Higher Education: Implementation of Culturally Sensitive Support. In P. Pangelinan & T. McVey (Eds.), *Learning and Reconciliation Through Indigenous Education in Oceania* (pp. 254–266). IGI Global. https://doi.org/10.4018/978-1-7998-7736-3.ch016

Cannaday, J. (2017). The Masking Effect: Hidden Gifts and Disabilities of 2e Students. In P. Dickenson, P. Keough, & J. Courduff (Eds.), *Preparing Pre-Service Teachers for the Inclusive Classroom* (pp. 220–231). Hershey, PA: IGI Global. doi:10.4018/978-1-5225-1753-5.ch011

Cederquist, S., Fishman, B., & Teasley, S. D. (2022). What's Missing From the College Transcript?: How Employers Make Sense of Student Skills. In Y. Huang (Ed.), *Handbook of Research on Credential Innovations for Inclusive Pathways to Professions* (pp. 234–253). IGI Global. https://doi.org/10.4018/978-1-7998-3820-3.ch012

Cockrell, P., & Gibson, T. (2019). The Untold Stories of Black and Brown Student Experiences in Historically White Fraternities and Sororities. In P. Hoffman-Miller, M. James, & D. Hermond (Eds.), *African American Suburbanization and the Consequential Loss of Identity* (pp. 153–171). IGI Global. https://doi.org/10.4018/978-1-5225-7835-2.ch009

Cohen, M. (2022). Leveraging Content Creation to Boost Student Engagement. In T. Driscoll III, (Ed.), *Designing Effective Distance and Blended Learning Environments in K-12* (pp. 223–239). IGI Global. https://doi.org/10.4018/978-1-7998-6829-3.ch013

Contreras, E. C., & Contreras, I. I. (2018). Development of Communication Skills through Auditory Training Software in Special Education. In M. Khosrow-Pour, D.B.A. (Ed.), Encyclopedia of Information Science and Technology, Fourth Edition (pp. 2431-2441). Hershey, PA: IGI Global. doi:10.4018/978-1-5225-2255-3.ch212

Cooke, L., Schugar, J., Schugar, H., Penny, C., & Bruning, H. (2020). Can Everyone Code?: Preparing Teachers to Teach Computer Languages as a Literacy. In J. Mitchell & E. Vaughn (Eds.), *Participatory Literacy Practices for P-12 Classrooms in the Digital Age* (pp. 163–183). IGI Global. https://doi.org/10.4018/978-1-7998-0000-2.ch009

Cooley, D., & Whitten, E. (2017). Special Education Leadership and the Implementation of Response to Intervention. In F. Topor (Ed.), *Handbook of Research on Individualism and Identity in the Globalized Digital Age* (pp. 265–286). Hershey, PA: IGI Global. doi:10.4018/978-1-5225-0522-8.ch012

Cosner, S., Tozer, S., & Zavitkovsky, P. (2017). Enacting a Cycle of Inquiry Capstone Research Project in Doctoral-Level Leadership Preparation. In I. Management Association (Ed.), Educational Leadership and Administration: Concepts, Methodologies, Tools, and Applications (pp. 1460-1481). Hershey, PA: IGI Global. doi:10.4018/978-1-5225-1624-8.ch067

Crawford, C. M. (2018). Instructional Real World Community Engagement. In M. Khosrow-Pour, D.B.A. (Ed.), Encyclopedia of Information Science and Technology, Fourth Edition (pp. 1474-1486). Hershey, PA: IGI Global. doi:10.4018/978-1-5225-2255-3.ch127

Crosby-Cooper, T., & Pacis, D. (2017). Implementing Effective Student Support Teams. In P. Dickenson, P. Keough, & J. Courduff (Eds.), *Preparing Pre-Service Teachers for the Inclusive Classroom* (pp. 248–262). Hershey, PA: IGI Global. doi:10.4018/978-1-5225-1753-5.ch013

Curran, C. M., & Hawbaker, B. W. (2017). Cultivating Communities of Inclusive Practice: Professional Development for Educators – Research and Practice. In C. Curran & A. Petersen (Eds.), *Handbook of Research on Classroom Diversity and Inclusive Education Practice* (pp. 120–153). Hershey, PA: IGI Global. doi:10.4018/978-1-5225-2520-2.ch006

Dass, S., & Dabbagh, N. (2018). Faculty Adoption of 3D Avatar-Based Virtual World Learning Environments: An Exploratory Case Study. In I. Management Association (Ed.), Technology Adoption and Social Issues: Concepts, Methodologies, Tools, and Applications (pp. 1000-1033). Hershey, PA: IGI Global. https://doi.org/ doi:10.4018/978-1-5225-5201-7.ch045

Davison, A. M., & Scholl, K. G. (2017). Inclusive Recreation as Part of the IEP Process. In C. Curran & A. Petersen (Eds.), *Handbook of Research on Classroom Diversity and Inclusive Education Practice* (pp. 311–330). Hershey, PA: IGI Global. doi:10.4018/978-1-5225-2520-2.ch013

DeCoito, I. (2018). Addressing Digital Competencies, Curriculum Development, and Instructional Design in Science Teacher Education. In M. Khosrow-Pour, D.B.A. (Ed.), Encyclopedia of Information Science and Technology, Fourth Edition (pp. 1420-1431). Hershey, PA: IGI Global. https:// doi.org/ doi:10.4018/978-1-5225-2255-3.ch122

DeCoito, I., & Richardson, T. (2017). Beyond Angry Birds™: Using Web-Based Tools to Engage Learners and Promote Inquiry in STEM Learning. In I. Levin & D. Tsybulsky (Eds.), *Digital Tools and Solutions for Inquiry-Based STEM Learning* (pp. 166–196). Hershey, PA: IGI Global. doi:10.4018/978-1-5225-2525-7.ch007

Delmas, P. M. (2017). Research-Based Leadership for Next-Generation Leaders. In R. Styron Jr & J. Styron (Eds.), *Comprehensive Problem-Solving and Skill Development for Next-Generation Leaders* (pp. 1–39). Hershey, PA: IGI Global. doi:10.4018/978-1-5225-1968-3.ch001

Demiray, U., & Ekren, G. (2018). Administrative-Related Evaluation for Distance Education Institutions in Turkey. In K. Buyuk, S. Kocdar, & A. Bozkurt (Eds.), *Administrative Leadership in Open and Distance Learning Programs* (pp. 263–288). Hershey, PA: IGI Global. doi:10.4018/978-1-5225-2645-2.ch011

Dickenson, P. (2017). What do we Know and Where Can We Grow?: Teachers Preparation for the Inclusive Classroom. In P. Dickenson, P. Keough, & J. Courduff (Eds.), *Preparing Pre-Service Teachers for the Inclusive Classroom* (pp. 1–22). Hershey, PA: IGI Global. doi:10.4018/978-1-5225-1753-5.ch001

Ding, Q., & Zhu, H. (2021). Flipping the Classroom in STEM Education. In J. Keengwe (Ed.), *Handbook of Research on Innovations in Non-Traditional Educational Practices* (pp. 155–173). IGI Global. https://doi.org/10.4018/978-1-7998-4360-3.ch008

Dixon, T., & Christison, M. (2021). Teaching English Grammar in a Hybrid Academic ESL Course: A Mixed Methods Study. In K. Kelch, P. Byun, S. Safavi, & S. Cervantes (Eds.), *CALL Theory Applications for Online TESOL Education* (pp. 229–251). IGI Global. https://doi.org/10.4018/978-1-7998-6609-1.ch010

Donne, V., & Hansen, M. (2017). Teachers' Use of Assistive Technologies in Education. In L. Tomei (Ed.), *Exploring the New Era of Technology-Infused Education* (pp. 86–101). Hershey, PA: IGI Global. doi:10.4018/978-1-5225-1709-2.ch006

Donne, V., & Hansen, M. A. (2018). Business and Technology Educators: Practices for Inclusion. In I. Management Association (Ed.), Business Education and Ethics: Concepts, Methodologies, Tools, and Applications (pp. 471-484). Hershey, PA: IGI Global. https://doi.org/ doi:10.4018/978-1-5225-3153-1.ch026

Dos Santos, L. M. (2022). Completing Student-Teaching Internships Online: Instructional Changes During the COVID-19 Pandemic. In M. Alaali (Ed.), *Assessing University Governance and Policies in Relation to the COVID-19 Pandemic* (pp. 106–127). IGI Global. https://doi.org/10.4018/978-1-7998-8279-4.ch007

Dreon, O., Shettel, J., & Bower, K. M. (2017). Preparing Next Generation Elementary Teachers for the Tools of Tomorrow. In M. Grassetti & S. Brookby (Eds.), *Advancing Next-Generation Teacher Education through Digital Tools and Applications* (pp. 143–159). Hershey, PA: IGI Global. doi:10.4018/978-1-5225-0965-3.ch008

Durak, H. Y., & Güyer, T. (2018). Design and Development of an Instructional Program for Teaching Programming Processes to Gifted Students Using Scratch. In J. Cannaday (Ed.), *Curriculum Development for Gifted Education Programs* (pp. 61–99). Hershey, PA: IGI Global. doi:10.4018/978-1-5225-3041-1.ch004

Egorkina, E., Ivanov, M., & Valyavskiy, A. Y. (2018). Students' Research Competence Formation of the Quality of Open and Distance Learning. In V. Mkrttchian & L. Belyanina (Eds.), *Handbook of Research on Students' Research Competence in Modern Educational Contexts* (pp. 364–384). Hershey, PA: IGI Global. doi:10.4018/978-1-5225-3485-3.ch019

Ekren, G., Karataş, S., & Demiray, U. (2017). Understanding of Leadership in Distance Education Management. In I. Management Association (Ed.), Educational Leadership and Administration: Concepts, Methodologies, Tools, and Applications (pp. 34-50). Hershey, PA: IGI Global. https://doi.org/ doi:10.4018/978-1-5225-1624-8.ch003

Elmore, W. M., Young, J. K., Harris, S., & Mason, D. (2017). The Relationship between Individual Student Attributes and Online Course Completion. In K. Shelton & K. Pedersen (Eds.), *Handbook of Research on Building, Growing, and Sustaining Quality E-Learning Programs* (pp. 151–173). Hershey, PA: IGI Global. doi:10.4018/978-1-5225-0877-9.ch008

Ercegovac, I. R., Alfirević, N., & Koludrović, M. (2017). School Principals' Communication and Co-Operation Assessment: The Croatian Experience. In I. Management Association (Ed.), Educational Leadership and Administration: Concepts, Methodologies, Tools, and Applications (pp. 1568-1589). Hershey, PA: IGI Global. https://doi.org/ doi:10.4018/978-1-5225-1624-8.ch072

Everhart, D., & Seymour, D. M. (2017). Challenges and Opportunities in the Currency of Higher Education. In K. Rasmussen, P. Northrup, & R. Colson (Eds.), *Handbook of Research on Competency-Based Education in University Settings* (pp. 41–65). Hershey, PA: IGI Global. doi:10.4018/978-1-5225-0932-5.ch003

Farmer, L. S. (2017). Managing Portable Technologies for Special Education. In V. Wang (Ed.), *Encyclopedia of Strategic Leadership and Management* (pp. 977–987). Hershey, PA: IGI Global. doi:10.4018/978-1-5225-1049-9.ch068

Farmer, L. S. (2018). Optimizing OERs for Optimal ICT Literacy in Higher Education. In J. Keengwe (Ed.), *Handbook of Research on Mobile Technology, Constructivism, and Meaningful Learning* (pp. 366–390). Hershey, PA: IGI Global. doi:10.4018/978-1-5225-3949-0.ch020

Ferguson, B. T. (2019). Supporting Affective Development of Children With Disabilities Through Moral Dilemmas. In S. Ikuta (Ed.), *Handmade Teaching Materials for Students With Disabilities* (pp. 253–275). IGI Global. doi:10.4018/978-1-5225-6240-5.ch011

Fındık, L. Y. (2017). Self-Assessment of Principals Based on Leadership in Complexity. In I. Management Association (Ed.), Educational Leadership and Administration: Concepts, Methodologies, Tools, and Applications (pp. 978-991). Hershey, PA: IGI Global. https://doi.org/ doi:10.4018/978-1-5225-1624-8.ch047

Flor, A. G., & Gonzalez-Flor, B. (2018). Dysfunctional Digital Demeanors: Tales From (and Policy Implications of) eLearning's Dark Side. In I. Management Association (Ed.), The Dark Web: Breakthroughs in Research and Practice (pp. 37-50). Hershey, PA: IGI Global. https://doi.org/ doi:10.4018/978-1-5225-3163-0.ch003

Floyd, K. K., & Shambaugh, N. (2017). Instructional Design for Simulations in Special Education Virtual Learning Spaces. In T. Kidd & L. Morris Jr., (Eds.), *Handbook of Research on Instructional Systems and Educational Technology* (pp. 202–215). Hershey, PA: IGI Global. doi:10.4018/978-1-5225-2399-4.ch018

Freeland, S. F. (2020). Community Schools: Improving Academic Achievement Through Meaningful Engagement. In R. Kronick (Ed.), *Emerging Perspectives on Community Schools and the Engaged University* (pp. 132–144). IGI Global. https://doi.org/10.4018/978-1-7998-0280-8.ch008

Ghanbarzadeh, R., & Ghapanchi, A. H. (2019). Applied Areas of Three Dimensional Virtual Worlds in Learning and Teaching: A Review of Higher Education. In I. Management Association (Ed.), *Virtual Reality in Education: Breakthroughs in Research and Practice* (pp. 172-192). IGI Global. https://doi.org/10.4018/978-1-5225-8179-6.ch008

Giovannini, J. M. (2017). Technology Integration in Preservice Teacher Education Programs: Research-based Recommendations. In M. Grassetti & S. Brookby (Eds.), *Advancing Next-Generation Teacher Education through Digital Tools and Applications* (pp. 82–102). Hershey, PA: IGI Global. doi:10.4018/978-1-5225-0965-3.ch005

Good, S., & Clarke, V. B. (2017). An Integral Analysis of One Urban School System's Efforts to Support Student-Centered Teaching. In J. Keengwe & G. Onchwari (Eds.), *Handbook of Research on Learner-Centered Pedagogy in Teacher Education and Professional Development* (pp. 45–68). Hershey, PA: IGI Global. doi:10.4018/978-1-5225-0892-2.ch003

Guetzoian, E. (2022). Gamification Strategies for Higher Education Student Worker Training. In C. Lane (Ed.), *Handbook of Research on Acquiring 21st Century Literacy Skills Through Game-Based Learning* (pp. 164–179). IGI Global. https://doi.org/10.4018/978-1-7998-7271-9.ch009

Hamidi, F., Owuor, P. M., Hynie, M., Baljko, M., & McGrath, S. (2017). Potentials of Digital Assistive Technology and Special Education in Kenya. In C. Ayo & V. Mbarika (Eds.), *Sustainable ICT Adoption and Integration for Socio-Economic Development* (pp. 125–151). Hershey, PA: IGI Global. doi:10.4018/978-1-5225-2565-3.ch006

Hamim, T., Benabbou, F., & Sael, N. (2022). Student Profile Modeling Using Boosting Algorithms. *International Journal of Web-Based Learning and Teaching Technologies*, *17*(5), 1–13. https://doi.org/10.4018/IJWLTT.20220901.oa4

Henderson, L. K. (2017). Meltdown at Fukushima: Global Catastrophic Events, Visual Literacy, and Art Education. In R. Shin (Ed.), *Convergence of Contemporary Art, Visual Culture, and Global Civic Engagement* (pp. 80–99). Hershey, PA: IGI Global. doi:10.4018/978-1-5225-1665-1.ch005

Hudgins, T., & Holland, J. L. (2018). Digital Badges: Tracking Knowledge Acquisition Within an Innovation Framework. In I. Management Association (Ed.), Wearable Technologies: Concepts, Methodologies, Tools, and Applications (pp. 1118-1132). Hershey, PA: IGI Global. https://doi.org/doi:10.4018/978-1-5225-5484-4.ch051

Hwang, R., Lin, H., Sun, J. C., & Wu, J. (2019). Improving Learning Achievement in Science Education for Elementary School Students via Blended Learning. *International Journal of Online Pedagogy and Course Design*, *9*(2), 44–62. https://doi.org/10.4018/IJOPCD.2019040104

Jančec, L., & Vodopivec, J. L. (2019). The Implicit Pedagogy and the Hidden Curriculum in Postmodern Education. In J. Vodopivec, L. Jančec, & T. Štemberger (Eds.), *Implicit Pedagogy for Optimized Learning in Contemporary Education* (pp. 41–59). IGI Global. https://doi.org/10.4018/978-1-5225-5799-9.ch003

Janus, M., & Siddiqua, A. (2018). Challenges for Children With Special Health Needs at the Time of Transition to School. In I. Management Association (Ed.), Autism Spectrum Disorders: Breakthroughs in Research and Practice (pp. 339-371). Hershey, PA: IGI Global. doi:10.4018/978-1-5225-3827-1.ch018

Jesus, R. A. (2018). Screencasts and Learning Styles. In M. Khosrow-Pour, D.B.A. (Ed.), Encyclopedia of Information Science and Technology, Fourth Edition (pp. 1548-1558). Hershey, PA: IGI Global. doi:10.4018/978-1-5225-2255-3.ch134

John, G., Francis, N., & Santhakumar, A. B. (2022). Student Engagement: Past, Present, and Future. In S. Ramlall, T. Cross, & M. Love (Eds.), *Handbook of Research on Future of Work and Education: Implications for Curriculum Delivery and Work Design* (pp. 329–341). IGI Global. https://doi.org/10.4018/978-1-7998-8275-6.ch020

Karpinski, A. C., D'Agostino, J. V., Williams, A. K., Highland, S. A., & Mellott, J. A. (2018). The Relationship Between Online Formative Assessment and State Test Scores Using Multilevel Modeling. In M. Khosrow-Pour, D.B.A. (Ed.), Encyclopedia of Information Science and Technology, Fourth Edition (pp. 5183-5192). Hershey, PA: IGI Global. doi:10.4018/978-1-5225-2255-3.ch450

Kats, Y. (2017). Educational Leadership and Integrated Support for Students with Autism Spectrum Disorders. In I. Management Association (Ed.), Educational Leadership and Administration: Concepts, Methodologies, Tools, and Applications (pp. 101-114). Hershey, PA: IGI Global. https://doi.org/doi:10.4018/978-1-5225-1624-8.ch007

Kaya, G., & Altun, A. (2018). Educational Ontology Development. In M. Khosrow-Pour, D.B.A. (Ed.), Encyclopedia of Information Science and Technology, Fourth Edition (pp. 1441-1450). Hershey, PA: IGI Global. doi:10.4018/978-1-5225-2255-3.ch124

Keough, P. D., & Pacis, D. (2017). Best Practices Implementing Special Education Curriculum and Common Core State Standards using UDL. In P. Dickenson, P. Keough, & J. Courduff (Eds.), *Preparing Pre-Service Teachers for the Inclusive Classroom* (pp. 107–123). Hershey, PA: IGI Global. doi:10.4018/978-1-5225-1753-5.ch006

Kilburn, M., Henckell, M., & Starrett, D. (2018). Factors Contributing to the Effectiveness of Online Students and Instructors. In M. Khosrow-Pour, D.B.A. (Ed.), Encyclopedia of Information Science and Technology, Fourth Edition (pp. 1451-1462). Hershey, PA: IGI Global. doi:10.4018/978-1-5225-2255-3.ch125

Koban Koç, D. (2021). Gender and Language: A Sociolinguistic Analysis of Second Language Writing. In E. Hancı-Azizoglu & N. Kavaklı (Eds.), *Futuristic and Linguistic Perspectives on Teaching Writing to Second Language Students* (pp. 161–177). IGI Global. https://doi.org/10.4018/978-1-7998-6508-7.ch010

Konecny, L. T. (2017). Hybrid, Online, and Flipped Classrooms in Health Science: Enhanced Learning Environments. In I. Management Association (Ed.), Flipped Instruction: Breakthroughs in Research and Practice (pp. 355-370). Hershey, PA: IGI Global. https://doi.org/ doi:10.4018/978-1-5225-1803-7.ch020

Kupietz, K. D. (2021). Gaming and Simulation in Public Education: Teaching Others to Help Themselves and Their Neighbors. In N. Drumhiller, T. Wilkin, & K. Srba (Eds.), *Simulation and Game-Based Learning in Emergency and Disaster Management* (pp. 41–62). IGI Global. https://doi.org/10.4018/978-1-7998-4087-9.ch003

Kwee, C. T. (2022). Assessing the International Student Enrolment Strategies in Australian Universities: A Case Study During the COVID-19 Pandemic. In M. Alaali (Ed.), *Assessing University Governance and Policies in Relation to the COVID-19 Pandemic* (pp. 162–188). IGI Global. https://doi.org/10.4018/978-1-7998-8279-4.ch010

Lauricella, S., & McArthur, F. A. (2022). Taking a Student-Centred Approach to Alternative Digital Credentials: Multiple Pathways Toward the Acquisition of Microcredentials. In D. Piedra (Ed.), *Innovations in the Design and Application of Alternative Digital Credentials* (pp. 57–69). IGI Global. https://doi.org/10.4018/978-1-7998-7697-7.ch003

Llamas, M. F. (2019). Intercultural Awareness in Teaching English for Early Childhood: A Film-Based Approach. In E. Domínguez Romero, J. Bobkina, & S. Stefanova (Eds.), *Teaching Literature and Language Through Multimodal Texts* (pp. 54–68). IGI Global. https://doi.org/10.4018/978-1-5225-5796-8.ch004

Lokhtina, I., & Kkese, E. T. (2022). Reflecting and Adapting to an Academic Workplace Before and After the Lockdown in Greek-Speaking Cyprus: Opportunities and Challenges. In A. Zhuplev & R. Koepp (Eds.), *Global Trends, Dynamics, and Imperatives for Strategic Development in Business Education in an Age of Disruption* (pp. 126–148). IGI Global. https://doi.org/10.4018/978-1-7998-7548-2.ch007

Lovell, K. L. (2017). Development and Evaluation of Neuroscience Computer-Based Modules for Medical Students: Instructional Design Principles and Effectiveness. In J. Stefaniak (Ed.), *Advancing Medical Education Through Strategic Instructional Design* (pp. 262–276). Hershey, PA: IGI Global. doi:10.4018/978-1-5225-2098-6.ch013

Maher, D. (2019). The Use of Course Management Systems in Pre-Service Teacher Education. In J. Keengwe (Ed.), *Handbook of Research on Blended Learning Pedagogies and Professional Development in Higher Education* (pp. 196–213). IGI Global. https://doi.org/10.4018/978-1-5225-5557-5.ch011

Makewa, L. N. (2019). Teacher Technology Competence Base. In L. Makewa, B. Ngussa, & J. Kuboja (Eds.), *Technology-Supported Teaching and Research Methods for Educators* (pp. 247–267). IGI Global. https://doi.org/10.4018/978-1-5225-5915-3.ch014

Mallett, C. A. (2022). School Resource (Police) Officers in Schools: Impact on Campus Safety, Student Discipline, and Learning. In G. Crews (Ed.), *Impact of School Shootings on Classroom Culture, Curriculum, and Learning* (pp. 53–70). IGI Global. https://doi.org/10.4018/978-1-7998-5200-1.ch004

Marinho, J. E., Freitas, I. R., Leão, I. B., Pacheco, L. O., Gonçalves, M. P., Castro, M. J., Silva, P. D., & Moreira, R. J. (2022). Project-Based Learning Application in Higher Education: Student Experiences and Perspectives. In A. Alves & N. van Hattum-Janssen (Eds.), *Training Engineering Students for Modern Technological Advancement* (pp. 146–164). IGI Global. https://doi.org/10.4018/978-1-7998-8816-1.ch007

McCleskey, J. A., & Melton, R. M. (2022). Rolling With the Flow: Online Faculty and Student Presence in a Post-COVID-19 World. In S. Ramlall, T. Cross, & M. Love (Eds.), *Handbook of Research on Future of Work and Education: Implications for Curriculum Delivery and Work Design* (pp. 307–328). IGI Global. https://doi.org/10.4018/978-1-7998-8275-6.ch019

McCormack, V. F., Stauffer, M., Fishley, K., Hohenbrink, J., Mascazine, J. R., & Zigler, T. (2018). Designing a Dual Licensure Path for Middle Childhood and Special Education Teacher Candidates. In D. Polly, M. Putman, T. Petty, & A. Good (Eds.), *Innovative Practices in Teacher Preparation and Graduate-Level Teacher Education Programs* (pp. 21–36). Hershey, PA: IGI Global. doi:10.4018/978-1-5225-3068-8.ch002

McDaniel, R. (2017). Strategic Leadership in Instructional Design: Applying the Principles of Instructional Design through the Lens of Strategic Leadership to Distance Education. In V. Wang (Ed.), *Encyclopedia of Strategic Leadership and Management* (pp. 1570–1584). Hershey, PA: IGI Global. doi:10.4018/978-1-5225-1049-9.ch109

McKinney, R. E., Halli-Tierney, A. D., Gold, A. E., Allen, R. S., & Carroll, D. G. (2022). Interprofessional Education: Using Standardized Cases in Face-to-Face and Remote Learning Settings. In C. Ford & K. Garza (Eds.), *Handbook of Research on Updating and Innovating Health Professions Education: Post-Pandemic Perspectives* (pp. 24–42). IGI Global. https://doi.org/10.4018/978-1-7998-7623-6.ch002

Meintjes, H. H. (2021). Learner Views of a Facebook Page as a Supportive Digital Pedagogical Tool at a Public South African School in a Grade 12 Business Studies Class. *International Journal of Smart Education and Urban Society, 12*(2), 32–45. https://doi.org/10.4018/IJSEUS.2021040104

Melero-García, F. (2022). Training Bilingual Interpreters in Healthcare Settings: Student Perceptions of Online Learning. In J. LeLoup & P. Swanson (Eds.), *Handbook of Research on Effective Online Language Teaching in a Disruptive Environment* (pp. 288–310). IGI Global. https://doi.org/10.4018/978-1-7998-7720-2.ch015

Meletiadou, E. (2022). The Use of Peer Assessment as an Inclusive Learning Strategy in Higher Education Institutions: Enhancing Student Writing Skills and Motivation. In E. Meletiadou (Ed.), *Handbook of Research on Policies and Practices for Assessing Inclusive Teaching and Learning* (pp. 1–26). IGI Global. https://doi.org/10.4018/978-1-7998-8579-5.ch001

Memon, R. N., Ahmad, R., & Salim, S. S. (2018). Critical Issues in Requirements Engineering Education. In I. Management Association (Ed.), Computer Systems and Software Engineering: Concepts, Methodologies, Tools, and Applications (pp. 1953-1976). Hershey, PA: IGI Global. doi:10.4018/978-1-5225-3923-0.ch081

Mendenhall, R. (2017). Western Governors University: CBE Innovator and National Model. In K. Rasmussen, P. Northrup, & R. Colson (Eds.), *Handbook of Research on Competency-Based Education in University Settings* (pp. 379–400). Hershey, PA: IGI Global. doi:10.4018/978-1-5225-0932-5.ch019

Mense, E. G., Griggs, D. M., & Shanks, J. N. (2018). School Leaders in a Time of Accountability and Data Use: Preparing Our Future School Leaders in Leadership Preparation Programs. In E. Mense & M. Crain-Dorough (Eds.), *Data Leadership for K-12 Schools in a Time of Accountability* (pp. 235–259). Hershey, PA: IGI Global. doi:10.4018/978-1-5225-3188-3.ch012

Mense, E. G., Griggs, D. M., & Shanks, J. N. (2018). School Leaders in a Time of Accountability and Data Use: Preparing Our Future School Leaders in Leadership Preparation Programs. In E. Mense & M. Crain-Dorough (Eds.), *Data Leadership for K-12 Schools in a Time of Accountability* (pp. 235–259). Hershey, PA: IGI Global. doi:10.4018/978-1-5225-3188-3.ch012

Mestry, R., & Naicker, S. R. (2017). Exploring Distributive Leadership in South African Public Primary Schools in the Soweto Region. In I. Management Association (Ed.), Educational Leadership and Administration: Concepts, Methodologies, Tools, and Applications (pp. 1041-1064). Hershey, PA: IGI Global. doi:10.4018/978-1-5225-1624-8.ch050

Monaghan, C. H., & Boboc, M. (2017). (Re) Defining Leadership in Higher Education in the U.S. In V. Wang (Ed.), *Encyclopedia of Strategic Leadership and Management* (pp. 567–579). Hershey, PA: IGI Global. doi:10.4018/978-1-5225-1049-9.ch040

Morall, M. B. (2021). Reimagining Mobile Phones: Multiple Literacies and Digital Media Compositions. In C. Moran (Eds.), *Affordances and Constraints of Mobile Phone Use in English Language Arts Classrooms* (pp. 41-53). IGI Global. https://doi.org/10.4018/978-1-7998-5805-8.ch003

Mthethwa, V. (2022). Student Governance and the Academic Minefield During COVID-19 Lockdown in South Africa. In M. Alaali (Ed.), *Assessing University Governance and Policies in Relation to the COVID-19 Pandemic* (pp. 255–276). IGI Global. https://doi.org/10.4018/978-1-7998-8279-4.ch015

Muthee, J. M., & Murungi, C. G. (2018). Relationship Among Intelligence, Achievement Motivation, Type of School, and Academic Performance of Kenyan Urban Primary School Pupils. In M. Khosrow-Pour, D.B.A. (Ed.), Encyclopedia of Information Science and Technology, Fourth Edition (pp. 1540-1547). Hershey, PA: IGI Global. https://doi.org/ doi:10.4018/978-1-5225-2255-3.ch133

Naranjo, J. (2018). Meeting the Need for Inclusive Educators Online: Teacher Education in Inclusive Special Education and Dual-Certification. In D. Polly, M. Putman, T. Petty, & A. Good (Eds.), *Innovative Practices in Teacher Preparation and Graduate-Level Teacher Education Programs* (pp. 106–122). Hershey, PA: IGI Global. doi:10.4018/978-1-5225-3068-8.ch007

Nkabinde, Z. P. (2017). Multiculturalism in Special Education: Perspectives of Minority Children in Urban Schools. In J. Keengwe (Ed.), *Handbook of Research on Promoting Cross-Cultural Competence and Social Justice in Teacher Education* (pp. 382–397). Hershey, PA: IGI Global. doi:10.4018/978-1-5225-0897-7.ch020

Nkabinde, Z. P. (2018). Online Instruction: Is the Quality the Same as Face-to-Face Instruction? In J. Keengwe (Ed.), *Handbook of Research on Digital Content, Mobile Learning, and Technology Integration Models in Teacher Education* (pp. 300–314). Hershey, PA: IGI Global. doi:10.4018/978-1-5225-2953-8.ch016

Nugroho, A., & Albusaidi, S. S. (2022). Internationalization of Higher Education: The Methodological Critiques on the Research Related to Study Overseas and International Experience. In H. Magd & S. Kunjumuhammed (Eds.), *Global Perspectives on Quality Assurance and Accreditation in Higher Education Institutions* (pp. 75–89). IGI Global. https://doi.org/10.4018/978-1-7998-8085-1.ch005

Nulty, Z., & West, S. G. (2022). Student Engagement and Supporting Students With Accommodations. In P. Bull & G. Patterson (Eds.), *Redefining Teacher Education and Teacher Preparation Programs in the Post-COVID-19 Era* (pp. 99–116). IGI Global. https://doi.org/10.4018/978-1-7998-8298-5.ch006

O’Connor, J. R. Jr, & Jackson, K. N. (2017). The Use of iPad® Devices and “Apps” for ASD Students in Special Education and Speech Therapy. In Y. Kats (Ed.), *Supporting the Education of Children with Autism Spectrum Disorders* (pp. 267–283). Hershey, PA: IGI Global. doi:10.4018/978-1-5225-0816-8.ch014

Okolie, U. C., & Yasin, A. M. (2017). TVET in Developing Nations and Human Development. In U. Okolie & A. Yasin (Eds.), *Technical Education and Vocational Training in Developing Nations* (pp. 1–25). Hershey, PA: IGI Global. doi:10.4018/978-1-5225-1811-2.ch001

Pack, A., & Barrett, A. (2021). A Review of Virtual Reality and English for Academic Purposes: Understanding Where to Start. *International Journal of Computer-Assisted Language Learning and Teaching, 11*(1), 72–80. https://doi.org/10.4018/IJCALLT.2021010105

Pashollari, E. (2019). Building Sustainability Through Environmental Education: Education for Sustainable Development. In L. Wilson, & C. Stevenson (Eds.), *Building Sustainability Through Environmental Education* (pp. 72-88). IGI Global. https://doi.org/10.4018/978-1-5225-7727-0.ch004

Paulson, E. N. (2017). Adapting and Advocating for an Online EdD Program in Changing Times and "Sacred" Cultures. In I. Management Association (Ed.), Educational Leadership and Administration: Concepts, Methodologies, Tools, and Applications (pp. 1849-1876). Hershey, PA: IGI Global. https://doi.org/ doi:10.4018/978-1-5225-1624-8.ch085

Petersen, A. J., Elser, C. F., Al Nassir, M. N., Stakey, J., & Everson, K. (2017). The Year of Teaching Inclusively: Building an Elementary Classroom for All Students. In C. Curran & A. Petersen (Eds.), *Handbook of Research on Classroom Diversity and Inclusive Education Practice* (pp. 332–348). Hershey, PA: IGI Global. doi:10.4018/978-1-5225-2520-2.ch014

Pfannenstiel, K. H., & Sanders, J. (2017). Characteristics and Instructional Strategies for Students With Mathematical Difficulties: In the Inclusive Classroom. In C. Curran & A. Petersen (Eds.), *Handbook of Research on Classroom Diversity and Inclusive Education Practice* (pp. 250–281). Hershey, PA: IGI Global. doi:10.4018/978-1-5225-2520-2.ch011

Phan, A. N. (2022). Quality Assurance of Higher Education From the Glonacal Agency Heuristic: An Example From Vietnam. In H. Magd & S. Kunjumuhammed (Eds.), *Global Perspectives on Quality Assurance and Accreditation in Higher Education Institutions* (pp. 136–155). IGI Global. https://doi.org/10.4018/978-1-7998-8085-1.ch008

Preast, J. L., Bowman, N., & Rose, C. A. (2017). Creating Inclusive Classroom Communities Through Social and Emotional Learning to Reduce Social Marginalization Among Students. In C. Curran & A. Petersen (Eds.), *Handbook of Research on Classroom Diversity and Inclusive Education Practice* (pp. 183–200). Hershey, PA: IGI Global. doi:10.4018/978-1-5225-2520-2.ch008

Randolph, K. M., & Brady, M. P. (2018). Evolution of Covert Coaching as an Evidence-Based Practice in Professional Development and Preparation of Teachers. In V. Bryan, A. Musgrove, & J. Powers (Eds.), *Handbook of Research on Human Development in the Digital Age* (pp. 281–299). Hershey, PA: IGI Global. doi:10.4018/978-1-5225-2838-8.ch013

Rell, A. B., Puig, R. A., Roll, F., Valles, V., Espinoza, M., & Duque, A. L. (2017). Addressing Cultural Diversity and Global Competence: The Dual Language Framework. In L. Leavitt, S. Wisdom, & K. Leavitt (Eds.), *Cultural Awareness and Competency Development in Higher Education* (pp. 111–131). Hershey, PA: IGI Global. doi:10.4018/978-1-5225-2145-7.ch007

Richards, M., & Guzman, I. R. (2020). Academic Assessment of Critical Thinking in Distance Education Information Technology Programs. In I. Management Association (Ed.), *Learning and Performance Assessment: Concepts, Methodologies, Tools, and Applications* (pp. 1-19). IGI Global. https://doi.org/10.4018/978-1-7998-0420-8.ch001

Riel, J., Lawless, K. A., & Brown, S. W. (2017). Defining and Designing Responsive Online Professional Development (ROPD): A Framework to Support Curriculum Implementation. In T. Kidd & L. Morris Jr., (Eds.), *Handbook of Research on Instructional Systems and Educational Technology* (pp. 104–115). Hershey, PA: IGI Global. doi:10.4018/978-1-5225-2399-4.ch010

Roberts, C. (2017). Advancing Women Leaders in Academe: Creating a Culture of Inclusion. In S. Mukerji & P. Tripathi (Eds.), *Handbook of Research on Administration, Policy, and Leadership in Higher Education* (pp. 256–273). Hershey, PA: IGI Global. doi:10.4018/978-1-5225-0672-0.ch012

Rodgers, W. J., Kennedy, M. J., Alves, K. D., & Romig, J. E. (2017). A Multimedia Tool for Teacher Education and Professional Development. In C. Martin & D. Polly (Eds.), *Handbook of Research on Teacher Education and Professional Development* (pp. 285–296). Hershey, PA: IGI Global. doi:10.4018/978-1-5225-1067-3.ch015

Romanowski, M. H. (2017). Qatar's Educational Reform: Critical Issues Facing Principals. In I. Management Association (Ed.), Educational Leadership and Administration: Concepts, Methodologies, Tools, and Applications (pp. 1758-1773). Hershey, PA: IGI Global. https://doi.org/ doi:10.4018/978-1-5225-1624-8.ch080

Ruffin, T. R., Hawkins, D. P., & Lee, D. I. (2018). Increasing Student Engagement and Participation Through Course Methodology. In M. Khosrow-Pour, D.B.A. (Ed.), Encyclopedia of Information Science and Technology, Fourth Edition (pp. 1463-1473). Hershey, PA: IGI Global. doi:10.4018/978-1-5225-2255-3.ch126

Sabina, L. L., Curry, K. A., Harris, E. L., Krumm, B. L., & Vencill, V. (2017). Assessing the Performance of a Cohort-Based Model Using Domestic and International Practices. In I. Management Association (Ed.), Educational Leadership and Administration: Concepts, Methodologies, Tools, and Applications(pp. 913-929). Hershey, PA: IGI Global. https://doi.org/ doi:10.4018/978-1-5225-1624-8.ch044

Samkian, A., Pascarella, J., & Slayton, J. (2022). Towards an Anti-Racist, Culturally Responsive, and LGBTQ+ Inclusive Education: Developing Critically-Conscious Educational Leaders. In E. Cain-Sanschagrin, R. Filback, & J. Crawford (Eds.), *Cases on Academic Program Redesign for Greater Racial and Social Justice* (pp. 150–175). IGI Global. https://doi.org/10.4018/978-1-7998-8463-7.ch007

Santamaría, A. P., Webber, M., & Santamaría, L. J. (2017). Effective School Leadership for Māori Achievement: Building Capacity through Indigenous, National, and International Cross-Cultural Collaboration. In I. Management Association (Ed.), Educational Leadership and Administration: Concepts, Methodologies, Tools, and Applications (pp. 1547-1567). Hershey, PA: IGI Global. https://doi.org/ doi:10.4018/978-1-5225-1624-8.ch071

Santamaría, L. J. (2017). Culturally Responsive Educational Leadership in Cross-Cultural International Contexts. In I. Management Association (Ed.), Educational Leadership and Administration: Concepts, Methodologies, Tools, and Applications (pp. 1380-1400). Hershey, PA: IGI Global. https://doi.org/ doi:10.4018/978-1-5225-1624-8.ch064

Segredo, M. R., Cistone, P. J., & Reio, T. G. (2017). Relationships Between Emotional Intelligence, Leadership Style, and School Culture. *International Journal of Adult Vocational Education and Technology*, *8*(3), 25–43. doi:10.4018/IJAVET.2017070103

Shalev, N. (2017). Empathy and Leadership From the Organizational Perspective. In Z. Nedelko & M. Brzozowski (Eds.), *Exploring the Influence of Personal Values and Cultures in the Workplace* (pp. 348–363). Hershey, PA: IGI Global. doi:10.4018/978-1-5225-2480-9.ch018

Siamak, M., Fathi, S., & Isfandyari-Moghaddam, A. (2018). Assessment and Measurement of Education Programs of Information Literacy. In R. Bhardwaj (Ed.), *Digitizing the Modern Library and the Transition From Print to Electronic* (pp. 164–192). Hershey, PA: IGI Global. doi:10.4018/978-1-5225-2119-8.ch007

Siu, K. W., & García, G. J. (2017). Disruptive Technologies and Education: Is There Any Disruption After All? In I. Management Association (Ed.), Educational Leadership and Administration: Concepts, Methodologies, Tools, and Applications (pp. 757-778). Hershey, PA: IGI Global. https://doi.org/doi:10.4018/978-1-5225-1624-8.ch037

Slagter van Tryon, P. J. (2017). The Nurse Educator's Role in Designing Instruction and Instructional Strategies for Academic and Clinical Settings. In J. Stefaniak (Ed.), *Advancing Medical Education Through Strategic Instructional Design* (pp. 133–149). Hershey, PA: IGI Global. doi:10.4018/978-1-5225-2098-6.ch006

Slattery, C. A. (2018). Literacy Intervention and the Differentiated Plan of Instruction. In *Developing Effective Literacy Intervention Strategies: Emerging Research and Opportunities* (pp. 41–62). Hershey, PA: IGI Global. doi:10.4018/978-1-5225-5007-5.ch003

Smith, A. R. (2017). Ensuring Quality: The Faculty Role in Online Higher Education. In K. Shelton & K. Pedersen (Eds.), *Handbook of Research on Building, Growing, and Sustaining Quality E-Learning Programs* (pp. 210–231). Hershey, PA: IGI Global. doi:10.4018/978-1-5225-0877-9.ch011

Souders, T. M. (2017). Understanding Your Learner: Conducting a Learner Analysis. In J. Stefaniak (Ed.), *Advancing Medical Education Through Strategic Instructional Design* (pp. 1–29). Hershey, PA: IGI Global. doi:10.4018/978-1-5225-2098-6.ch001

Spring, K. J., Graham, C. R., & Ikahihifo, T. B. (2018). Learner Engagement in Blended Learning. In M. Khosrow-Pour, D.B.A. (Ed.), Encyclopedia of Information Science and Technology, Fourth Edition (pp. 1487-1498). Hershey, PA: IGI Global. doi:10.4018/978-1-5225-2255-3.ch128

Storey, V. A., Anthony, A. K., & Wahid, P. (2017). Gender-Based Leadership Barriers: Advancement of Female Faculty to Leadership Positions in Higher Education. In V. Wang (Ed.), *Encyclopedia of Strategic Leadership and Management* (pp. 244–258). Hershey, PA: IGI Global. doi:10.4018/978-1-5225-1049-9.ch018

Stottlemyer, D. (2018). Develop a Teaching Model Plan for a Differentiated Learning Approach. In *Differentiated Instructional Design for Multicultural Environments: Emerging Research and Opportunities* (pp. 106–130). Hershey, PA: IGI Global. doi:10.4018/978-1-5225-5106-5.ch005

Stottlemyer, D. (2018). Developing a Multicultural Environment. In *Differentiated Instructional Design for Multicultural Environments: Emerging Research and Opportunities* (pp. 1–27). Hershey, PA: IGI Global. doi:10.4018/978-1-5225-5106-5.ch001

Swagerty, T. (2022). Digital Access to Culturally Relevant Curricula: The Impact on the Native and Indigenous Student. In E. Reeves & C. McIntyre (Eds.), *Multidisciplinary Perspectives on Diversity and Equity in a Virtual World* (pp. 99–113). IGI Global. https://doi.org/10.4018/978-1-7998-8028-8.ch006

Swami, B. N., Gobona, T., & Tsimako, J. J. (2017). Academic Leadership: A Case Study of the University of Botswana. In N. Baporikar (Ed.), *Innovation and Shifting Perspectives in Management Education* (pp. 1–32). Hershey, PA: IGI Global. doi:10.4018/978-1-5225-1019-2.ch001

Swanson, K. W., & Collins, G. (2018). Designing Engaging Instruction for the Adult Learners. In M. Khosrow-Pour, D.B.A. (Ed.), Encyclopedia of Information Science and Technology, Fourth Edition (pp. 1432-1440). Hershey, PA: IGI Global. doi:10.4018/978-1-5225-2255-3.ch123

Swartz, B. A., Lynch, J. M., & Lynch, S. D. (2018). Embedding Elementary Teacher Education Coursework in Local Classrooms: Examples in Mathematics and Special Education. In D. Polly, M. Putman, T. Petty, & A. Good (Eds.), *Innovative Practices in Teacher Preparation and Graduate-Level Teacher Education Programs* (pp. 262–292). Hershey, PA: IGI Global. doi:10.4018/978-1-5225-3068-8.ch015

Taliadorou, N., & Pashiardis, P. (2017). Emotional Intelligence and Political Skill Really Matter in Educational Leadership. In I. Management Association (Ed.), Educational Leadership and Administration: Concepts, Methodologies, Tools, and Applications (pp. 1274-1303). Hershey, PA: IGI Global. https://doi.org/ doi:10.4018/978-1-5225-1624-8.ch060

Tandoh, K. A., & Ebe-Arthur, J. E. (2018). Effective Educational Leadership in the Digital Age: An Examination of Professional Qualities and Best Practices. In J. Keengwe (Ed.), *Handbook of Research on Digital Content, Mobile Learning, and Technology Integration Models in Teacher Education* (pp. 244–265). Hershey, PA: IGI Global. doi:10.4018/978-1-5225-2953-8.ch013

Tobin, M. T. (2018). Multimodal Literacy. In M. Khosrow-Pour, D.B.A. (Ed.), Encyclopedia of Information Science and Technology, Fourth Edition (pp. 1508-1516). Hershey, PA: IGI Global. doi:10.4018/978-1-5225-2255-3.ch130

Torres, K. M., Arrastia-Chisholm, M. C., & Tackett, S. (2019). A Phenomenological Study of Pre-Service Teachers' Perceptions of Completing ESOL Field Placements. *International Journal of Teacher Education and Professional Development*, *2*(2), 85–101. https://doi.org/10.4018/IJTEPD.2019070106

Torres, M. C., Salamanca, Y. N., Cely, J. P., & Aguilar, J. L. (2020). All We Need is a Boost! Using Multimodal Tools and the Translanguaging Strategy: Strengthening Speaking in the EFL Classroom. *International Journal of Computer-Assisted Language Learning and Teaching*, *10*(3), 28–47. doi:10.4018/IJCALLT.2020070103

Torres, M. L., & Ramos, V. J. (2018). Music Therapy: A Pedagogical Alternative for ASD and ID Students in Regular Classrooms. In P. Epler (Ed.), *Instructional Strategies in General Education and Putting the Individuals With Disabilities Act (IDEA) Into Practice* (pp. 222–244). Hershey, PA: IGI Global. doi:10.4018/978-1-5225-3111-1.ch008

Toulassi, B. (2017). Educational Administration and Leadership in Francophone Africa: 5 Dynamics to Change Education. In S. Mukerji & P. Tripathi (Eds.), *Handbook of Research on Administration, Policy, and Leadership in Higher Education* (pp. 20–45). Hershey, PA: IGI Global. doi:10.4018/978-1-5225-0672-0.ch002

Umair, S., & Sharif, M. M. (2018). Predicting Students Grades Using Artificial Neural Networks and Support Vector Machine. In M. Khosrow-Pour, D.B.A. (Ed.), Encyclopedia of Information Science and Technology, Fourth Edition (pp. 5169-5182). Hershey, PA: IGI Global. doi:10.4018/978-1-5225-2255-3.ch449

Vettraino, L., Castello, V., Guspini, M., & Guglielman, E. (2018). Self-Awareness and Motivation Contrasting ESL and NEET Using the SAVE System. In M. Khosrow-Pour, D.B.A. (Ed.), Encyclopedia of Information Science and Technology, Fourth Edition (pp. 1559-1568). Hershey, PA: IGI Global. doi:10.4018/978-1-5225-2255-3.ch135

Wiemelt, J. (2017). Critical Bilingual Leadership for Emergent Bilingual Students. In I. Management Association (Ed.), Educational Leadership and Administration: Concepts, Methodologies, Tools, and Applications (pp. 1606-1631). Hershey, PA: IGI Global. doi:10.4018/978-1-5225-1624-8.ch074

Wolf, F., Seyfarth, F. C., & Pflaum, E. (2018). Scalable Capacity-Building for Geographically Dispersed Learners: Designing the MOOC "Sustainable Energy in Small Island Developing States (SIDS)". In U. Pandey & V. Indrakanti (Eds.), *Open and Distance Learning Initiatives for Sustainable Development* (pp. 58–83). Hershey, PA: IGI Global. doi:10.4018/978-1-5225-2621-6.ch003

Woodley, X. M., Mucundanyi, G., & Lockard, M. (2017). Designing Counter-Narratives: Constructing Culturally Responsive Curriculum Online. *International Journal of Online Pedagogy and Course Design*, 7(1), 43–56. doi:10.4018/IJOPCD.2017010104

Yell, M. L., & Christle, C. A. (2017). The Foundation of Inclusion in Federal Legislation and Litigation. In C. Curran & A. Petersen (Eds.), *Handbook of Research on Classroom Diversity and Inclusive Education Practice* (pp. 27–52). Hershey, PA: IGI Global. doi:10.4018/978-1-5225-2520-2.ch002

Zinner, L. (2019). Fostering Academic Citizenship With a Shared Leadership Approach. In C. Zhu & M. Zayim-Kurtay (Eds.), *University Governance and Academic Leadership in the EU and China* (pp. 99–117). IGI Global. https://doi.org/10.4018/978-1-5225-7441-5.ch007

About the Authors

Muhammad Shahzad Aslam is a young high-performing professional with more than five years of experience in higher education. He is currently working as Assistant Professor in the School of Traditional Chinese Medicine, Xiamen University Malaysia. He completed his PhD in October 2017 from Universiti Malaysia Perlis, Malaysia, under a scholarship awarded by the Government of Malaysia under the Ministry of Higher Education Malaysia categorized as Malaysian International Scholarship. He had completed M.Phil in Pharmaceutical Chemistry from Bahauddin Zakariya University, Multan, Pakistan. He has graduated as a Doctor of Pharmacy (Pharm-D) from Baqai Medical University, Karachi, Pakistan. He has been working with a multi-disciplinary attitude in digital health, mental health, psychopharmacology, public health, natural product chemistry, green chemistry, novel extraction prototype, extraction, fractionation and isolation of bioactive compounds, stabilities studies of pharmaceuticals, standardization of herbal product, pre-clinical trials, and health informatics.

Saima Nisar PhD in Information Technology from Universiti Utara Malaysia with IBM certified Data Scientist with experience in various aspects of Data science and analytics including Python, Machine Learning, data analysis, statistical analysis and predictive modelling. Saima Nisar has published eleven articles and has an h-index (3).

Index

O

P

Q

R

S

T

U

W

Y

www.ingramcontent.com/pod-product-compliance
Lightning Source LLC
LaVergne TN
LVHW061536290926
849162LV00004B/807